SOURDOUGH
CULTURE

SOURDOUGH CULTURE

A HISTORY OF BREAD MAKING FROM ANCIENT TO MODERN BAKERS

ERIC PALLANT

FOREWORD BY PETER REINHART

AGATE

CHICAGO

First printed in September 2021
Printed in the United States

9 8 7 6 5 4 3 2 1   21 22 23 24 25

Cover design by Morgan Krehbiel
Author photo by John Mangine

Library of Congress Cataloging-in-Publication Data

Names: Pallant, Eric, author.
Title: Sourdough culture : a history of bread making from ancient to modern
bakers / Eric Pallant ; foreword by Peter Reinhart.
Description: [Chicago] : Surrey, [2021] | Summary: "An exploration of the
history of sourdough, accompanied by a selection from the author's own
favorite recipes"-- Provided by publisher.
Identifiers: LCCN 2021010845 (print) | LCCN 2021010846 (ebook) | ISBN
9781572843011 (hardcover) | ISBN 9781572848535 (ebook)
Subjects: LCSH: Sourdough bread. | Bread--History. | Cooking (Sourdough)
Classification: LCC TX770.S66 P35 2021 (print) | LCC TX770.S66 (ebook) |
DDC 641.81/5--dc23
LC record available at https://lccn.loc.gov/2021010845
LC ebook record available at https://lccn.loc.gov/2021010846

Surrey Books is an imprint of Agate Publishing.
Agate books are available in bulk at discount prices.
Single copies are available prepaid direct from the publisher.

AgatePublishing.com

For my family, past, present, and future,
related and unrelated.

"How can a nation be great if its bread tastes like Kleenex?"
ATTRIBUTED TO JULIA CHILD

Cripple Creek sourdough culture (1893) preparing to start a loaf.

CONTENTS

FOREWORD

BREAD HAS BECOME A CROWDED CATEGORY FOR food books these past few years. Each time a new bread book comes out, I find myself asking, "Is there really anything new that can be said on the subject?" And along comes another and yet another terrific book. Bread, it must be concluded, is a fathomless subject, from a scientific, historical, technological, craft, or even literary perspective. In fact, there is now so much written about bread that what we really need is a way to tie it all together, to integrate it into a cohesive fabric, to connect the dots. And this, I am pleased to see, is exactly what Eric Pallant has done in this lively, beautifully written tome about the six-thousand-year journey of sourdough from the Fertile Crescent to our twenty-first-century kitchens.

"Connecting the dots" is the key phrase here. Bread, more than just about any subject—and certainly in any culinary sense—is totally about connectedness, both as a universal symbol and as a literal thing. Sourdough cultures are a living embodiment of connectivity, transmitting traditions, rituals, beliefs, knowledge, flavor, and living organisms from friend to friend and from parent to child. The most effective means of transmitting this kind of knowledge from person to person and generation to generation is through celebrations and through stories, and bread has a long, important, celebratory story to tell. We yearn for stories, especially when they're well told, because they engage and work on us on multiple levels. This story of sourdough is the ideal medium through which to explore our interconnectedness—our history, the development of our technology, and our humanity.

Eric Pallant has paved the way for us to traverse the deeper meanings of bread by guiding us through its outer crust. He does this with the well-crafted use of a central story thread, the chronicle of his personally archived one-hundred-plus-year-old Cripple Creek sourdough starter, and he shows us how this piece of living microbe-infused dough informed and added meaning to his life.

Writing about bread at the literal level, especially bread science, can easily become dry and overly technical. But the Cripple Creek starter's lineage is a joyride into the everything-ness of bread. In a contemporary voice and to a more bread-savvy readership, Eric carries the torch that H. E. Jacobs took up more than seventy years ago with his seminal book *Six Thousand Years of Bread: Its Holy and Unholy History*. Eric's book invites us to ride along and see how scientists, theologians, laborers, bakers, soldiers, and bread lovers have interacted with sourdough since the dawn of Western civilization.

As you can tell, I am impressed by both the content and the structure of this book. The passing on from hand to hand of the Cripple Creek sourdough starter throughout the years beautifully parallels the meta-theme of the transmission of knowledge from one generation to the next. I learned so much more than I, a fellow bread geek, imagined I would. The book's structure is also intrinsically satisfying because the writer in me loves to be in the presence of a story well told, and great story structure provides good bones for every literary work. I also appreciate the nuanced tone, the ironic little asides, even the catty moments where the personal, necessarily subjective narrative weaves itself around and through the necessarily objective science and facts.

It is no easy task to hold a reader's attention when diving into the intricacies of a single subject, but I believe that Eric, whom I have now known and corresponded with for the past few years—since 2018, when he presented at the annual International Symposium on Bread that I host at Johnson & Wales University—has, by virtue of this book, expanded and deepened the many levels of my understanding of a subject we both care about fervently. But even more important is that reading about Eric's journey has allowed me to get to know him, my fellow traveler, even more deeply.

—Peter Reinhart
March 2020, Charlotte, North Carolina

INTRODUCTION

I F IT WEREN'T FOR THE GENTLE PERSISTENCE OF my wife, I would avoid most social gatherings. I would have found an excuse not to attend a picnic hosted by Milosz Mamula, director of financial aid at Allegheny College, and his wife, Quimby, and I would have missed my opportunity to begin a relationship with a sourdough starter that has now stretched more than thirty years.

I was a new assistant professor of environmental science at Allegheny College, and the Mamulas had invited us to a get-to-know-the-new-couple summer picnic in their backyard. It was 1988. In the countryside outside Meadville, Pennsylvania, the sun was bright, the sky was cloudless, and their lawn expanded like an endless ocean of green. There were hardwood forests in the valleys.

Susan and I arrived at the Mamulas' as we often do when approaching gatherings: Susan was smiling and looking forward to an afternoon conversing with people, and I was in quite the opposite state. My heart was beating too quickly, my hands were leaving damp marks on the steering wheel, and my appetite had been displaced by mild nausea.

I do not recall what we had for lunch, but I do remember enjoying the bread that was served and using that fact to break my discomfiture. The bread had oatmeal in it, so in addition to its home-baked warmth and golden crust, there was an overture of comfort about it.

"Hey, this is great bread," I said, or something equally witty.

"It's sourdough bread. I just baked it," Quimby said.

"Oh, I bake bread, but I've never used sourdough," I told her.

"Would you like some of my starter? I can give you some now. Come on in. I have some growing in the kitchen."

Though none of us knew it at the time, the bread we ate with lunch was baked from a sourdough starter that I would later find out was nearing its one hundredth birthday and had a history I would trace back as far as the gold rush, in Cripple Creek, Colorado, in 1893. It was also the beginning of my love affair with sourdough.

I took the Mamulas' starter more on impulse than because of any particular ideological commitment or cooking goal. When I was young, my dad made bread. He was a big man, over six feet tall, more than two hundred pounds. His hands were the size of catcher's mitts. He made eggy brioche with noses that protruded like his and shiny tops like his own bald head. I liked brioche because it was sweet and rich. He made sourdough, too, but because of its overwhelming dissimilarity to the Wonder Bread I had grown up with and preferred, I did not take to it at the time.

There was something magical about Quimby Mamula's bread that infused me with a spirit to learn how to work with sourdough. I looked at a few recipes but mostly experimented, making a thousand mistakes and accumulating just as many observations. As the first decade of the 2000s neared its end, one day I pulled my sourdough culture from the refrigerator, pausing just before feeding it fresh water and flour. Staring into my bottle of culture, I thought to myself that my Cripple Creek starter had been with me longer than my children, both of whom were then teenagers capable of consuming large quantities of bread. It had outlived multiple computers, numerous cell phones, a toaster, a refrigerator, and a washing machine. It was one of my oldest possessions. And unlike the few things that I had inherited from my grandparents, my sourdough starter was a *living* heirloom. If I had kept this starter alive for twenty years, and it was alive in the Mamula household before coming to me, how old *was* it? My need to know more was greater than my fear of cold-calling the Mamulas.

After our picnic, we had not stayed in touch, and Milosz had since retired from Allegheny. To my great relief, within seconds of answering the phone, they recalled our long-ago luncheon and even who gave them the starter. It had belonged to Douglas Steeples, a friend of theirs from when they lived in Indiana, in the 1970s. Steeples had inherited it from his grandmother. Already, I understood our starter to be very old. Finding Douglas Steeples and asking what he could recall was my next step.

At one time, Steeples had been a professor of history at Earlham College. He had retired and was well into his seventies and living in North Carolina when I first reached him. Just as the Mamulas had requested a sample of starter when I called them out of the blue, Steeples asked if he could have a sample returned to him. Both had let their starters die some ten years prior. I packed a jarful into a FedEx box with some ice packs and sent it on its way.

About the starter Steeples could say only one thing with assurance: it didn't originate with his grandmother. He was confident the starter he gave to the Mamulas was from the Cripple Creek gold rush of 1893. Steeples was not sure exactly how the starter had gotten to him. For more than a year, he and I corresponded as he fed me clues.

I was now the owner of a Gold Rush starter from 1893, a starter with a proud history. After a little research, I learned that sourdough and gold mining were more than metaphorically synonymous. Legend states that gray-bearded, bandy-legged miners protected personal starters at gunpoint. When it got cold at night, they slept with pouches of starter inside their bedclothes to keep their starters from freezing. According to some accounts, living with a sourdough starter next to their skin meant that some miners began to smell like it. (No one has ever written much about what a sourdough starter smelled like after cozying up to an unbathed miner night after night.) By 1898, at the height of the Klondike Gold Rush in Alaska, a miner coming in from the wild for provisions not only smelled like sourdough but also was called a Sourdough. For many years, any loaf of bread I baked was served with a story about a lonely miner in the Rocky Mountains who had once baked with the same sourdough starter I was now using.

Remarkably, it seemed my starter had survived for more than 125 years and had apparently escaped the most common demises: it had not been accidentally baked, contaminated, infected, or ignored. Was it possible to discover the origins of my miner's starter? Had my miner arrived in the West with a pouch of starter from his mother's kitchen? Maybe it was even a starter that had been in his family since before they'd arrived in North America from somewhere in Europe. My imagination ran wild, but the seeds of a book—this book—were beginning to germinate. I had studied microbiology as a PhD student and knew I needed to broaden my inquiry: was there any way to know if the bacteria and yeast now living in my refrigerator were descendants of microscopic organisms from more than a century prior? Did it matter if they were?

For the better part of a year, Douglas Steeples tried to recall who, exactly, had given him the starter. He sent me names of former colleagues and students, and I did my best to locate them to ask if they were once sourdough bakers. While I followed Steeples's leads, I recognized that my investigation would eventually grow cold; sooner or later I would reach a point in history that no one who was still around could remember. In order to deduce how a starter might have first arrived in Cripple Creek, Colorado, I began searching for the origin of bread. My plan was to work forward from that history in the hope that at some point my investigation would intersect with the history of my starter. Beginning with the first known bread makers, I would trace sourdough through millennia until I found at least one viable route that led to Cripple Creek, Colorado.

I wanted to learn who invented bread and who invented sourdough. How did bread come to be the staple upon which so much of Western civilization came to depend? What experiments led scientists to reveal that living species were growing and reproducing inside a sourdough starter? Did gold miners really sleep with sourdough starters inside their clothes? What happened when they rolled over? And why, after six thousand years, have so many people given up on sourdough in favor of bread designed by engineers to exit a factory line with all the reliability and taste of a Model T? My attempt to answer these questions is this book.

The paradox of a sourdough starter is that while each cell responsible for raising a loaf of bread is but a few hours old when it is cooked, the ability of people to harness the microbial power of yeast and bacteria to leaven is as old as civilization itself. I wanted to know who first domesticated the microscopic organisms now slumbering in my refrigerator to reveal the life my starter had lived and, in effect, to learn the culture of my culture. The birth of my sourdough culture, it turns out, was intertwined with the birth of agriculture and earth's first civilizations.

CHAPTER 1

IN THE BEGINNING

W

HEN I MADE MY FIRST SOURDOUGH BREAD
with the starter from Quimby Mamula, I plunged in
with both hands. Diving into history felt much the same.
First, there was unconvincing glop: a sticky, fermenting concoction
of stories about people and places, some living and some long gone.
I kneaded until strands of history began to align, like filaments of
gluten, into coherency. But I was a long way from prepping and
assembling all the ingredients necessary to tell a good story. I had
to locate two people: someone making sourdough bread in Cripple Creek, Colorado, and the person who, for the first time in history, put two hands into a fermenting bowl of gruel and baked it.

I set off in two directions. While I worked back in time through
Douglas Steeples's growing list of people who might have been Cripple Creek's personal carrier, I also sought out the trailhead for a path
forward toward Cripple Creek. Someone had to gather or cultivate
plants from which bread could be made—and then they had to use
grindstones and pestles to pound those plants into rudimentary
flour. The earliest evidence of this can be found among Stone Age
inhabitants of what is today Mozambique. Their excavated tools

contain grains of starch. The grasses collected were 105,000 years old when archaeologists discovered them. While this evidence likely represents a first step, smashed grass is still a long way from bread.[1]

Mortars and pestles have also been found among archaeological sites that are thirty thousand years old, in what is known today as Italy, Russia, and the Czech Republic, and archaeologists have deduced the presence of flour from tiny grains of starch adhered to their grinding surfaces.[2] A variety of modern microscopes have been used to compare those extracted starch grains to a library of modern plant-specific starches. From these, scientists were able to ascertain that across Europe, even at a time when the bulk of the human diet was presumed to be animal based, people made rudimentary flour. They mashed the fleshy roots of cattails between two stones. They added roots and seeds of another dozen plants. Archaeologists don't have proof that they *cooked* the flour at that time—they may have drunk it like a smoothie or eaten it raw. But cooking a gruel of flour and water seems a likely possibility, and porridge the likely outcome. To bake bread, dough would have been placed on heated stones to bake, and archaeologists cannot say with any certainty whether these early European cooks made the transition from porridge to bread.

Move forward about ten thousand years and drift southeast to the Sea of Galilee in northern Israel, and there is clear evidence that people baked. An archaeological site called Ohalo II, located on the southeastern shore of the sea, dates back more than twenty thousand years. Fortunately, the locale has been beneath six to ten feet of water for around 23,000 years and covered by fine sediments and in anoxic conditions that have prevented decomposition. Finding intact organic remains that are that old is very unusual.[3]

When Ohalo II's scientists removed starch grains from the grinding stones found on-site, they were able to identify remnants of more than thirty species of plants, including wild barley and wild emmer wheat, an ancestor of modern bread wheat.[4] Wheat and barley belong to the plant family of grasses. The use of grasses is important because grasses—oats, corn, rye, millet, sorghum, and rice—became the staples upon which nearly all of humanity depended for its caloric sustenance.

Among the half acre of carefully excavated artifacts at Ohalo II are several hearths. The hearths are arrangements of stones in circles or ovals. They contain charcoal and ash deposits that are usually ten to twenty inches in diameter and a few inches thick. A few of the seeds recovered at Ohalo have been burned, but only a very few, suggesting that roasted grains were not a staple. Rather, bread was. Scientists at Ohalo have suggested that bread-making techniques along the shores of Galilee were similar to those employed by modern groups in southwest Asia, the Sahara, and Australia. Grasses and seeds were ground between two stones. A rough dough was made by mixing flour with water, and the dough was cooked on stones heated by hearths.[5]

Thus, twenty thousand years ago, on beaches near the Sea of Galilee, the smell of fresh bread would have mingled in the air alongside the wafting aromas of barbecued meat and seared fish. There was not yet farming, and the breads were almost certainly unleavened, but the path to both agriculture and a recognizable loaf of bread was underway.

Before flatbreads could be transformed into risen ones, however, a few additional developments were still in order. Wheat, with its high gluten content and gluten's ability to hold on to gas bubbles, had to be prized above the dozens of other grasses common in a field of wild plants. Other grains and legumes, such as barley, maize, lentils, and rice, which were all domesticated around the same time as wheat, may also be ground to flour, mixed with water, kneaded, and baked. Maize, for example, is good for preparing something the thickness of a tortilla, but not a loaf. Rice and lentils can be soaked long enough that bacteria and yeast similar to those that grow on wheat to make sourdough will take up residence. In a few days, a bubbly, slightly sour mash will form, but if you cook that batter, you will make paper-thin dosas, not a loaf of bread. Barley dough can be kneaded and shaped into a thick, dense loaf and baked, but it remains so heavy that soldiers in ancient Rome's army who were forced to eat it considered it punishment rations.[6]

Ah, but wheat. At some point in history, early cooks placing pats of dough on heated rocks made the discovery that dough made from wheat flour puffed when it was heated. The resulting bread was light and deliciously airy compared with the dense, flat cakes made from other grains. Preferentially gathering wheat seeds from fields would have been the next step toward intentional bread making. The practice of saving and storing some of those seeds for replanting had to follow.

Though there is still considerable debate among archaeologists about where, when, and why agriculture replaced hunting and gathering, there are nonetheless some general points of agreement. About ten thousand years ago, pretty much all over the world, some plants—and animals, too—altered by human intervention began to replace wild varieties. Archaeologists who have analyzed seeds extracted from ancient settlements have observed that, with time, people were first gathering, and later planting, tastier and more productive varieties of plants. They have also surmised that a seed's ability to care for itself began to diminish.

Consider reproduction. In the wild, a seed must put distance between itself and its parent if it is going to thrive. There is no benefit for a young seedling to compete for light, water, and essential minerals with its progenitor. In order to live, it must land on fertile soil, but before that, it must first survive the digestive tract of an animal, fly on the wind, or spring readily from the seed head as it is brushed by a gust or an animal. Ancient wheat bundled its seeds atop a tall stalk. If the head or stalk was jostled while the seeds were mature, progeny shattered in all directions, increasing the chances of a seedling beginning life in unencumbered earth.

From there, a pair of awns, the spiky hairs at the top of each seed, took control. They stuck into the ground and directed the seed toward the soil. As the humidity rose, the hairs bent, much like some human hair frizzes in the same conditions. Tiny silica hairs on each awn acted as anchors so that the only direction the seed could travel was down, into the soil. Nighttime humidity in the desert rose while the temperature rapidly dropped, and in this way, wild wheat planted itself.[7]

To early gatherers ranging from the Balkans to modern-day Iran,[8] however, shattering meant that, for a collector moving through a field shaking or cutting stalks of wheat, disaggregating grains were cussingly difficult to capture. Experiments performed in the late 1980s showed exactly how hard it might have been for an ancient gatherer to collect wheat seeds by hand. By counting the number of captures and comparing it with the number of seeds that got away, scientists calculated that a decent reaper could at best take 80 percent of a wild grain. The norm was a harvest rate of only 50 percent.[9]

It's easy to understand why, when an early gatherer found a plant that had evolved to produce seeds that clung tightly to its stalk when its stem was cut with a flint sickle, she set those seeds aside. Instead of eating them, she replanted them the next season.[10] This represents a first step toward the codependence of plant and human. Humans benefited because the seeds they wished to eat stayed atop the stalks they were cutting. In exchange, domesticated wheat needed a human to transport its seeds to a bare patch of soil.

Archaeologists and plant biologists can observe additional changes as, with time, humans honed their skills related to soil preparation, weeding, watering, and harvesting. Seeds became larger, and they germinated soon after planting, rather than sprouting when an environmental cue, such as a decent rainstorm, triggered their physiology. They ripened around the same time and positioned their seeds at the same height, which made them easier to harvest. Plants that produced the best-quality food—good-tasting, high-rising bread, for example—displaced less desirable variants.[11]

Archaeologists are in general agreement that agriculture began fifteen to twenty thousand years ago, when hunter-gatherers first began cultivating soil, broadcasting seeds, and weeding out unwanted invaders. Ten thousand years ago, the transition from wild to domesticated was well underway for plants and animals around the world. As the last ice age ended, plants and animals associated with sedentary human habitations were readily distinguishable from their wild forebears.[12]

Domesticated seeds became so heavy that they dropped right at their parent's feet, if they even dropped at all. There was not much dispersal. They also developed a tenderness that made them even tastier to crawling insects and animals. The very stuff that rendered seeds such a valuable food source to humans was a physiological trade-off with self-defense. Toss a domesticated wheat seed, corn kernel, or grain of rice into a field of wild grasses, and it will be overwhelmed by the mass of plants that, for generation upon generation, have had to do their business in a very tough neighborhood. A crop plant's chances for survival would be no higher than that of a domesticated chicken in a barn full of wild raccoons.

The development of agriculture meant that human civilizations employed select members among their citizenry to plant, hoe, water, fertilize, defend, harvest, and store their growing menagerie of domesticated plants. In exchange for the assistance required to nurture helpless seedlings, domesticated plants returned sustenance without which humans and their domesticated animals would surely starve.

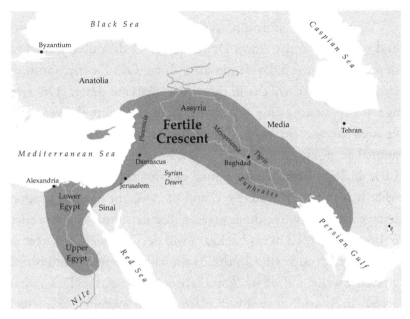

The Fertile Crescent.

By 8000 BCE, give or take, across the arc of the Fertile Crescent, agriculture was well established. Among the seeds resting in archaeologists' sieves were lentils, peas, barley, bitter vetch (a lentil-like legume, only significantly more astringent), and two species of wheat: einkorn (*Triticale monococcum*) and emmer (*Triticale dicoccum*), the wheat that went on to dominate agriculture in central Asia and western Europe.[13]

IN 2002, I taught classes on sustainable development at the Arava Institute for Environmental Studies in southern Israel. The Arava Institute is in the Fertile Crescent, midway between the Jordanian and Egyptian borders, just east of Sinai, and about 175 miles south of Ohalo. Uzi Avner, an Israeli archaeologist and fellow instructor, invited me to join his class on a field trip to the desert to reconnoiter the remains of ancient farm sites.

Very early one morning, Avner drove about a dozen students and me out into the Arava Desert to the Uvda Valley, a shallow depression in the Eilat Mountains. The Arava Desert, south of Israel's Negev, is what is known as an extreme desert. On average, it experiences only thirty millimeters of rainfall a year, just enough to wet the middle knuckle on your little finger. The annual evaporation rate is 4,500 millimeters. By contrast, where I live in Pennsylvania, the annual evaporation rate is one-tenth what it is in the Arava Desert, and the amount of precipitation in a year is thirty-five times greater. The net result is that a slice of bread discarded in my backyard will decompose in a matter of months; that same slice in the Arava will become a mummified cracker by the end of its first afternoon. The Arava Desert has always been arid, an unlikely place to find evidence of ancient agronomy. When we arrived, steppe eagles and honey buzzards were just beginning to ride the spring thermals north for the summer. As I looked around at my tawny stone surroundings, I did not see much of anything except rocks and boulders. As far as I could see, nothing was growing.

Avner's skin was leathery from years of desert sand, wind, and sun. His broad, brimmed hat was as craggy and tan as weathered limestone, and his attitude matched. He took off like a missile across the desert, leaving the rest of us to trot to keep up. When he finally stopped, he explained how he knew that some of the very first agriculture in the world had taken place there.[14] Farming was practiced in the Uvda Valley beginning six thousand years ago, soon after wheat was first domesticated. According to Avner, the population in the valley at that time was three thousand people.[15] He was going to have to prove it to me.

Avner showed me and the students, some of whom were still waking up, how to read the stones in the desert. Standing just inside a knee-high wall of rocks laid by primitive herdsmen, he picked up a fine powder that looked like cocoa and let the wind blow it from his palm. It was animal dung. Avner had drilled test bores into the dung pile and discovered that it was three feet deep. Ordinarily, a three-foot pile of six-thousand-year-old animal dung is not worth so much attention, but this dung was created by the first ever domesticated goats and sheep. Outside the corral, Avner showed us a leopard trap set up by ancient inhabitants to prevent wily predators from eating their stock.[16]

Avner's diggings in nearby sites had also uncovered the oldest dyed wool in the world, a piece of fabric dating from 4000 BCE. Red and yellow threads were woven in opposite directions. He proceeded to show us a few of the 154 habitation sites, all located within a few square miles: 32 corrals, 40 tent camps, 32 threshing floors, 1,200 hectares of cultivated fields, dams, wells, grain storage halls, and many cult sites. I started to see how the place had supported a population of three thousand.

It was apparent that the ancient civilization had planted and harvested, despite the Arava's extreme aridity and what must have been a terribly harsh climate to endure. On previous trips, Avner had found flint plow tips used to plow the site's unique combination of silt and lime sand.[17] Avner had also uncovered numerous sickles once used to harvest crops. These soils were intentionally irrigated with floodwater. Only after Avner walked the length of one could I see a small dam just a few stones high built across a low-gradient ravine. A tiny pile of rocks ran perpendicular to the wash and would have stopped cross-surface runoff, allowing time for silt to accumulate and water to drain into the porous subsurface. Looking up the valley, I saw that ancient farmers had engineered several tiny dams at regular intervals.

Once Avner had shown us what we were looking at, threshing floors became distinguishable as broad circular patches of bedrock cleared of all surface debris. Draft animals pulling sledges would have trampled the chaff that protected each seed. Analysis of tiny grains of fossilized pollen indicated that more than 50 percent of the grain residues excavated from the threshing floors and silos were domesticated wheat and barley. In addition, pollen grains indicated the presence of pesky agricultural weeds.[18]

The bases of grain silos were recognizable as cubicles of stones tightly chinked together to keep out hungry desert rodents. Avner showed us grinding stones for turning seeds into flour and offering stones where animal sacrifices were offered to the gods. Burn marks were still visible at their bases.

What Avner did not show us, however, was how ancient farmers ate their grains or cooked their flour. Porridge or bread? He surmised that they also ate goat meat, drank goat's milk, and probably preserved some goat's milk as yogurt, or labneh. However, he has not yet excavated a bread oven.

THE FIRST EVIDENCE archaeologists have of bread baking is the primitive ovens of Babylon, a city located in the heart of the Fertile Crescent, which date from approximately 4000 BCE. Babylonian bread was rudimentary: dense, unleavened barley rolls. I found one reference to breads that were baked in Switzerland about two hundred years later, but the Swiss site is small, and the technique was probably not widespread.[19] In any case, under the Pharaonic dynasties of ancient Egypt, large-scale bread production took off.

Archaeologists are confident that several thousand years after the residents of Ohalo II ground seeds of wild grasses and, later still, after early farmers planted wheat and barley in the Arava Desert, fields of wheat burgeoned three hundred miles due west of the Arava along the Nile River. Pictures and artifacts left behind by early Egyptian civilizations suggest that bread making was fully underway by 2500 BCE. As I read about these digs, I hoped for some evidence that Egyptian bread was leavened—an initial link in the chain of sourdough history.

The Amarna Workmen's Village, located in the modern province of Minya on the eastern bank of the Nile River, holds many clues about ancient bread making. Built during the reign of King Akhenaten in 1353 BCE and abandoned shortly after his death seventeen years later, the site is unique because it was not a tomb of elites. It was, as the archaeological nomenclature suggests, a place where regular people lived. During a dig at the site in 1986, in a house designated by archaeologists as Gate Street 9, lead archaeologist Delwen Samuel turned her attention from an earlier preoccupation with kings, tombs, sphinxes, and pyramids to the more practical question of how ordinary Egyptians produced their food.

Emmer wheat.

Samuel's work took her inside Gate Street 9's kitchen.[20] She examined ancient Egyptian storage bins and discovered that though barley was plentiful in the Middle East and was used widely to produce beer, the grain used for bread in the Amarna was emmer wheat, which by that point had been fully domesticated and widely cultivated in the Fertile Crescent for several thousand years. Still, Samuel's discovery that emmer wheat was used to make Egyptian bread was something of a surprise. By the time of the earliest Pharaonic dynasties, approximately five thousand years ago, farmers in the Fertile Crescent had already domesticated a new species of wheat called bread wheat (*Triticum aestivum*) by crossing emmer with wild goat grass.[21] By the time

Amarna's bakers were making bread, bread wheat had been around for nearly two thousand years and was being grown by Egypt's trading partners. Archaeologists can safely assume that Egyptian bakers were aware of bread wheat's existence.

Bread wheat held several advantages over emmer. When emmer was threshed, its seeds broke from the spike still wearing their coats, or hulls. In contrast, bread wheat was free threshing, meaning that its stalks released naked seeds when beaten. Free-threshing wheats relieved millers from the task of threshing to separate chaff from grain.

Yet Egyptians eschewed free-threshing bread wheat in favor of the more difficult and less glutenous emmer. The best explanation is that they preferred its taste, and there is one surviving clue to back this assertion. Herodotus, who lived in Greece during the fifth century BCE and was called the Father of History because he was the first historian to systematically collect data, said that the Egyptians believed "emmer is the only fit cereal for bread."[22]

Consequently, mortars—the stone basins into which a wooden pole could be rammed to separate wheat from chaff—would have been of particular importance for processing emmer. It's no surprise that, inside the Amarna kitchen, excavators uncovered two complete limestone mortars, each about the size of a very large flowerpot.

To understand how ancient Egyptians might have baked bread, Samuel constructed a replica kitchen. Because the excavated rock mortars had not deteriorated in the intervening millennia, Samuel moved one to her replica room and used it. Models in the Egyptian Museum in Cairo and tomb paintings show workers hammering away with long-handled pestles. Samuel built one out of pine to a size and height that suited her, approximating the ones in the pictures. "The pestle was easy to use," Samuel stated in an article titled "Their Staff of Life."[23]

It did not require much force to release grains from their hulls. She learned the secret of dehulling emmer by watching people in

Wall painting showing ancient Egyptian harvesting grain, tomb of Sennedjem Sinjun, Deir el-Medina, Thebes, ca. 1295 to 1213 BCE.

Turkey debran whole grains. The secret was water.[24] She added just enough to create dampness, encouraging grains to slide past one another without breaking. The hulls stripped right off. She dried the mixture of damp grain and soggy chaff in the sun and then winnowed. No clear archaeological evidence has been discovered regarding whether Egyptian winnowing was done with a sieve, by wind, or with fans, but the goal was to keep the grains in a basket while chaff blew off to the side.

Even when well cleaned, sacks of grain contained small stones, clods of earth, pieces of straw, weed seeds, and chaff. An offering basket found in King Tut's tomb contained all these things. While it is conceivable that the tomb preparers did not put a great deal of effort into packaging the highest-quality wheat—Tut was dead, after all—there is an extant painting to suggest otherwise. The Egyptian Museum houses a baking and brewing scene from the Fifth Dynasty (2494–2345 BCE) tomb of Saleh and Sourouzian. The fifth person from the right sits at a table, a heap of grain piled before him. He holds one cupped hand outstretched. With the other, he uses his thumb and forefinger to carefully remove impurities.

To grind winnowed and cleaned wheat seeds into flour, an early baker relied upon a quern: a stone platform upon which seeds could be placed with a second stone that could be pushed across the top of the first to crush the seeds. Some querns required a miller to kneel upon the ground pushing one stone across another. Samuel constructed a saddle quern typical of Amarna's bakeries that allowed millers to stand with their heels supported by a wall and their thighs supported by the quern. The quern was a flat or slightly curved slab of stone embedded in the "seat" of what resembled a squat armless chair made of brick. "I found fallen bricks from the derelict house," wrote Samuel. "They were very convenient to use since they were originally ancient mud bricks of the right dimensions. I made a thick mud paste to cement the bricks together." To mill flour with the Egyptian quern, Samuel stood with her back to a wall, the large stone quern two feet in front of her. With her raised heels on the wall, she pressed her thighs against the "chair back" of the quern, leaning over it to push the handstone down the stone slope to the "chair seat."

The ingenuity of the apparatus was the miller's flexed position. Bending over the chair, she put her arms directly over the quern. Its surface was rough, and it gripped the tiny kernels of wheat she placed upon it as she pushed a separate handstone over its top, crushing the kernels into flour. Her back was in exactly the right position to be free of strain.

The process of grinding was quick, Samuel found. "It took me about two minutes to grind meal into fine-textured flour. The concertina position of my body let me really apply a lot of power to the grinding stone. I could rock back and forth at the hips. The longer I ground, the finer the flour," she reported in "Their Staff of Life." "It was not easy to catch the flour. I used a basin beneath the stone's lip to catch flour and flour either fell or I brushed it into the basin. A cloth extending from the lip to the basin would have made it a lot easier." Catching falling flour was not the only obstacle to overcome.

Only a small number of grains could be placed beneath the grinding stone. Add too many, and they rolled off the base. The time it took to make flour was not in the grinding, but in the limited quantity that could be processed at one time. A single handful of grains. Grind. Brush off the platform. Repeat. A day's repast for an Egyptian village likely required a small army of cleaners, pounders, millers, and bakers. The gentle ringing of pestles in mortars and the rhythmic passage of saddle querns must have been the daily soundtrack. To an Egyptian, bread made of emmer wheat must have evinced the taste of home for all the extra effort it took to thresh and winnow. Bread wheat was so much easier.

Microscopic examination of extant loaves from Egyptian tombs has proven that many loaves contained sand as one of their ingredients, and enough ancient Egyptian skulls have been examined to show that their teeth were unusually worn down by it. One explanation was provided by Frank Filce Leek, who practiced dentistry and archaeology in the Dental School at King's College Hospital beginning in 1930.

His interest in teeth extended to the archaeology of ancient Egypt: Leek examined skulls of ancient Egyptians from predynastic times through Ptolemy, roughly the three thousand or more years of Egyptian domination of the eastern Mediterranean. Leek was struck by the nearly complete absence of cavities in Egyptian teeth, a stark contrast to his observation of patients in his King's College dental clinic. What Egyptian teeth of both young and old did exhibit, however, was significant attrition on the biting surfaces. Even young adults had ground their teeth down to the pulpy interior. Once the chewing surface was lost, pathogens readily infected soft tissue inside the teeth. Abscesses were common.[25]

Using X-rays and an acid dissolution technique, Leek went hunting for sand inside fossilized loaves. After hitting small samples of preserved museum loaves with concentrated sulfuric acid and 50 percent hydrogen peroxide, his X-rays turned up grains of quartz, feldspar, amphibole, mica, and probably hornblende.[26] From that observation came the theory that sand was sprinkled on querns to enhance the milling process, as experiments have demonstrated that a little bit of sand goes a long way in making very fine flour.

Delwen Samuel thought otherwise. She found it pretty easy to grind wheat into flour without the addition of sand. Her hypothesis was that sand simply blew in. Seems likely enough, given the volume of sand in the surrounding environment and frequency of sandstorms in the weather forecast. Even modern bread in Egypt, milled by machine and baked in a village bakery, can be very gritty.

Frank Filce Leek was not the only archaeologist to examine fossilized Egyptian loaves. Because the climate was so dry, many loaves of bread were well-preserved, and today, a lot of museums around the world store ancient Egyptian breads and make them available for study. I hoped archaeologists, in addition to confirming the presence of sand, would be able to tell if Egyptian bread had been leavened.

Archaeologists are certain that yeast was present in beer produced in ancient Egypt, in part because yeast cells have been scraped from extant urns. The same species of yeast that carbonates beer, *Saccharomyces cerevisiae*, will also leaven bread, so there is reason to speculate that Egyptian breads were not simply flat pitas, but rather doughs that were allowed to rise before baking.

Unfortunately, yeast cells do not survive temperatures found inside bread ovens, so analysis of museum loaves cannot prove that leavening agents were used, intentionally or otherwise. Barley and emmer flours contain low levels of gluten compared with bread wheat, too, so even if breads were infected with sourdough or yeast cells transferred from beer foam, their rise would have been limited. Conversely, an unleavened dough of wheat flour can puff like a pita even if it has never been leavened.[27] Simply put, archaeologists cannot discern whether an ancient bread was leavened from studying the flour, poofy structure, or some other postmortem analysis of fossilized loaves.

However, archaeologists do know the shape of a loaf. The overwhelming majority of early Egyptian breads were shaped by hand. Some were shaped like fish, and some looked like humans. Others were slashed, pricked, poked with holes, or decorated with bands of appliquéd dough. By New Kingdom times (1550–1069 BCE), molded breads had replaced hand-formed loaves.

In addition to the wide array of shapes, the ingredients used—on top of emmer wheat and some barley flour—were nearly as varied as those that might be found in a modern artisanal bakery. Bakers precooked and soaked whole and cracked grains before adding them to their breads. At least a few semicircular loaves from King Tut's tomb contained ground coriander seeds; other loaves contained fig.[28] Loaves from three different Egyptian eras contained the lichen *Evernia furfuracea*, which was used as a spice or perhaps to assist in leavening. Lichen bread was an interesting discovery because the particular species did not grow in Egypt and was likely imported from Greece and Ethiopia.[29]

Once she had replicated Egyptian techniques for flour preparation, Delwen Samuel wanted to see if she could bake like an Egyptian. She was primarily interested in whether her oven and cooking technique would work and did not put a great deal of effort into her bread formula. Because she was unable to acquire emmer wheat in 1987, the year of her experiment, she simply imported whole wheat and barley flours from Great Britain.[30] Samuel built an oven modeled on those uncovered in the Amarna Workmen's site. She fired it with palm fronds and cakes of animal dung and rigged her replica with a thermometer. Her oven reached a temperature of 1,184 degrees Fahrenheit in eight minutes. Forty-six minutes later, roughly the time it would take to bake a three-pound loaf, the oven temperature had dropped to 212 degrees Fahrenheit, still a reasonable temperature to finish baking.

To perform a test bake, Samuel modeled her technique on tomb paintings from the Middle and Old Kingdoms that suggested that breads were baked in hefty cylindrical molds, clay pots roughly the size and shape of paper towel tubes. Samuel built a flight of crude clay cylinders, each slightly less than a foot long and three-fourths of an inch thick. The inner diameter was only a couple of inches, requiring careful insertion of her dough.[31]

Her breads did indeed shrink away from the sides of their cylinders when they were cooked, as most cooked breads will do, but still stuck. She needed a hammer to shatter each mold, but there was no question about it: a preheated clay pot surrounded by burning palm and dried donkey doo makes bread.

The Egyptians did bread historians many favors. They left loaves, diagrams, models, and cooking utensils for future archaeologists to find. They placed their remains in tombs, and they lived in one of the driest climates on the planet, which provided the greatest likelihood that their grains and flours would survive until the present day. Delwen Samuel's research could not tell me if Egyptian bakers used sourdough. She did make it clear to me, however, how important bread was to the kingdoms of ancient Egypt.

Wall painting of ancient Egyptians making bread, from the tomb of Qenamun, West Thebes, 1550 to 1292 BCE.

RENOWNED EGYPTOLOGIST MARK Lehner has been piecing together the lives of ancient Egyptians for more than three decades, one tiny fragment of pottery at a time. Like Delwen Samuel, Lehner looked beyond the monumental pyramids and the Sphinx, the subjects of most public fascination, to ask questions regarding daily life.

In fall 1999, Lehner and his crew began a thirty-five-month excavation of approximately one-tenth of a site located about a quarter mile south of the Sphinx. It is known as the Lost City of Giza, a major urban complex from the third millennium BCE; Lehner has published numerous books and articles detailing his discoveries.[32] His team found barracks, houses, manors, administrative offices, fish-processing stalls, and royal buildings. One portion of the dig was referred to as Gallery Set III; it contained eight long rectangular rooms, some storage space, and a double-wide hypostyle hall, a term that means its ceiling was once supported by limestone columns.

Down the center of each long, narrow gallery was a low mud wall that divided the room into halves, each about two meters wide. The floor sloped, just slightly, toward the central divider wall, and Lehner was astute enough to recognize that the floor's angle and distance from footer (the low end) to header (slightly uphill) would be exactly right for a man to lie on his back, snoring. The low dividing wall, upon closer inspection, was just about the height of a man's feet if he were lying on his back and wide enough to hold his toothbrush, shaving kit, dress-up kaftan, and framed photograph of his girlfriend.

Lehner suspected that he had located sleeping quarters for the workers who built the Sphinx and pyramids. To test his theory, he lined up his graduate students, assistants, and day laborers and asked them to lie side by side on the dusty ground. It sure looked like a bunk room. The slope in the floor was probably designed to make sleeping with your head higher than your feet a comfort feature. Then he did the math. The two sections could comfortably handle forty to fifty workers. Lehner multiplied that by the number of galleries per set and the number of sets on the site and estimated that a workforce of 1,600 to 2,000 laborers could have easily been sheltered there. Lehner went on to calculate that with the addition of all the people necessary for support, such as carpenters, potters, metalworkers, quarriers, haulers, masons, and setters, the total labor force might have been in the range of twenty thousand.[33]

But what did they eat? It was likely a combination of meat, fish, and bread that provided the energy needed to build one of history's commanding civilizations. There were several clues. Lehner's team unearthed the bones of enough sheep, goats, and cattle to have fed several thousand consumers for a period of sixty years. One attendant archaeologist estimated that eleven cattle and thirty sheep or goats were slaughtered every day. Excavated containers, low benches for working surfaces, and column bases that supported the roof all pointed to a major operation for drying Nile River fish. I have to hand it to the scrupulous archaeologists who located a few fish bones beneath five thousand years of accumulated sand and rubble. And I cannot help but wonder—where did they go to the bathroom? Lehner wondered about sewage, too, but has not figured that out yet.

Lehner's army of archaeologists also unearthed more than five hundred thousand fragments of pottery, more than 50 percent of which came from bread molds. A lot of baking must have been going on. Behind the double walls of an administrative building, probably guarded by royal sentries back in the day, the archaeological team uncovered seven, or possibly eight, mud brick silos. The base of each measures five cubits in diameter, or roughly nine feet. They were probably storage silos for grain. There were querns for grinding flour in other locations, as well as hearths, huge ash piles, storerooms of bread molds, and several bakeries.

While many of the bake sites scattered about the Lost City were of the small household variety, two industrial-size bakeries were extensively excavated on the south side of the hypostyle hall. They appear to be the oldest in ancient Egypt. Lehner and his team unearthed enough baking accoutrements to suggest how bread was made, even without existing recipes or the means to determine if leavening was used.

Inside each bakery he found massive round-bottomed ceramic vats, about the size you would choose for a movie set if you wanted to tie a hero and heroine together in a cooking pot for cannibals preparing to boil them into soup, maybe chest high with a wide enough diameter to float some whole onions and carrots around the ensnared duo. These vats were buried halfway into the shop floor, perhaps to make them easier to lean into. Where their bases had cracked, they had been repaired with pieces of limestone and granite.

Lehner thought that the broken vat bottoms might have come from overexuberant kneading. Lehner wondered if workers hopped in to knead with their feet. I emailed Lehner later to ask if the buried vats might also have made stirring easier. He dug through his memories and agreed: stirring or scraping the vats was very likely. "In at least one, maybe two, instances we found large triangular flint scrapers, which the bakers might have used for scraping the interior walls of the vats. [The scrapers were] shoved right down into the ash against the exterior wall of the vat," he told me. "But we also found, tucked into the dark ash at the base of the fieldstone walls, large bivalve shells, which might work better as scoops."[34]

The artistic and ceramic evidence from the era suggests that baking was accomplished in large, crude ceramic cones, larger, in fact, than those discovered in the Amarna Workmen's site. Labeled *bedja* in tomb scenes, hundreds of thousands of them were discovered at the Lost City of Giza. They were heavy and unwieldy. Empty, the largest weighed 26.5 pounds, about the same weight as three gallons of water. Evidence from other archaeological digs from Elephantine Island in southern Egypt all the way to Palestine in the north suggests that *bedja* were used in bread baking across the region for nearly five hundred years throughout the second half of the 2000s BCE. Their bell-like shape, however, meant that when filled with dough, they could not stand up on their pointy ends or lie on their sides without losing their contents. It was a puzzle that took Lehner some time to unravel.

Ancient tomb scenes show workmen pouring batter-like dough into *bedja*. Other scenes depict *bedja* stacked upside down preheating over an open fire. Lehner discovered upside-down *bedja* inside Giza fireplaces. In the Giza bakeries, two rows of depressions, looking like oversize egg cartons, had been dug into the floor to serve as receptacles for the heated *bedja*, holding them plumb. The preheated cones, full of dough, were covered with preheated covers, probably inverted *bedja*, and then covered with heated coals.

Lehner answered one more question that had gnawed at me from the earliest days of my research. When was salt added to the recipe for bread? According to Lehner, ancient Egyptians "could have easily had salt from saline lake beds, especially in the desert. Limestone, which made up the major part of the Egyptian table-land, is naturally laden with salt, as is sedimentary rock from sea sediments."[35] Nearly all the pieces were in place: flour, salt, water, and bread molds. But was there sourdough?

I N T H E F A L L of 1991, after reading a short inner-page article in the *Idaho Statesman* about Mark Lehner's discovery of the ancient Giza bakeries, Dr. Ed Wood, a retired pathologist, micro-biologist, and sourdough enthusiast, asked the same question I was asking: were ancient Egyptian bakers using sourdough?

Wood thought that sourdough bread in ancient Egypt was not only possible, it was likely. In the introduction to his book *World Sourdoughs from Antiquity*, Wood described how he dialed direct to Cairo to propose to Lehner a sourdough bake-off using the techniques of ancient Egypt and contemporary native Egyptian microbes.[36]

First, Wood secured fifty pounds of emmer flour, which was no easier for Wood than it had been for Samuel. Emmer, then and now, is grown sparingly around the world. Wood sourced his from Turkey. Next, he needed to sterilize the flour; he wanted to be pos-itive that he was raising his bread with genuine wild Giza bacteria and yeast, not with organisms that were clinging to tiny specks of Turkish flour. He couldn't precook the flour, a technique certain to toast any existing yeast to death, because that would ruin what little gluten the emmer wheat contained. His solution was to nuke it.

To test his technique for sterilizing emmer, Wood placed samples of flour in glass jars and exposed them to 50,000, 100,000, and 150,000 rads of cesium radiation, enough to eliminate cells found in blood. He tested his results by placing samples of irradiated flour on petri dishes with nutrient solutions. It took several days for microscopic organisms to get going—about the same amount of time it takes to launch a sourdough starter in a mash of flour and water—and to Wood's surprise, not a single sample was sterile. Every petri dish grew something.

Finally, Wood determined that if he exposed his full bag of flour to 500,000 rads for twelve hours and then sealed it tight, he would arrive in Egypt with sterile flour. It was a level of radiation, he reported in his book, just below that which changed the color of his glass jars from clear to brown. He tested his flour, too, by making bread with it afterward and was satisfied that the flour itself remained unaltered.

After Wood arrived in Egypt, Wood and Lehner constructed a replica of the Giza bakeries in the fields beneath the Saqqara bluffs. In so doing, they discovered that the internal walls of the ancient bakery, which were low and flat and roughly equivalent to the perfect height for a modern countertop, provided ideal work surfaces. Wood employed a Cairo ceramicist to construct a series of cones to approximate *bedja*. Then he grew some sourdough.

In *World Sourdoughs from Antiquity*, Wood described a large date palm growing above the balcony of an upper-level room of the Mena House Oberoi, the hotel where he was staying. "Huge succulent clumps of ripening dates oozed juices and odors that wafted by on the hot, incoming breezes," he wrote of the spot he selected. "I have never seen a more fertile or lush environment." Wood was confident that his balcony dates would be coated with wild yeast.

Wood exposed a mixture of boiled water and sterile flour to the elements beneath the tree and waited. By the second day, he had bubbles. By the third, he was dealing with a "first-rate active culture." Making authentic Giza bread was pretty straightforward after that. With Lehner looking on, Wood mixed water, salt, and a dozen different ratios of emmer and barley flour, an experimental range he hoped would approximate what Gizan bakers might have used. No written recipes have ever been uncovered by archaeologists. He infected each mixture with a glob of his House Oberoi sourdough.

Tomb wall paintings and excavations reveal a much clearer understanding of how bread was baked than how dough was prepared. With these tomb wall directions in mind, Wood placed dough into thirteen *bedja* and waited for the dough to rise. When each *bedja* was nearly full, he placed hot coals into dimples he had dug into a field near the Saqqara bluffs and lowered the cones into them. He then carefully placed tightly fitted, preheated cones over the cooking dough, packed additional radiating coals around the pots, and waited.

As a practicing scientist, Wood could not resist two additional items. He made one loaf of white bread as a control, using a starter he had worked with before. That one had to work. He also heated an empty *bedja* with a tiny hole in the lid, through which he inserted a thermocouple. How else to know at what temperature he was cooking? The internal temperature rose to 350 degrees Fahrenheit. Perfect.

The loaves cooked for ninety minutes. When Wood pulled them from their pots, he had thirteen golden, aromatic, conical breads made from varying combinations of emmer and barley. The freshly emergent bread crackled and emitted the delectable smell of warm baked wheat. At the time, it was as close as anyone had ever come to reenacting bread-baking practices that had taken place at that exact location five thousand years prior. With the exception of the pure barley loaf, which unsurprisingly failed to rise at all,

Wood wrote, "All the breads were proclaimed entirely edible by an enthusiastic audience [of archaeologists and field workers], and the demonstration a complete success."

Ancient Egypt could have supported the world's first sourdough bakeries, but Wood's experiment was not exactly proof that it did. Comparable loaves could also have been made without leavens. As far as I know, no one has tried to make an unleavened bread in a replica of an Egyptian clay pot. Nevertheless, Ed Wood's experiment made it clear that sourdough emmer bread was entirely possible. His breads looked right and, to him, tasted right.

In a newsletter he issued in which he described the experiment, Lehner was less keen. "The bread that we made in our bakery model was a heavy sourdough loaf," he wrote. "It was less-than-delightful to eat and more importantly, it obviously was not quite the right formula. We let the dough stand too long and the lactobacilli, which live alongside the yeast, took over and made the sourdough bread too sour."[37]

I once ran an experiment of my own that reflected the conflicting reports of Wood and Lehner. My daughter, Leah, purchased a Saudi Arabian starter from Ed Wood and gave it to me as a gift. The advertisement for the starter said, "The Saudi sourdough is as desert as its Bedouin baker. It rises moderately well and has one of the most distinctive flavors of all the cultures." It is conceivable that there is something distinctive about Middle Eastern bacteria that Wood appreciated and Lehner did not.

I followed Wood's instructions. I placed the talcum-like contents in a mason jar with three-fourths of a cup of water and one cup of organic white flour. I set the jar on the floor of my oven; the pilot light in my 1950s Chambers stove kept the cooking space at approximately 90 degrees Fahrenheit—an ideal temperature, according to Wood, to foster the growth of bacteria, which sprang to life before the yeast. The lactobacilli rapidly acidified the culture, preventing contamination by non-sourdough organisms.

It worked, but I understood Lehner's complaint about the flavor of the bread that Wood made for him in Giza. In the first twenty-four hours, the mixture smelled like muck that had ripened between my toes and then mated with bacteria from a sewage treatment plant. The concoction had separated into loose curds and a whey-colored liquid, like moldy vichyssoise. Small bubbles appeared at the top and popped occasionally. The whole thing looked and smelled like a Superfund site. At the end of the first day, as my eyes watered, I removed one-half of the original mixture and funneled it into an empty seltzer bottle that I resealed as quickly as I could.

On the second day, according to the directions suggested by Wood, the wild yeast in the mixture was supposed to flourish. By the time forty-eight hours had passed, I was greeted by baby vomit. I gagged. My son gagged. My daughter had to feed it for me.

I repeated the feeding every twelve hours for three days: three-fourths of a cup of water and one cup of white flour. Finally, I was ready to bake bread. I poured half my starter into a bowl and kept half in a jar. By this stage the microscopic cells in my jar were most definitely alive; they had converted my flour and water into a stretchy, single-minded mass. Imagine pizza dough tossed high into the air, expanding with each circle but never ripping. It was that tight. In my case, however, Saudi Arabia smelled like watery yogurt, stained my fingers with that odor, and existed as one girthy cable of dough, even when poured. I was expecting a loaf that was chewy, authentic, and hearty.

Six hours after assembling my dough, I had almost no rise. I baked it anyway and was relieved when the house smelled only like baking bread, rather than like the inside of a yogurt maker. The bread goldened and expanded slightly in the oven. It tasted a bit like cheese and was as dense as a foam bat. It was not nearly as good as the two loaves of beer-corn-rye-potato-molasses bread I made at the same time with my Cripple Creek starter.

After a month of getting to know one another, I cooked my first real success with Saudi Arabia. I made flawless injera, an Ethiopian flatbread. It is interesting to note that nearly all modern injera recipes attempt to create the taste of sourdough; either the recipe calls for yeast and asks the cook to wait three days for the batter to become sour, or it shortcuts the process with acid additions of lemon or vinegar. Injera, like most breads before the advent of commercial yeast, was meant to be made from sourdough. While a spicy Ethiopian chicken stew boiled away on the back burner, I ladled sourdough batter into a heated frying pan. Each flatbread was done in five minutes, thin as a crepe, white as a cloud, porous as a sponge, soft as a down pillow, and stretchy as a boll of cotton. Many years later, now that its flavors have mellowed, my Saudi Arabian starter is my go-to for pitas, fry breads, and pizza crusts.

There has been a recent attempt to make authentic sourdough bread that might really taste like bread eaten in ancient Egypt. In 2019, Jonathan "Seamus" Blackley, inventor of the Xbox, partnered with a biologist and an archaeologist to bake their version. They extracted dormant yeast adhered to ancient Egyptian ceramics stored at Boston's Museum of Fine Arts and Harvard University's Peabody Museum. The yeast, they discovered, would revive only when grown on emmer, which strongly suggested that their technique had in fact captured cells that were thousands of years old. Like Ed Wood before him, Blackley baked in a clay *bedja* surrounded by hot coals. "I've made a fuck-ton of sourdough," said Blackley, "but this was different." The ancient loaves were sweeter and chewier than the standard modern sourdough, with a smooth crumb like that of white bread.[38]

Even if DNA evidence confirms that Blackley's sourdough bread was leavened by yeast that gave its last exhalations five thousand years ago, the scientific and archaeological evidence of a first sourdough remains difficult to pin down. At this point, I knew how wheat was domesticated, how it was made into flour, and where and when the first breads that were not simply porridge poured onto a hot rock were first baked. But proof of the first sourdough culture in the form of writings or hieroglyphics was going to have to wait for the Greeks.

A note on recipes in this book: *The sourdough recipes in this book should be considered approximations, difficult as it is for cooks who are precisionists, like my dad was. Some starters act quickly; others are slow and methodical. Experiment. If your bread does not meet your expectations on the first try, do something a little different the next time you try it. You will observe that some measurements are in US customary, some in metric, and some recipes are without any measurements at all to reflect the intentions of the original recipe developer and the age in which the recipe was prepared.*

STARTING A STARTER
Yield: 1 sourdough starter

To make your own sourdough starter, you need only repeat what ancient bakers discovered entirely by accident. The precise measurements are not essential. You are reproducing a technique that is six thousand years old. Because microbial populations increase rapidly, demanding more and more food to stay alive, most modern descriptions for starting a starter advise you to discard some mixture daily to avoid doubling your feedings as the size of your microbial population also doubles.

> 500 grams white bread flour
> 500 grams whole wheat flour
> Water, room temperature or 80°F (to speed things along)

Day 1. In a large bowl, mix together the white bread flour and whole wheat flour. This will be the food stock for your growing population of microbes. To rouse your microbes from their dormancy, place 100 grams of the flour mixture and 100 grams of water into a small bowl. Use your hands to mix them together.

Cover the bowl with a porous cloth or paper towel, held in place with a rubber band. Place the bowl in a warm location, out of direct sunlight, for three days, or until bubbles form on top of the mixture and the dough puffs. This will happen more quickly in warm temperatures.

Day 3. Remove the covering from the bowl. Discard or compost about 80 percent of the mixture. Feed it with 50 grams of the reserved flour mixture and 50 grams of water. Stir or mix by hand.

Cover the bowl with a cloth or paper towel. Place in a warm location, out of direct sunlight, for 24 hours.

Days 4–10 (more or less). At about the same time every day, repeat the steps from day 3. Depending on the temperature of your house and the serendipity of the species of yeast and bacteria that colonize your starter, after a week has passed, your culture should start to rise and fall every day. There will be bubbles of carbon dioxide visible throughout the starter and on the surface and a black liquid called *hooch* may begin to collect. It should begin to smell sour.

To bake or store. When your starter rises and falls with regularity and smells sour, it is time to take a couple of tablespoons of starter and infect a roughly 3:2 ratio of flour to water. For example, in a 1-quart mason jar, mix 1 cup of water with your starter. Stir. Then add 1½ cups of flour. Mix. In 12 hours, it will be ready to use in a recipe. You may also put it in the refrigerator until you are ready to bake with it. Alternatively, you may divide it: use some to bake and store some for later.

OPEN-FLAME SOURDOUGH FLATBREADS WITH OLIVE OIL
Yield: 2 dozen flatbreads

This recipe encourages you to cook over an open flame, as the ancient Egyptians might have, or as Bedouin and people throughout the Middle East do to this day. You will need a *saj,* or wok; these flatbreads can also be made in a cast-iron pan or on a griddle. If your flatbreads are firm enough (which depends upon the initial hydration of your starter and the kind of flour you use), you can fry your flatbreads on a slatted grill. The finished flatbreads are crisp where bubbles have formed, very chewy, lightly coated with oil, and slightly smoky from the fire. They are excellent for tearing apart and dipping into hummus, roasted eggplant spreads, za'atar, or additional olive oil. They taste best when they are still warm.

Sourdough starter, refrigerated
3½ cups water, divided
4 cups white flour, divided
3 cups whole wheat flour, divided
2 heaping teaspoons kosher salt
Olive oil, for brushing

Morning, Day 1. Remove the mason jar of starter from the refrigerator. If a black liquid has accumulated on top, pour it off, stir it in, or drink it. (The hooch is slightly alcoholic, but mostly tastes like sourdough starter.)

To the jar of cold starter, add ¾ cup of the water and shake or stir to disperse the starter. Add 1 cup of the white flour and shake or stir until the freshly added flour is combined and no lumps remain. Screw down the cover to the mason jar *loosely.*

Set the jar of mixture on a plate to proof at room temperature for about 12 hours. The mixture should rise substantially inside the jar. If you look through the glass, you should see many bubbles forming. Depending upon the temperature of your kitchen and how frequently you use your starter, it may sink back upon itself by the end of the day, leaving a foam of bubbles on top. As the active starter rises, it may also overflow. Placing the jar with its loose lid on a plate makes for easier cleanup if it does.

Evening, Day 1. Pour the contents from the mason jar into a large bowl. Add 2 cups of the water and stir to combine. Add the remaining 3 cups of white flour and stir to combine. Transfer 1 cup of the loose dough to a clean 1-quart mason jar. Screw the cap on loosely. The bacteria and yeast will feed on the fresh flour overnight and be returned to the refrigerator in the morning. This will be your saved starter for your next bake.

Cover the bowl with plastic wrap and leave the mixture alone to proof at room temperature until morning, about 12 hours.

Morning, Day 2. Refrigerate the mason jar containing your saved starter.

To the bowl, add the salt and the remaining ¾ cup of water. Add 2 cups of the whole wheat flour, 1 cup at a time. Knead with a spoon after each addition to incorporate. Flour a clean work surface with the remaining 1 cup of whole wheat flour. When the dough is too stiff to mix by hand, transfer it to the floured work surface and knead again.

Knead the dough for 20 minutes. Transfer it to a lightly oiled bowl to prevent sticking, then cover in plastic wrap. Allow to rise for 4 to

6 hours, until the dough feels soft and puffy. It will not double in size but will grow by at least half. A finger pressed gently into its surface will leave an indentation.

Grease a baking sheet. Gently scrape the dough onto a clean countertop.

While keeping the bulk of the dough covered with plastic to keep it from drying out, cut off hunks larger than a golf ball but smaller than a tennis ball. Gently roll into a ball shape and place on the prepared baking sheet with about 1 inch of open space around each ball to accommodate spreading. You should be able to fit 8 to 10 balls on one sheet.

Cover with plastic. Let rise for 1 to 2 hours, until the balls are pillowy and soft and have increased in size by about 50 percent.

Create a fire that is stinking hot. It can be an open flame in a firepit or a barbecue grill. Place a saj or wok, curved-side up, over the flame. Or bake on a barbecue grill over an open flame or in a cast-iron pan, right-side up.

Using floured hands and a well-floured surface, pat the balls flat on the countertop or between your palms. Brush one side of the flattened bread with olive oil and place it, oil-side down, on the saj. Cook for 1 to 2 minutes, until the bread bubbles. Brush the top of the bread with more oil, then flip and cook for 1 more minute. Remove the breads from the heat and serve warm.

CHAPTER 2

BREAD AND HUNGER

ALMOST A YEAR TO THE DAY AFTER MY FIRST PHONE
call to Douglas Steeples asking if he could recall who had
brought him a sourdough starter, he sent me an excited
email. The subject line read, "I've finally gotten to the bottom of
our search." Steeples told me that while he was teaching history at
Earlham College in Richmond, Indiana, a former Air Force pilot
named Dale Noyd joined Earlham's faculty sometime in the late
1960s or early 1970s. According to Steeples, just before coming to
Earlham, the US Air Force had held Noyd under house arrest in
Colorado Springs after his opposition to the Vietnam War led him
to refuse orders handed to him by his superiors. Noyd arrived in
Indiana with a sourdough starter and a story of its origins: the 1893
Gold Rush in Cripple Creek, which is only an hour's drive from the
Air Force Academy. Together, Noyd and Steeples used to lead wil-
derness expeditions for students. They did a lot of outdoor cooking,
and Noyd's Cripple Creek sourdough was part of their repertoire.

Finding information about Dale Noyd was not difficult. He
had died in 2007 at the age of seventy-three, and several obituaries
were available on the internet. Even the *New York Times* recounted

a brief description of his life. Noyd's opposition to America's war in Vietnam was so groundbreaking in its novelty that his court case reached both the highest military tribunal (he lost, which is why the US Air Force imposed his house arrest) and the US Supreme Court.

I was on the trail again. First, I had to figure out how and when Noyd was released by the Air Force and then what he was doing in a defunct gold-mining town called Cripple Creek. I also hoped to figure out who gave him a sourdough starter and who kept it alive from 1893 until Noyd's arrival. If I could trace the starter back to gold rush days, there seemed a chance I might identify the miner hoping to make a fortune who had brought it to Cripple Creek in the first place. While I sought out Dale Noyd's family to hear what they might recall, I carried on with my research into the movement of bread making from the Fertile Crescent westward, toward North America.

In 332 BCE, Greece conquered ancient Egypt. One would think ancient Greeks, aware of Egyptian baking techniques and smart as they were, would have relied upon a similar diet. However, most Greeks were poor—peasants, farmers, field hands, and their children, everyone except a small handful of elites—and did not consume much wheat bread. They survived instead on dense barley cakes called *maza*. Wealthy Athenians, on the other hand, ate wheat breads, and their philosophers and dieticians made it quite clear that it was good stuff. In *Problems*, Aristotle pronounced wheat far more nourishing than barley. In the early third century BCE, the dietician Diphilus of Siphnos called wheat bread "superior for nourishment and digestibility and altogether better."[1] Greek philosophers, alas, did not mention whether bread for the wealthy was leavened.

If bread was good and *maza* was just something you ate to stay alive, why didn't the ancient Greeks eat more bread? The answer lies in their soil or, more accurately, their rather imprudent disposal of soil. Greek denudation was so complete, and in many places so repetitive, that in most of Greece, there wasn't enough topsoil remaining to grow the wheat necessary to make decent bread. Varro (116–27 BCE), Virgil (70–19 BCE), and Lucretius (ca. 99–55 BCE) all blamed soil loss on overgrazing herds of goats and sheep and shepherds who burned down high forests to expand grazing grounds.[2] Additional timber was felled for fuel to heat the kilns that made Greek ceramics, pottery, bricks, tiles, statues, utensils, and weapons. Net result? Bare mountains.

Plato described what were to him the olden days, when Greece's hillsides were carpeted in forests and its homes carried roofs of timber. When the trees were cut and deluges descended from above, he lamented the fate of Greece's ancient topsoil:

> *The earth has fallen away all round and sunk out of sight. The consequence is, that in comparison of what then was, there are remaining only the bones of the wasted body, as they may be called, as in the case of small islands, all the richer and softer parts of the soil having fallen away, and the mere skeleton of the land being left.[3]*

No soil, no wheat. In contrast to wheat, barley is a plant that can take a joke, getting by with less water and fewer nutrients than wheat. As far as grains go, barley is a wild goat while wheat is a pampered dairy cow. Wheat breads were around in ancient Greece, but they were not a dietary staple unless you could pay big drachmas.[4]

T HE ANCIENT EMPIRE of Rome, located across the Adriatic Sea from Greece and the next great dynasty on the Mediterranean, faced the same constraints as its Greek predecessor: much of Italy's landscape includes steep slopes and highly erodible soil, and it suffers torrential winter rains. Romans, however, did not waste their time on philosophy any more than they did on barley gruel. They reckoned a solution to the wheat problem. They were so awash in wheat that they could distribute huge sacks of golden wheat berries to the freemen of Rome.

Where did all that grain come from? Even more puzzling is how it got there and how Rome's leaders managed to gather enough wheat that Roman bakers churned out seemingly endless supplies of bread. Juvenal, a Roman satirist and poet (first century to early second century CE), noticing the surfeit of bread in Rome, hurled an insult at Roman leaders that lives on to this day. He suggested that old codgers were buying votes for office with offers of *panem et circenses*, bread and circuses.[5] According to historians and archaeologists, the bread exchanged for votes was sourdough.

I did the math. At year 0 on the Christian calendar, the best estimate of Rome's population was between 750,000 and 1 million people.[6] Rome's bureaucrats reported that both Julius Caesar and Augustus gave free bread to 320,000 citizens per month at the rate of five modii—the equivalent of about a peck, or ten gallons—per capita. Typically, wheat at 13.5 percent moisture content weighs fifteen pounds a peck. Run out all the multiplications, and each person's free allotment was seventy-five pounds of wheat a month, enough to feed an extended family. Continue the arithmetic of five modii every month for 320,000 men, and nineteen million modii a year were needed. That is more than 120,000 tons.

Professor G. E. Rickman, a British scholar of ancient Rome, was so intrigued by the question of bread supplies, he wrote two books and numerous articles about grain in ancient Rome. In one, Rickman wrote, "Whatever its other drawbacks, and grain is seriously deficient in vitamins A, C, and D, it was supremely important as fuel for humans. . . . It had to be eaten in quantity throughout the year by the majority of people, sometimes with very little else by way of supplement, simply to keep them alive."[7]

Bringing bread to Roman masses was not simply a question of volume; it was also a question of how to transport a truly finicky product. Without modern preservatives, bread develops mold too quickly to withstand being transported a long distance, so wheat berries, the seeds of wheat, were shipped instead. Except wheat is heavy and does not stack well. If piled loosely, wheat berries can flow like liquid. If placed in a box to a height of six feet, wheat exerts a pressure of 240 pounds per square foot on the floor. Because the berries are round and have a tendency to flow outward, they also exert up to two-thirds that much pressure on the walls of a vessel.

Still, bread was so important, Roman historian Titus Flavius Josephus (37–ca. 100 CE) wrote in *Bellum Judaicum* that Africa fed Rome for two-thirds of the year, while Egypt's Nile River basin was the breadbasket for the remaining third.[8] Moving wheat berries from Africa to Rome was best done by ship, as both stone-lined roads and ox-drawn wheeled carts were impractical forms of conveyance for that much tonnage.

The Roman Empire and its sources of grain.

Some of the ships coming from Alexandria loaded with wheat nourished by the Nile's floodwaters were gigantic, capable of carrying one thousand tons. Rickman calculated the number of ships destined for the Italian coast to have been in the thousands. Analysis of inscriptions, pictures, and statuettes suggests that every year porters hauled six million sacks up ship gangplanks to Roman storehouses.[9]

The trip from Egypt went like this: as soon as spring wheat was harvested in the Nile River Valley, it was put into containers, which were carried by pack animals to a village threshing floor. Once threshed and winnowed, some wheat berries were stored for next year's planting, but most were transported on donkey trains or camel caravans to the closest port along the Nile. Small boats ferried bags of grain to larger boats anchored midriver, which when fully loaded, journeyed downstream to Alexandria. It was important to move quickly and keep the grain dry. Roman procurators waited anxiously to fill great granaries in the Neapolis and Mercurium neighborhoods of the coastal city of Alexandria, whereupon the deliverer was handed a Roman receipt.[10]

Nothing more accurately describes Rome's maddening efficiency than this shipper's receipts from 211 to 212 CE. It is clear from the following how Western bureaucracies—think the Internal Revenue Service—can trace their roots to ancient Rome.

Given to Didymus, strategos of the Oxyhynchite name, by Posidonius also called Triadelphus, master of eight boats carrying 40,000 artabae [an artaba is an Egyptian dry measurement equivalent to approximately twenty-nine to thirty-nine liters] in the Neaspoleos administration, I have received and had measured out to me the amount ordered by the strategos (named) and by the basilicogrammateus (named) of the same name, from the stiologoi (named) of the Psobthis district, in accordance with the order of his excellency of the procurater Neaspoleos, from public granaries of the said village at the river Tomis (a specified amount of) wheat, produce of the year (specified), unadulterated, with no admixture of earth or barley, untrodden and sifted, which I will carry to Alexandria and deliver to the officials of the administration safely, free of all risk, and damage by ship. This receipt is valid, there being three copies of it, of which I have issued two to you the strategos and one to the sitologoi. Date.[11]

Surprisingly, nothing in the archaeological record explains how grain was packaged for its Mediterranean crossing. The grain had to be kept dry; moistened grain, in addition to running the risk of spoiling, swells to twice its original size, enough to split the sides of a ship. It had to be stored above the bilgewater, but well protected from wave splashes. Under no circumstances could it be permitted to shift. Once rolling in one direction, flowing grain can easily capsize a boat. Rickman's best guess, based on partial evidence but mostly on logic, was that the grain remained in sacks, the hold was filled to capacity, and there were probably partitions so that in the event of settling or a slightly underfilled ship, loose grain was not free to flow a very long distance.

Sailing 1,200-ton freighters from Alexandria to Italy was painstaking. The prevailing winds of the Mediterranean are westerly, blowing predominantly out of the north and west. Sailboats cannot sail into the wind, and square-rigged sailboats can get to within only seven points of the wind. The trip was best accomplished by either hugging the north coast around Cyprus and along Turkey or poking along the north coast of Africa. Either way, it was a journey requiring at least a month, sometimes two. The time and effort were worth it. Historically speaking, a well-fed population is far more docile than a hungry one.

Grain ships were off-loaded in the ports of Ostia or the aptly named city of Portus. From the granaries in the port, sacks of wheat were transferred to smaller boats especially designed to carry goods up the Tiber River. If one of these rivercraft could carry sixty to seventy tons, Rickman calculated that there must have been four thousand boatloads annually, or about eleven daily, headed upstream. One ship per hour, every day of the year, would have unloaded grain just for the city of Rome. Near the Aventine Hill in Rome, the grain was distributed to markets, where it was purchased by bakers.

A second- or third-century wall painting from Ostia depicting a Roman merchant ship being loaded with grain.

According to Pliny the Elder, Roman bread was leavened with sourdough. Born in 23 CE, Pliny the Elder was among the Roman scholars who studied and recorded everything he believed was known or knowable to a Roman of his generation. Between 77 and 79 CE, he published the *Naturalis Historia*, which to this day remains the most voluminous written work to survive from the era. His encyclopedia runs to thirty-seven books arranged into ten volumes.

Book XI, chapters 26 and 27, describes various kinds of bread and how to make them. Here we learn things such as the whiter the flour, the higher its cost. Coarsely ground wheat, heavy with bran, or wheat mixed with inferior flours, like barley, was food for peasants and slaves; wholemeal and bran bread was called *sordidus*; unleavened and probably very dense bread resembling today's health bars was called *athletarum*; rustic breads, aptly called *panis plebeius*, were concocted from crudely sifted flour containing milling waste; and *panis secondaris* was prepared from second-rate-quality flour.[12] *Panis palatius*, made from the finest flours that passed through the thinnest of gauzes after milling, was reserved for imperial households.

Pliny also described oyster bread, cake bread, hurry bread, oven bread, tin bread, mold bread, and new to Rome, Parthian bread. "Parthian bread is remarkably light and full of holes," he wrote.[13] I wish he had more to say, but with many more volumes to write and his desire to remain dispassionate, I can only suppose that he liked Parthian bread nearly as much as he coveted desserts. Regarding enriched doughs, Pliny wrote, "Some persons knead the dough with eggs or milk, and butter even has been employed for the purpose by nations that have had leisure to cultivate the arts of peace, and to give their attention to the art of making pastry."[14]

Pliny devoted all of chapter 26 (of book XVIII, *The Natural History of Grain*) to various kinds of leaven, and here is where sourdough makes its first incontrovertible appearance in historical texts. He wrote that mixing millet with freshly crushed wheat and letting it soak for three days can make leaven. The crushed wheat berries release a syrupy liquid highly desirable to yeast, and three days is, incidentally, the amount of time necessary for establishing a sourdough culture of yeast and bacteria. While this method, by his accounting, made the best bread, it could be used only at the time of what he called "vintage." Without refrigeration or regular feedings, no sourdough will live very long.

According to Pliny, barley leaven, in contrast to millet and wheat cultures, could be made at any time. Barley was first baked and stored as two-pound cakes. When it was called for, it was mixed with water, sealed in a vessel until it turned quite sour, and then blended with flour appropriate to the kind of bread about to be baked. All of this must have been a kind of magic to Pliny. Good as he was at writing encyclopedias, it was another two millennia before a self-taught Dutch scientist named Antonie van Leeuwenhoek peered through a microscope to observe the organisms capable of raising bread. I'll get to van Leeuwenhoek in due time.

Almost as an afterthought, Pliny described a porridge-like mixture of meal, barley leaven, and salt that turned sour and was used by most bakers of his day. He wrote that "in most cases, however, they do not warm it at all, but only make use of a little of the dough that has been kept from the day before. It is very evident that the principle which causes the dough to rise is of an acid nature, and it is equally evident that those persons who are dieted upon fermented bread are stronger in body." Though he did not name it, Pliny the Elder described sourdough culture.

A GREAT DEAL IS known about bread baking in ancient Rome from archaeologists working in Pompeii, 160 miles southeast of the capital. There are several reasons Pompeii serves as the archetype for what we know about bread production in the Roman Empire. First, the city's bakeries were entombed, in the middle of their morning production schedule, by the volcanic blast of Mount Vesuvius in 79 CE. Second, a PhD student produced a detailed study of everything associated with every bakery in the city. And third, what they said about Pompeii was written on the front of a travel lodge in Nuceria: "Traveler, you enjoy bread at Pompeii. But at Nuceria you drink."[15]

On August 20, 79 CE, small earthquakes deep inside Mount Vesuvius were no longer ignorable. The cobbled streets of the city swayed unnervingly; thunder boomed from the mountaintop. On

August 24, rising pressure created by growing pockets of steam blew the peak from the swollen mountain, not unlike a baking loaf of bread insufficiently slashed for expansion. A turbulent mixture of gases, ash, cinders, and pulverized rock at more than 1,400 degrees Fahrenheit exploded into the atmosphere. It swirled fifty thousand to one hundred thousand feet above the summit, reaching the upper stratosphere.[16] One toxic swirl raced across the ground surface with such force that it rose up and over hills and down slopes at boiling speeds in excess of sixty miles an hour, destroying the town of Herculaneum in a front of poison gas.[17] Among the victims of the blast was Pliny the Elder.

When Mount Vesuvius finally finished emptying its gut of excess bile and gas, Pompeii was encapsulated beneath nearly ten feet of debris. More than one thousand dead have been unearthed, many in futile poses; some skeletons were found holding their skulls in their hands in an attempt to protect themselves against the falling ash. Pompeiian archaeologists also uncovered thirty-three bakeries. Inside one of them, eighty-five loaves of bread were severely overcooked when the baker ran away and the bakery was covered in smoldering ash.

Archaeologist Betty Jo Mayeske analyzed Pompeii's bakeries in her PhD thesis, which contained a full description of the baking process, from the arrival of wheat at the miller to the salesclerk handing warm bread to the customer.[18] According to Mayeske, the delivery of grain in Pompeii was the same as it was in Rome. Pompeii was a port city, so whole wheat berries arrived on board ships. Bags of grain were carried to market stalls, where bakers haggled with sellers over quality and prices. From the market, slaves hauled modii of wheat to one of the city's thirty-three bakeries.

First, the wheat needed to be milled. In this regard, Pompeiian bakers made advances on the saddle querns used by their Egyptian forebears. The eruption of Vesuvius in 79 CE was not the region's first volcanic explosion, which meant that basalt, perfect for millstones, was abundant in Pompeii. As minerals go, basalt is hard. Even as its face was gradually worn, a bumpy, bubbly, basaltic millstone tended to renew itself as fresh stone was newly exposed. Other rocks used for milling self-polish into smooth, comparatively useless planes.

Huge mills were constructed to provide milling capacity far beyond what a hand quern could process. The bottom millstone, called a *meta*, was placed on a pile of rubble larger than the stone it held. Mayeske noted the dimensions of the foundation: nine feet, six inches in diameter by one foot, six inches high.[19] The upper millstone, called a *catillus*, was also formerly lava but was shaped like an hourglass, narrow at the waist and wider at the shoulder and hips. A double cone shape was achieved with two stones of identical form, one inverted on the other. They were both hollow, so the upper stone could serve as a hopper, a hollow tube for funneling grain toward the grinding surface.

The most important features of the *catillus* were the two square sockets into which long wooden poles could be affixed. The poles were harnessed to donkeys or pushed by slaves who were driven around in a circle. Grain was poured into the hopper, and flour was taken from the surface of the *meta*.

Adjacent to the mill station was evidence of kneading machines. This confirmed that the substance being baked was wheat bread, which contains gluten that needs to be massaged if the bread is to rise. And if it is going to rise, as Pliny noted in his *Naturalis Historia*, there needs to be the addition of a leavening agent: a little bit of dough taken from a previous batter. The kneading machine found in one Pompeiian bakery was an ingenious device.[20] A shaft of wood was inserted into a round lava bowl with a socket in its center. The shaft had horizontal arms for the baker to apply torque; at its base, inside the bowl, the shaft had wooden teeth that pushed, pulled, and stretched the dough.

Pompeiian mills. Oven in background, last operating 79 CE.

The ovens of Pompeii were not much different than brick pizza ovens of today. A flat stone slab rested over a firebox. A brick arch retained heat, and a wooden peel was used to introduce breads to the heart of the oven and then withdraw them as they finished. Risen dough ready for baking arrived from the kneading room, where it was passed to the baker. He slid uncooked breads into the oven and waited for them to swell as steam trapped inside tiny bubbles of dough expanded like volcanic gases in the heat. Adjacent to many of the ovens were water basins. Though Mayeske was not certain what the water was used for, the addition of water to the oven would surely have increased oven spring, the rapid expansion of breads deep inside hot ovens, yielding lighter and larger loaves. The baker then handed finished breads to a receiver in a storage room opposite the kneading room without ever leaving the front of the oven.

In addition to breads, Mayeske reported that Pompeiians liked fanciful designs and sweets. Mayeske found pastry molds shaped like a pig, a griffin's head, Medusa, a dressed hare, and a ham. There were even three intact pastries that survived the volcano. One looked like a slice of loaf cake, the second looked like a miniature bread with an amply configured crust, and the third sure looked like a jelly donut. Think of it: at the end of a long day of work in Pompeii, a person could lace up his leather sandals and pick up a dozen jelly donuts on the way home. Not a bad life, if you ignore the smoking mountaintop just outside the city.

One piece of evidence suggested that miller-bakers thought of themselves as he-men. They managed donkeys—notoriously stubborn, self-righteous animals—and slaves, sieved flour, kneaded scores of loaves of bread, fired their ovens, kept the temperature reliably constant, and stood before an open furnace for hours on end. Additionally, commercial bakers the world over worked at night so that warm bread was available first thing in the morning. Over the arch of many a Pompeiian oven there was what one archaeologist simply referred to as "a regular oven appurtenance": a phallus.[21] That's one way to let customers know what kind of man bakes their bread.

B EFORE DEPARTING THE Mediterranean basin to follow the track of sourdough into Europe, it pays to make one last stop in the Middle East, where sourdough bread was infused with religious significance. Here, a little more than two thousand years ago, in an eastern outpost of a sea monitored by Rome, a baby was born of a virgin mother. His birthplace is now a UNESCO-nominated World Heritage site, the Church of the Nativity in Bethlehem. Interestingly, one translation of Bethlehem, *Bet Lechem*, from Hebrew to English means House of Bread. The life of Jesus is as intertwined with bread as the braids of a Sabbath challah.

I once visited the church while leading a trip for students, and though sourdough research was not part of my agenda, stopping for local bread and food was very much part of my itinerary and was first up after the church. I had warned the women among us to dress modestly, but I did not realize that men wearing shorts would not be tolerated. We purchased scarves from vendors in the court-yard and wrapped ourselves in skirts as best we could. Our hairy ankles and calves peeked above our hiking boots as we entered the rather lightless church.

I brought my students to the fourteen-point silver star on the floor that marks the spot above the grotto where Mary supposedly placed her newborn child. Hanging above the star burned fifteen silver lamps: six maintained by Greeks, five by Armenians, and four by Latins—a division of standpoints that extends to their perspectives on Jesus's relationship to bread.

As at most tourist destinations, crowds of people were battling for the best angle at which to aim their camera phones. My students joined the fray. Afterward, we left the church and navigated loaded pushcarts, shouting merchants, mothers, toddlers, and young men carrying large crates and made our way to a bakery. I wanted to offer everyone the opportunity to switch from sight and sound to taste and smell.

Today, Bethlehem's bread is round, hand formed, warm, earthy, and deeply pungent, with the aroma of freshly harvested local wheat. It somehow tastes even more rewarding when you have just stepped out of Bethlehem's crowded souk into a tiny storefront bakery. Palestinian bakers are not immune to modernization, and their bread today is leavened with yeast. What it has going for it that Western yeasted breads do not is that it is fresh from an oven.

Arabic coffee rivals freshly baked bread for the finest aroma of Bethlehem. The beans used are roasted nearly to the color of charcoal, then mixed just before being ground with handfuls of pungent pods of cardamom. The best location for a cup of Arabic coffee in Bethlehem—maybe in the entire Middle East—is in the

King Solomon Bazaar across from the city's main parking garage. What I learned from Adnan Al Korna, the bazaar's owner, is that making good coffee relies on the same key ingredient necessary for making good sourdough bread: patience.

Mr. Al Korna is lanky, dark skinned, and consummately erudite. On my first visit, he offered me coffee. When I told Adnan that his coffee was the best Arabic coffee I'd ever tasted, he readily concurred. His coffee was velvety. Its spicy bouquet lingered about my forehead rather than coating my mouth with the thick coffee paste so typical of coffee made with the grounds still present. "Making good coffee," he told me, "takes time." The pleasure of Arabic coffee is further enhanced if it is drunk slowly, as the locals do. The cups are tiny, but the conversation is long—the diametric opposite of Starbucks, where you can pick up a thirty-ounce trenta to go.

Revived by hot coffee and fresh bread, I considered what was known of Jesus of Bethlehem, about to become Jesus Christ. Palestine at the time of Jesus's birth was a post in Rome's vast mercantile network surrounding the Mediterranean. Jesus performed many miracles during his life, but only one, apart from his resurrection, was described in all four gospels: feeding the multitude. Jesus was grieving over the death of John the Baptist. He boarded a boat on the Sea of Galilee and docked at a remote location on the western shore to mourn by himself. Ignoring his desire to be alone, crowds of thousands seeking both spiritual and physical nourishment followed him. Jesus's disciples, concerned about crowd control as dusk approached, made a suggestion. "Jesus," they said, "send the crowds home that they may return to their towns to buy themselves food."

Jesus replied, "They do not need to go away. You give them something to eat."

"We have here only five loaves of bread and two fish," they answered.

"Bring them here to me," he said.[22]

Jesus gathered the crowd and asked them to sit. He directed the disciples to break the loaves, eat some, and pass the remainder to someone sitting near to him. In that way, five thousand men and an unknown number of women and children were divinely and corporally satisfied. In the end, there were still twelve baskets of leftover bread. John the Apostle summarized the importance of bread:

> *Jesus said to them, "It is my Father who gives you the true bread from heaven. For the bread of God is that which comes down from heaven and gives life to the world." They said to him, "Sir, give us this bread always." Jesus said to them, "I am the bread of life. Whoever comes to me will never be hungry, and whoever believes in me will never be thirsty."*[23]

It is also possible that the biblical story of loaves and fishes served as metaphor for a population fully familiar with the steps of making sourdough bread. Sourdough culture, like religious belief, can be expanded and shared indefinitely.

Juvenal's critique of Roman leadership, that politicians were buying favor with "bread and circuses," was as appropriate in ancient Palestine as it was in Rome. Palestine's Roman proxy, King Herod, had constructed a hippodrome in Caesarea on the Mediterranean coast. Evidently, neither betting on racing charioteers nor praying at Herod's newly constructed Temple Mount in Jerusalem satisfied a regional hunger for something more substantial. Again, Jesus made a case for spiritual salvation with bread as metaphor.

His disciples came to Jesus, pleading, "Teach us how to pray."[24] Preaching his Sermon on the Mount, Jesus delivered the Lord's Prayer, a prayer for bread:

> *Our Father in heaven,*
> *hallowed be your name,*

your kingdom come,
your will be done
on earth as it is in heaven.
Give us today our daily bread.
Forgive us our debts,
as we also have forgiven our debtors.
And lead us not into temptation,
but deliver us from the evil one.

Dr. Amy-Jill Levine is one of North America's foremost scholars of the historical Jesus. She is a feisty, fast-talking, exceptionally intelligent professor of New Testament studies at Vanderbilt University. She has spent much of her life working to find common language among Jews and Christians. She does it by focusing prodigious energy on researching and explaining the context within which Jesus actually lived. At the start of every lecture, she removes her high-heeled shoes to pad about in stocking feet.

Her interpretation of the central portion of the Lord's Prayer is that to hardworking Jews of the first century, heaven was going to be a feast. In stark contrast to their daily hunger, both spiritual and actual, heaven's table would be a banquet. Thus, "On earth as it is in heaven. Give us today our daily bread."

The Middle East is a land of surprising extremes. The summer produces blistering heat, but winter is bone-chilling, and when it is cold, warm bread can be terrifically satisfying. Jesus and his disciples would have known that. Jesus's many references to bread make more sense the longer you spend in the Middle East, which became clear to me while leading another tour, just north of the Sea of Galilee.

We were on a mountain overlooking the sea, along a spine of hills that includes the mount from which Jesus delivered a sermon blessing the meek—"For they shall," he said, "inherit the earth." It was a lot colder than any of us had expected. A tiny Druze woman huddled beneath a tattered blue tarpaulin was selling bread. She was bundled in a navy floor-length abaya and a white hijab splayed across her shoulders. Her modest blue apron did nothing to keep her clothing from being coated in flour dust.

As she took our order, she beamed a mostly toothless smile and grabbed a handful of white, stretchy dough from a red plastic basin. She patted and stretched and pulled it across a pillowy cushion until she had a floured disk of dough as thin as fabric and wide as a pizza crust. She turned the pillow over a *saj* and dropped the dough onto the heated steel. Within seconds it began to blister. With her bare fingers, she grabbed the bread and flipped it. The flatbread browned on the opposite side. While it was still steaming, she whipped the finished bread onto a piece of foil and poured olive oil over it from a repurposed dish soap dispenser. She slapped on a huge dollop of labneh, a cultured yogurt-like product that is richer and creamier than American yogurt, and sprinkled it with a generous handful of za'atar. With a magician's sleight of hand, she wrapped the sandwich, now warm inside its foil wrapper, and passed it to a customer. The concoction tasted sour, and I suspected that her dough was made from an old sourdough starter, but I do not speak Arabic and had no way of asking.

Warm bread, fresh olive oil, creamy labneh, and za'atar, an indigenous spice mix of thyme, sumac, salt, and sesame seeds, were heavenly and filling. It satisfied the otherworldly craving that emerges when you are cold and tired and standing on the side of a road, feeling vaguely bereft. Jesus and his disciples were fully aware of the fulfillment bread provides.

Bread appeared again in the Last Supper and as sourdough in the Eucharist. As the final days of Jesus's life on earth approached, he was joined by twelve disciples. What he said to them has probably engendered as much writing, analysis, philosophy, and divisiveness as anything else he ever said. Matthew (14:22–24), Mark (26:26–28), Luke (22:19–20), and 1 Corinthians (11:23–25) all reported the same thing: Jesus lifted the bread, gave thanks to God, broke off a piece, and declared, "Take. Eat. This is my body." He lifted a cup of wine, again offered a prayer of thanks, and reinforced, "Drink it all, this is my blood of the covenant."

The first-century letters of Saint Ignatius carried an allusion that many Christian historians consider one of the earliest written references to the Eucharist: "I desire the bread of God, the heavenly bread, the bread of life, which is the flesh of Jesus Christ, the Son of God, who became afterwards of the seed of David and Abraham; and I desire the drink of God, namely his blood, which is incorruptible love and eternal life."[25] In the second century, practice of the Eucharist continued.[26] Saint Justin, who wrote in Palestine in the year 150, and Saint Irenaeus, the bishop of Lyons, France, in the 180s and 190s, both asserted that followers of Christ should make their beliefs physical in addition to metaphysical by taking sanctified wine and bread, the blood and body of their savior.[27]

My addition to the myriad of scholarly texts dedicated to the origins and significance of the Eucharist is a sourdough perspective. Jesus selected two foods that matured, flourished, and were transformed, as if by empyrean power. The transfiguration of grape juice into wine, dough into bread, and that wine and bread into the blood and body of Christ was all the work of the divine.

By specifying that his body was bread, Jesus implied the following: consume me and you, too, can be as eternal as your sourdough starters. And like your starters, pass me from one kitchen to the next, share me with a friend, and they, too, can have immortality that is warm, comfortingly aromatic, and satiating. Eastern branches of early Christianity concurred with this perspective. According to their liturgical history, Eucharistic breads offered to this day as the body of Christ are from sourdoughs that are two thousand years old with origins that can be traced to Christ on the cross.

As Christ's apostles fanned out from the Middle East to spread his word, the Nestorian Church (also known as "Church of the East," "Persian Church," "East Syrian Church," "Chaldean Syrian Church," "Holy Apostolic Catholic Assyrian Church of the East," and "Assyrian Church of the East") burgeoned eastward and flourished in what is today Iraq, Iran, Turkey, and Syria. It also spread to Turkmenistan, India, and China. Nestorians consider their doctrine to be as pure as any Christian faith on the planet can be. Nestorian scriptures were recorded in original Aramaic; today, Nestorians proudly claim that the scriptures have not changed since Christ's first followers wrote them down.[28]

Nestorians would have been considered good Catholics by Rome if it were not for a fierce schism that erupted in the 430s. Western Catholics were quite clear: Jesus was concurrently man and God. John Nestorius, the archbishop of Constantinople in the late 420s, who incidentally neither was Nestorian nor spoke any Aramaic, was concerned that the Virgin Mary was being worshipped as a goddess herself. Fearing her excessive veneration, he suggested that Jesus Christ was *not* simultaneously man and God, but rather two separate natures. He reasoned that the father of Jesus was indeed God, but his mother, Mary, was human, in which case she would not have been a deity. Nestorius was consequently called in front of the First Council of Ephesus, where he was condemned for heresy by a majority of bishops and removed from his see.[29]

The split between Nestorianism and Roman Catholicism was so complete that little was known of Nestorian practices in the West until the 1840s, when European Christians rediscovered what Nestorians considered to be divine sourdough, Holy Leaven. The British explorer who reconnected with the Church of the East was George Percy Badger (1815–1888), a man largely buried by history. Undoubtedly, part of his obscurity lies with the fact that Badger never attended university. He was largely a self-taught Arabist who hung about with unusual friends. In the late 1830s, upon returning from his first trip to the Middle East, he joined a band of evangelists headed by a German, the reverend Christian Schlienz, who later went mad and tried to walk through the streets of Valletta naked.[30]

Nevertheless, Badger pieced together accounts from thirteenth-century Nestorian narratives that purport to be missives directly from Peter.[31] The author of the thirteenth-century texts swore in writing, "The account which I have read bore the sign of Peter."[32] Their subject matter was Holy Leaven.

It goes like this: upon emerging from the Jordan River, John the Baptist, having submerged Jesus, captured some drops from Christ's body. John the Baptist gave this vial of Holy Water to John the Apostle, who took it with him from the banks of the Jordan, over the mountains, and into Jerusalem for the Last Supper.

After declaring, "The Bread is my body; the wine is my blood of the covenant," Jesus gave each of his disciples a loaf of bread. To John the Apostle, however, he gave two loaves. Jesus advised John "to eat one and preserve the other, that it might serve as leaven to be retained by the Church for perpetual commemoration."[33]

When Jesus was seized and crucified, all the disciples hid in fear, save John the Apostle, who watched the horror unfold. Jesus was nailed to his cross among the thieves of the city. The Roman guards wanted to be certain all the bad guys were dead. "If they are still alive," they were ordered, "break their legs so they will die outright." When they got to Jesus, they found him already expired, so they did not need to break his legs. Instead, a guard pierced him in the side with a spear, and out came, separately, blood and water.

John the Apostle took his uneaten second loaf and let Christ's blood soak into it. He collected some of the water from his body in the same vial containing water from Jesus's baptism, given to him by John the Baptist.[34]

According to George Percy Badger, the Nestorian description went on to say that after rising from his grave and ascending into heaven, Christ sent his spirit to his disciples to endow them with wisdom, commanding them to ordain his church and spread his word. They were to use water captured at his baptism and leaven made with bread immersed in the blood of Christ at his crucifixion. Dispersing into Asia, each disciple carried with him a container of sourdough starter from which could be made the bread of the sacrament. Christ's eastern disciples divided their sourdough starter, mixed it with flour and water, and distributed it in separate vials so that every convert joining the church would take communion with bread painstakingly reconstituted from the body and blood of Christ.[35]

I N T H E F O U R centuries that passed between the crucifixion of Christ and the demise of the Roman Empire, Christianity and its Eucharist radiated outward from Jerusalem. My goal was to follow the bread. I had followed it from the Fertile Crescent to Egypt, on to Greece, and then to Rome, where I grew certain that it was leavened with sourdough. To continue the trail of sourdough from Rome toward a nineteenth-century date in the Rocky Mountains, I had to ascertain what transpired in Europe after Roman rule ended. European, notably British and French, explorers were the dominant colonizers of North America, and some of them surely brought the practice of sourdough cultures, if not actual vats of sourdough, with them.

In the fifth century CE, the capital of the Roman Empire moved from Rome to the city of Constantinople, Turkey. While the move did not officially end the Roman Empire, what followed is generally referred to as the Byzantine era, and most historians concur that by 476 CE, Roman rule had all but disappeared. Rome's famous centralized economy, carefully maintained transportation networks, exquisitely engineered water and sewage networks, and grain-to-bakery conveyor system fell into disrepair. The fall of Rome and rise of Byzantium in the East corresponded with the beginning of what is known as the Dark Ages, Middle Ages, or medieval era (roughly 500–1500 CE). For much of Europe, urban life disintegrated into myriad rural fiefdoms. Most Europeans were poor and illiterate and did not have a healthy diet. They spent their lives in service to feudal overlords. Roman art and science gave way to biblical doctrine, and eating enough bread became necessary for survival.

One account of a peasant household paints a very clear picture of life endured by the majority of the population during the Dark Ages. The Dutch humanist and theologian Desiderius Erasmus (ca. 1466–1536) wrote that a typical family lived in a single room beneath a thatch roof that also housed insects and mice. The dirt floor was covered in decomposing straw. He wrote, "The bottom layer is left undisturbed, sometimes for twenty years, harbouring expectorations, vomiting, the leakages of dogs and men, ale-droppings, scraps of fish, and other abominations not fit to be mentioned."[36]

Deducing what medieval Europeans ate, however, has not been an easy task for historians. In sharp contrast to the Romans, who kept scrupulous records of every kernel of grain moving through their extended empire, average citizens of the Dark Ages are not known for their extant writings. Part of the explanation goes back to the fragile balance between calories reaped and calories burned. Even if a worker was literate, a rarity throughout much of the millennium, the time needed to first eke out sufficient harvests from a parcel controlled by a lord in a castle and then preserve whatever he was permitted to take home did not leave a lot of additional energy for writing poetry or dictating legendarily delicious family recipes. If there is one thing nearly all researchers of the medieval agree upon, it is that there is little written documentation from which to infer daily diets.

One of the most capable historians on foodstuffs of the Dark Ages is Kathy L. Pearson, a professor of history at Old Dominion University in Norfolk, Virginia. For her work "Nutrition and the Early-Medieval Diet,"[37] she combined archaeological findings of plant, animal, and human remains with estate inventories, capitularies (acts of legislation), law codes, chronicles, and monastic rules to estimate food consumption patterns. The picture was not pretty. Women on average lived only twenty to thirty years, while most men expired by their midforties.[38]

Pearson suggested that as the Dark Ages closed in on Europe following the collapse of Roman authority, for around two hundred years until the 600s, many Europeans were pastoralists. Residents in what is today known as Spain, Germany, France, Austria, northern Italy, and Poland raised farm animals rather than grain. Relying upon livestock for sustenance, rather than bread as the Egyptians, Greeks, and Romans had, was possible because land was plentiful and people were not.

But as human populations grew, feeding fields of grass to cows, pigs, or sheep became inefficient; meat became a luxury. Growing a large warm-blooded animal to full size meant that for months, a cow, for instance, burned calories to stay warm, walk about, and think cow thoughts—calories that could have been given to a human to perform nearly identical activities.

Grain initially emerged as a replacement for meat at the base of the human food pyramid in the seventh century along the Rhine River and in Francia, north of the Loire River—an area that today is part of Germany, Belgium, and northern France. In that region, alluvial soils, growing populations, and landowners who knew how to increase production while simultaneously controlling their workers all combined to change farming practices.[39] Consolidation of landholdings by increasingly wealthy rulers, literally landlords, spread as the predominant form of agricultural management.

The unrelenting daily work of coaxing food from the earth was a matter of life and death for a millennium. Serfs worked fields from dawn to dusk, handed their landlords harvested grain, or paid them a tax with grain in lieu of cash. Serfs grew supplemental food, if they could, in household gardens, but for most of the Dark Ages, as pastoralism waned and field cropping replaced it, rich and poor alike relied upon very similar diets. Bread was their primary sustenance, accompanied by gruels and stewed vegetables of various sorts. Beer proved a clever means of preserving the nutrition captured by barley and was safer than water in a society without the capacity of Roman engineers to keep their sewage and drinking water separate. Rulers, nobility, and landlords, greater in wealth but only a tiny fraction of Europe's inhabitants, had access to greater quantities of meat and poultry.[40]

The bread upon which most people depended for calories was assembled from bread wheat (*Triticum aestivum*), although other grains were also used. By this point in history, approximately ever since Alexander the Great took control of Egypt for the Greeks in 332 BCE, bread wheat, with its free-threshing, naked seeds, had supplanted hull-encased emmer wheat, the species favored by Egyptians.[41] Of all the grains that could be grown, bread wheat was the tastiest and most gluten rich, and it produced the highest yield of useful grain per sown seed. It was also the most finicky: susceptible to cold, damp, heat, and drought in ways that sturdier grains like barley, oats, and rye were not. Smart farmers, who included anyone with half a desire to survive until next year, diversified their crops. So both landlords and women tending gardens at home also planted barley, spelt, rye, millet, oats, and emmer wheat. To further hedge their bets that something would thrive, they also planted einkorn wheat, which like emmer, is not free threshing.[42]

In addition to tending the household garden, according to the 1531 *Boke of Husbandry*, a woman was expected to begin her day sweeping floors—or at least those not covered in fresh rushes—tidying the dish board, and setting the house to good order. With the house put to rights, she tended calves, milked cows, and strained still-warm milk through a series of clean cloths to remove dirt and cow hair. Without refrigeration, she had to churn butter or make cheese within just a handful of hours. She sprouted and dried barley, which she brewed into ale.[43] If hops were not available, she had to make ale frequently, as beer without hops does not keep.[44] It was her responsibility to dress and "array" the children, prepare their food, and make meals for her husband.

To supply the daily base of household nutrition, a woman's first job was to acquire flour. In the unlikely instance that she had enough money to do so, she could purchase flour from a miller. More commonly, the woman of the house took the grain the family was able to grow, or permitted to keep as meager payment in exchange for labor, and carried it to the miller to be turned into flour. To her chagrin, the miller was also an employee of the landlord; he charged a monopoly fee. Many millers were routinely suspected of adulterating their flour with less expensive substitutes, even if a housewife handed him her own wheat. If she did not have wheat herself, she purchased or carried other grains and legumes, such as barley, oats, and even acorns, to the miller to mill for her. Barley, oat, and acorn breads are edible, but they are dense as stone.

Returning home, most women mixed what flour they had with water and leavened it either with yeast skimmed from fermenting ale or with sourdough saved from a previous round of baking.[45] Medieval beer, it should be noted, was sour because it was readily infected with bacteria. Consequently, a bread leavened with foam taken from a bubbling vat of ale would have produced a bread that was also likely to be sour—that is, a sour dough, not very dissimilar from a loaf leavened with an actual sourdough culture.

There was rarely enough time in a day to start and tend a household fire or enough wood to waste on an oven hefty enough to bake bread. If there was sufficient wood or even the human energy to harvest it, logs would have been stacked and saved for winter warmth. A few sticks could have been burned to heat stews or gruels, but good bread needed a lot of heat, a large stone oven, and a considerable amount of time. The medieval solution was a communal bakery located near the castle or manor, which served as the center of the village. Alas, the baker, like the miller, was also an employee of the landlord.

Communal ovens in the Dark Ages were domed, made of stone, clay, or brick, and often several feet tall and up to six feet in diameter—too large to be practically housed inside a hut with a mud floor and thatch roof. A woman handed her risen but uncooked doughs to the baker. Three-fourths of an hour later, after paying the nobleman's baker for his services, the woman hustled home to serve bread, cheese, bean stew, and ale to her hungry children and an exhausted husband returning from a day of plowing.

To earn grain that could be milled to flour that his wife would turn into bread, a man typically rose before dawn to feed his draft animals.[46] He grabbed a hunk of sourdough bread and a piece of cheese, ate even the moldy bits, and downed a pint of ale before heading to the fields to plow. He was expected at work by first sunlight.

Driving a pair of oxen or a team of horses was the dominant work of field hands. In regions where rainfall was plentiful—Great

A medieval woman visits the communal oven, fourteenth century.

Britain, Scandinavia, Germany, and parts of France—furrowing was the primary means of drainage. Multiple passes of the plow were needed to create ridges and drainage ditches. As late spring and early summer approached and fields dried out, plowmen drove their animals yet again to flatten winter ridges for warm-weather crops like peas, beans, and oats. During any season that was passable, plowmen urged their beasts forward, their animals straining to uproot weeds. In autumn, the cycle was repeated; the stubble of crops was plowed back into furrows for drainage, and ridges were raised for wheat and rye planting. Fallowing was practiced to rehabilitate fields in which the soil was exhausted from repetitive planting and harvesting, but this also meant that new fields had to be broken open with plows, as time allowed and as hunger necessitated or the landlord insisted.[47]

✑━━ **Serfs harvesting wheat, ca. 1340.**

At the beginning of summer, when wheat was ready for harvest, men swung scythes as long as there was sufficient light; wheat had to be harvested within a window that lasted less than a week. Women helped with the important work of bundling and tying. At day's end, coated in sweat, pollen, and kicked-up soil and wearing stained clothing that was washed only every few weeks, a field worker earned some grain to bring home and perhaps some cash.

This routine—rise before the sun, eat, work without pause until dark, then sleep—varied with the seasons, but not much over the years. It was a daily ritual followed by peasants for centuries, more or less from the fall of Rome in the fifth century until the age of exploration in the fifteenth.

It is important to consider what crops looked like 1,500 years ago. Today, for example, the average German farmer pulls six thousand to seven thousand kilograms of grain per hectare. In a great year, a medieval farmer working the same fields might have harvested almost one thousand kilograms, but the best historical estimates suggest that yields were more likely around five hundred kilograms, or less than 10 percent of a current yield. A British milk cow in the fourteenth century provided less than 10 percent of a modern cow's capacity.[48] Vegetable yields were equally wimpy, and though some may have been fertilized with animal manure, there would not have been enough to spread to all the plants. The labor to cart cow dung from where it fell to where it was needed was exhausting, and the calculus of removing it from one field to feed another was illogical.

Complicating prospects for a successful crop season was the wobbly and rather unstable climate that persisted throughout the Middle Ages. Between 400 and 900, the average mean temperature dropped by as much as 2 to 3 degrees centigrade,[49] which short-ened already tight growing seasons. Cool summers were especially common between 500 and 700. During the seventh, eighth, and tenth centuries, summers were dryer than normal and were often followed by very cold winters. The coldest winter in the past two thousand years started in 763 before finally warming up in April of 764. Four great winters in the ninth century caused the Rhine, Danube, and Seine to freeze solid for more than a month.[50] Live-stock did not fare well when temperatures were low and food was in short supply. Pigs and cows were taken into houses to keep their human owners warm, but many animals froze along with their starving human companions.

As the climate fluctuated, so did insect populations. Warm weather in eastern Europe brought a plague of locusts that devoured the grain supply of Germany and Francia during the years 873 and 874.[51] The battle to grow enough grain to turn into sourdough bread was lost.

Among populations with insufficient access to bread, disease exacerbated death tolls. Plagues of bubonic bacteria, rats, and crop rusts spread across the continent. The great Plague of Justinian swept through Europe in 541, killing so many field hands that there wasn't enough labor to harvest the grain. Famine reigned for nearly three generations.[52] The Iberian Peninsula suffered from famine and plague in 750. In 809, the weather was so cold, poor harvests led to famine throughout most of Europe, followed by additional famines from 1000 to 1100, and again in 1243, 1258, and 1314. As Europe moved through the middle of the fourteenth century, plague systematically claimed more than one in every three citizens. Fields of wheat were abandoned when no one was left to work them.[53] A wheat shortage, followed by an inevitable shortage of sourdough bread, sent village populations into viciously downward spirals of death and hunger.

Ergot, a dark fungus, first appeared in 857, in the Rhine Valley and infected the region's fields of rye, the dominant grain of northern Europe, where it is too cold and damp for wheat. (To this day, German and Scandinavian breads are overwhelmingly rye rather than wheat.) The fungal infection was easy to overlook on dark-seeded plants. The toxins released by ergot were not disarmed when baked, and the toxins were not affected in any way by sourdough cultures, the predominant method for making rye breads. Eating rye bread infected by ergot led to a set of symptoms you would not wish upon your worst enemy. It acted first as a vaso-constrictor so severe that limbs became gangrenous and had to be removed. Concurrently, fungal alkaloids went to work on the central nervous system, causing everything from uterine contractions and spontaneous abortions to vomiting, diarrhea, seizures, hallucinations, mania, unconsciousness, and death. Ergot intermittently plagued rye-growing countries for centuries and killed or maimed thousands of people. In 943 alone, some forty thousand people died of ergotism in Limoges, France.

As if an unreliable climate, swarms of insects, raiding rats, and unexplainable ailments were not enough of a drag on food production, the Catholic Church delivered an additional insult to nutrition. Perpetually concerned by sexual urges among its flock, Catholic leaders advised regular self-induced semistarvation to curb sexual desires.[54] Combine frequent fasts, vitamin and calorie deficiencies, and shortages of protein with tommy gun–like maternity, and suddenly the incredibly low life expectancy among women is much easier to understand.

Finally, even in acceptable years of production, there was one more problem associated with medieval diets: the absence of dental care. Though people wiped their teeth from time to time with a cloth dusted with wood ash or candle soot and picked large chunks from between them with thin pieces of wood or a knife, brushing was not common.[55] Archaeologists who have examined skulls from the early Dark Ages found teeth wracked by plaque. The winter brought scurvy, which included tooth loss among its sufferers. Abscesses and rampant periodontal disease led to the loss of many teeth and halitosis of such intensity that the household goats must have heaved when they were being milked. Pearson made clear that without teeth, some people would surely have gone hungry amid years of plenty.

Taken together, ignorance, famine, plague, warfare, theft, unscrupulous landlords, unnaturally cold winters, pests, malnourishment, and fatigue make it easy to understand Kathy Pearson's take on Dark Age nutrition: abundance was possible only when conditions were perfect. If the rains were on time, temperatures were moderate, what insects emerged were mostly of a variety the household chickens enjoyed, and the family cow discovered a hidden gold mine of nutritious grasses, a family could, in theory, enjoy a hearty month—or year—of bread, cheese, ale, and meat. Nevertheless, Pearson concluded, "Every egg counted as a precious part of the most basic element of human existence."[56]

What did not change throughout the Dark Ages was dependence upon bread as the primary source of sustenance for anyone who was not wealthy, which is to say nearly everyone. Ruth Goodman, a British historian, has done a marvelous job of placing bread in its central position in the medieval diet of the last centuries of the Dark Ages. Goodman's period of expertise is

Great Britain's Tudor period (1486–1603), and she has passed countless hours reading old manuscripts, lived for weeks as a Tudor, and run experiments to learn how Tudor men and women cooked, worked, played, washed, learned, and dressed.[57] Goodman was the expert to whom the BBC turned when it wanted to authenticate its filming of the television show *Wolf Hall*, based on Hilary Mantel's novels about Thomas Cromwell in the court of Henry VIII.

While England is not exactly contiguous with western Europe, Goodman's investigations and descriptions are nonetheless a decent generalization of much of the continent for much of the period between the decline of the Roman Empire and Europe's resuscitation in the Renaissance. In her book *How to Be a Tudor*, Goodman proposed a way of considering bread's importance in the medieval diet. Think back to every meal you've eaten this week and consider how many of those meals were accompanied by bread. In addition to toast and sandwiches, include any meal served in a bun or tortilla, pizza, and foods fried in a breaded coating. Now add in meals that included rice, pasta, or potatoes that were baked, french fried, or mashed. Replace those carbohydrates with bread. Next, think of all the foods that could not be grown in your hometown, except during a very short growing season. For me, every lemon, tomato, banana, and avocado would have been bread. In sum, as Goodman wrote, "Bread for breakfast, bread for dinner, bread for supper, day in and day out. Although it was often eaten with other foods, for the poorest it was bread alone."[58]

B Y THE SIXTEENTH century, Europe had at last displaced medievalism with an Age of Discovery. Telescopes scanned night skies, and by the seventeenth century, microscopes revealed a miniature universe hitherto unknown. Among the organisms magnified by microscopes would be yeast and bacteria living in sourdough cultures.

The physical geography of Europe was changing, too: towns were growing. Economies were slowly shifting from subsistence farming toward businesses that relied upon the flow of money. Blacksmiths, innkeepers, weavers, potters, carpenters, shoemakers, soap makers, and bakers grew into independent professions. Townspeople used their income to purchase at least some of their foodstuffs from bakers, butchers, and farm women selling surplus eggs, cheeses, and turnips in the market square.

Sourdough bread had nourished Western civilizations from the ancient Middle East across the Mediterranean Sea and spread throughout much of Europe. As the Dark Ages came to a close, European voyagers imposed their cultures on Indigenous peoples around the world, catalyzing the exchange of people, animals, crops, and microscopic organisms, many of which were diseases. In order to follow sourdough from Europe to what was for Europeans a "New World," the next leg of my journey focused on the earliest and most prolific colonizers of North America: France and England.

PLINY THE ELDER'S PICENUM BREAD

This description, taken verbatim from chapter 27 of *Naturalis Historia* by Pliny the Elder, is titled "The Method of Making Bread: Origin of the Art."[59] It is as close to a recipe as we have from this era. Picenum was a region of Rome's empire in the northeast of Italy located along the Adriatic Sea. Alica is a hulled wheat, probably emmer or spelt, that has had the hulls removed and has been pounded into grits and coarse flour. In Pliny the Elder's time, this work was done by "slaves working in chains," and the flour was whitened with chalk.[60]

Picenum still maintains its ancient reputation for making the bread which it was the first to invent, alica being the grain employed. The flour is kept in soak for nine days, and is kneaded on the tenth with raisin juice, in the shape of long rolls; after which it is baked in an oven in earthen pots, till they break. This bread, however, is never eaten till it has been well-soaked, which is mostly done in milk mixed with honey.

MEDIEVAL MASLIN BREAD
Yield: 1 loaf

Even though it was the main source of calories for the rich and poor alike, there are few surviving recipes for medieval bread. Maslin bread was made with a mixture of available flours, and the following directions are based on a recipe compiled by the Oakden Research Center,[61] an organization that specializes in medieval cooking and cookware in the British Isles. For the sake of authenticity, Oakden recommends seeking out traditional stone-ground flours. To maintain the spirit of the era, I have added chores to the recipe.

    200 grams sourdough starter
    200 grams rye flour
    100 grams barley flour
    350 grams whole wheat flour, plus more for dusting
    500 grams warm water
    1 teaspoon coarse sea salt

Place the starter, rye flour, barley flour, whole wheat flour, water, and salt in a bowl and mix.

When the dough becomes too difficult to mix, turn it onto a floured surface. Knead for 20 minutes.

Place the kneaded loaf in a bowl and cover with a damp towel. Let rise until it has increased in size by about half. Depending on the temperature inside your hut, this could take 6 to 10 hours.

Do your chores (card wool, make thread, gather eggs, sprout barley for ale, get the chickens out of the house, wrap a child's bloodied knee with cloth, churn butter).

Gently shape the dough into a ball. Try not to squish out too much of the air that has accumulated inside.

Allow to rise for another 90 minutes atop a cast-iron base or a baking sheet.

If you have your own oven and do not have to pay to use the oven of the communal baker, preheat it to 450°F.

Use a sharp knife to make a shallow cut all around the side at the bottom of the dough. Cut a cross into the top. Place the cast-iron skillet or baking tray into the preheated oven and bake for 40 to 50 minutes, or until your bread looks nicely browned and sounds hollow when tapped. Let cool for several hours before slicing, or the interior will likely be gummy.

CHAPTER 3

THE FRENCH CONNECTION

FRENCH AND BRITISH COLONIZERS ESTABLISHED
footholds in North America in the 1500s, so I set my sights
on understanding the relationships they each had to their
daily bread. The more I dug in, the more disparate they appeared.
Residents of the British Isles drank ale and, when they could, used
barm, the yeasty froth skimmed from ale, to leaven their breads
quickly. In contrast, Frenchmen relied upon slower, more aromatic
fermentations: vintage wine, aged cheese, and sourdough bread.

Because much of England's approach to both industrialization and entrepreneurship influenced the demise of sourdough in
the United States, I had to keep my eye on them. But it was the
French to whom I dedicated my initial inquiries, foremost because
I uncovered an article laying out a direct line from French sourdough to the bread eaten by gold miners.

In 1973, Peter Tamony wrote an article for *Western Folklore*
called "Sourdough and French Bread" in which he chronicled the
lives of French colonists in Mexican villages during the first half
of the nineteenth century. Frenchmen in Mexico baked and sold
sourdough bread, and according to Tamony, in 1848, when news

spread around the world that there was gold in California, Frenchmen from Mexico were among the first to arrive. They brought
their sourdough starters with them.[1] If French bakers were making
sourdough bread for the San Francisco Gold Rush by 1849, it
seemed plausible that an aging French baker or his son (women
were not yet welcome in commercial baking) might have plied
his craft at a gold rush in Cripple Creek forty-four years later. It is
unlikely, though not impossible, that the starter in my Meadville
kitchen was once used in San Francisco and Mexico. Nevertheless,
Tamony's assertion that bread baked with sourdough had arrived
in North America from France and that sourdough baking had
made its way into California in the middle of the nineteenth century caused me to aim my research directly into the heart of French
bread making.

    In the sixteenth, seventeenth, and eighteenth centuries, sour-
dough bread remained the primary source of calories for much
of Europe, just as it had for earlier cultures in Egypt, Greece,
Rome, and much of the continent mired in the Dark Ages. Dense
sourdough loaves made with rye and oats were the mainstay in
Germany, Holland, and Scandinavia, largely because northern
Europe was climatically inhospitable for wheat. But France was
wheat country, and as with wine and cheese, they baked uniquely
regional sourdough breads. By the end of the eighteenth century,
sourdough bread had become so central to French fare that the
average Frenchman consumed three pounds per day, making them
"the biggest eaters of bread in the whole world."[2]

    The French imbued their daily bread with such religious and
spiritual significance that the insult of a dropped loaf had to be
redressed with a kiss to its crust. The *Encyclopédie Méthodique*,
published between 1782 and 1832, reported that "the bulk of the
people believe that they are dying of hunger if they do not have
bread."[3] A Frenchman who was painfully ill was said to have "lost

his taste for bread." An elderly individual "has already baked more than half his bread." A sad or despondent Frenchman "has lost the bread in the oven." And a man who persuades his girlfriend to engage in premarital sex may discover that "it is not always he who heated up the oven who is the first to bite into the warm bread."[4]

Because France was central to the history of sourdough and its devotion to it is so historically entrenched, I traveled to France in 2014 with my wife to meet bakers, talk to them about their training and practices, visit their bakeries, explore the important sites of sourdough's history, and to the best of my ability, eat as much French bread as I could in two weeks. I made my first stop at Poilâne Bakery on the Left Bank in metropolitan Paris. Poilâne has been a family-owned business since 1932, and its five-pound round sourdough, called a *miche* (translated by some as "butt cheek"), is widely discussed, written about, argued over, and applauded.

When Susan and I entered the little shop with its wooden floor and open shelves of bread, we were greeted by the customary sing-song "bonjour." A middle-aged woman with her hair pulled back sat behind a raised counter. To her right, standing at attention, back against the wall, was her young assistant. Both wore starched beige and yellow uniforms that made them look a bit like early twentieth-century nurses in a convalescence ward. I scanned the shelves, and once I reached my decisions, I called upon the assistant, who jumped from her military posture to place my selections in individual bags.

I pointed to a raisin petit pain (sourdough, whole wheat), an open-faced, flaky pastry with sliced apples splayed across the bottom like a little round boat, and a pair of croissants. Then, because I did not want to carry a two-kilogram *miche* the size of a tire on a European Smart car, I instead requested four slices of their oak-fired, thick-crusted country loaf. Total cost for the coiled raisin roll, apple pastry, croissants, and bread was about eleven dollars.

We exited the store into a Parisian spring rain and raced for an apartment doorway with an overhanging canopy where, huddled beneath hood and umbrella, we ate the apple pastry and croissants. The taste of country fresh butter rang in every bite of croissant, and the crust was so flaky, a snowstorm of flecks fell at our feet. The bread lived up to its billing: substantive, aromatic, and bursting with a riot of flavors no yeasted bread baked in an ordinary oven could ever have achieved.

We drove to the South of France, where a distant cousin of mine had arranged for me to meet his neighborhood bakers in Saint-Rémy-de-Provence. I was surprised that one of the two bakers we met was a woman who looked to be in her early thirties, as men still dominate commercial baking in France. I thought of the Pompeiian bakers with phallic appurtenances affixed over their ovens who for centuries had dominated the craft. When I asked, she admitted she had to work much harder than her male colleagues in order to be recognized by her peers. Still, she harbored no rancor and was remarkably pleasant, considering she had been awake since four in the morning tending a 500-degree-Fahrenheit, gas-fired oven.

Bread competitions are a big deal and commonplace in France, and the older baker in the shop sliced a baguette from end to end in one swift stroke so that he could explain the difference between what I was looking at and an award winner. The distribution of large and small holes in the bread's crumb was key, and though I quickly recognized the exceptional quality of the baguette before me, I could not discern why the two bakers—the older gentleman and the younger woman—believed the cut loaf could never win an award. Only after I departed did I realize I had been so overwhelmed by their skill at making baguettes—the young woman had been training for twelve years, she said—that I forgot to ask anyone's name.

I did ask, however, to see their starter, which they happily presented in its five-gallon plastic bucket. At the time, I was convinced

 **The appropriate crumb in a baguette.**

that old sourdough starters were irreproducible and contained characteristics as rare as an heirloom tomato or disappearing breed of goat, so I asked the two bakers how old their starter was. Ten years, they told me with a shrug.

Over the years I have posed the same question to numerous professional bakers, and most claimed they didn't really know and didn't really care. Many bakers maintained that neither the age nor origin of a sourdough has more than a minor influence on the outcome of the bread's flavor, color, texture, or performance. The final product, they insisted, depended upon how the baker prepared the bread, the quality and moisture content of the flour, the size and shape of the loaf, mixing and rising time, rising temperature and duration, baking room humidity, and oven temperature. Sourdough matters, of course, just as do the type of salt, origin of the grains, purity of the water, and tenderness of additives like millet, flax, and nuts. Many professional bakers are orchestra conductors, bringing forth symphonies in which the ringing finales are not simply a function of the notes on a score but rather the culmination of practice, integration, and harmony.

Then again, it might be mostly bakeries that do not have old starters that suggest new starters are just as good as old ones. The only two bakeries I know that advertise the age of their starter are Boudin Bakery on the wharf in San Francisco and the Creative Crust, formerly of Meadville, Pennsylvania, to whom I gave a sample of Cripple Creek. I needed to learn a lot of modern science about sourdough before I could reach a conclusion.

In France, fresh bread really is everywhere—even gas stations. A US gas station or quick stop keeps cigarettes behind the counter; in France it's fresh baguettes warming beneath an orange glow. At one stop, Susan and I purchased, in addition to a tiny tankful of petrol, an apple-filled croissant, a croissant Suisse, and a baguette right from the oven. We waited two minutes for the timer to ding, or whatever a tiny oven in a gas station says *en français*, and walked out with bread that was too hot to hold even inside its paper bag.

The baguette might have been hot, but it was still 100 percent factory made. The crust was thin and brownish; its interior was white as paper. Unlike bread made by trained professional bakers, the crumb inside the gas station bread was perfectly uniform. Every tiny hole, produced by a cell of yeast raised in a lab by a multinational yeast corporation, was identical in size and shape to its neighbor. There was no hint of salt, leavening, or aroma. It tasted like it had come fresh from a photocopier, and hungry though we were, we threw it away and stopped in a town to buy a real bread to have with our Normandy Camembert.

M Y TRIP TO France helped put into perspective the century-spanning transition from medieval sourdough to insta-baguettes sold in filling stations. Castles and palaces of various ages are well-preserved throughout France, and while most tourists book castle tours with the intention of goggling at opulence, I was on the lookout for baking ovens, storage facilities for grain, gristmills, and surrounding fields that looked fertile. The Cité de Carcassonne in the South of France was a good place to begin. Nearly two miles of double walls and fifty-two towers surround the interior city and central castle. The city was founded just as the era of Roman dominance was drawing to a close in the fourth century, meaning that the city and castle itself served as an archetype of economics during the Dark Ages.

Constructing, maintaining, protecting, and provisioning a medieval castle or a town surrounded by defensive walls was an endeavor only wealthy aristocrats could afford.[5] To ensure that the whole operation—army, horses, stablemen, latrine emptiers, moat diggers, masonry repairmen, millers, bakers, and the like—ran smoothly required taxes, ordinarily paid in the form of grain.[6]

Close to the nobleman's manor house, inside his protective walls, the landlord kept the community oven and the mill for grinding grain. Grain had to be run through millstones by the nobleman's miller; bread had to be baked by the nobleman's baker. Bread, the caloric fuel that powered the entire operation, was managed by government monopoly. But in the sixteenth and seventeenth centuries, the relationships between monopolistic noblemen and their serfs changed dramatically, and new forms of government spread across the Western world. The Dark Ages came to a full stop.

The French word for a communal bakery owned and operated by the nobleman's baker is a *banal* oven. As you might surmise, the translation of *banal* to English is "commonplace, run-of-the-mill." (Not to go too far afield here, but, according to the Oxford English Dictionary, "run-of-the-mill" is an English metaphor for a routine, monotonous event, though the British etymology refers to the run of a textile, not grain, mill.) For multiple centuries the Dark Ages were marked, without much interruption or modification, by a regular trip to the *banal* oven.

A medieval landlord worried about food shortages not only because malnutrition and disease threatened his workforce but also because hungry French serfs resorted to riots. Food riots were subject to seasonal rhythms. The greatest danger, surprisingly, arrived with the growing season, March to September.[7] By that time, the average subsistence-level peasant had taken a considerable portion of his fall harvest and handed it over as taxes, dues, and tithes. What meager provisions he and his family managed to keep for winter survival were carefully rationed, and by springtime, the family's cupboards were vacant. There are few sounds more abrasive on the soul of a parent than the bleating of hungry children.

If winter was long and rations were low, hungry families had no choice but to eat seeds they were saving to plant in the spring. They ripped open their stored sacks of wheat they had hoped to plant for food in the following year, carrying what was necessary for survival in this year to the nobleman's miller to grind into flour for bread. When the weather warmed enough to begin sowing, farmers who had eaten all of their stored wheat were forced into the marketplace to dicker for replacement seeds. Seed merchants enjoyed doubled demand: planters who had eaten their planting stock needed to purchase seeds for their household plots *and* to grind into flour.

As brokers and suppliers raised prices in response to increased demand, the shortage of grain in the marketplace forced up the price of bread. Recognizing the annual springtime increase in demand, grain sellers were not averse to manipulating supplies. By holding back a little winter grain, merchants could push prices higher and then release their hoardings at the artificially elevated price. There was a fine balance to maintain between making extra profits by withholding grain and having your storehouse ransacked and your grain sacks unceremoniously shredded. That was April and May.[8]

Real desperation arrived in August and September, when crops in the field ripened and household supplies were nearly gone. Tension was palpable at the end of summer, when a late summer drought or a vicious hailstorm could demolish grain heads with comparable efficiency.[9]

Through the latter part of the Dark Ages and into the seventeenth and eighteenth centuries, hunger-induced irritability erupted, sending throngs of frustrated women toward landlords, noblemen, and monasteries, the very people to whom their families had paid taxes and tithes. Next on their list of warehouses to ransack were those under the economic thumb of the rich and powerful: millers, grain dealers, and bakers.

In the 1630s, food riots erupted in Caen in the province of Normandy, in Pertuis and Reillanne in Provence, and in Angers in Anjou. The number of riots increased through the seventeenth century so that during the thirty-year period of 1690 to 1720, France endured 182 food uprisings. Between 1760 and 1789, the years leading up to the French Revolution, that number nearly quadrupled. On 652 occasions the people of France took to the streets.[10]

In the 1700s, government bureaucrats displaced landlords. Local governors created *la police des grains* or *la police de subsistence*, charging the newly appointed government officials with maintaining civil order.[11] Put simply, the market price in France was arrived at by the following calculation made by sellers, buyers, and the local *police des grains*. Sellers asked for the highest price they could get without inciting a riot. If the price went too high, buyers ransacked. Ransacking held the benefit of ensuring food security; a poor person could scrounge grain from the ground even if she arrived late for the riot. Local police did their best to maintain reasonable prices for bread,[12] hoping to forestall civil unrest. It wasn't quite Rome's bread and circuses, but France's attempt to keep the price of bread within reach was nonetheless an endeavor to make sure most people could afford to eat.

As the French economy matured, however, farmers increasingly grew food where soils were fertile and rainfall reliable, and they shipped it to cities where workers and factories were plentiful. Food grown in one area of France, or in French colonies in the Caribbean, Americas, Africa, or India, was transported to markets in another. Mills were constructed beside the country's most powerful rivers, where large millstones could grind wheat most efficiently. It was a very logical system—unless you were a hungry peasant living in a region where the wheat you tended all through the long, sticky summer was shipped off to Paris. Just like their country counterparts, impoverished workers who lived in large villages and in cities were also easily perturbed if the price of bread rose above their means.

In the late 1700s, the interlocked stories of bread, castles, hunger, and politics moved to the country's most opulent palace: Versailles. In 1789, French commoners, like Egyptians, Greeks, Romans, and medieval Europeans before them, were still subsisting on bread, and lots of it. French bakers prepared large loaves that sometimes weighed as much as twelve pounds that bakers divided with a device that looked an awful lot like the French Revolution's infamous guillotines. But peasant bread was once again expensive and becoming more so.

It was a dry year. Not only was the harvest underwhelming, but rivers ran so low that millers did not have the power to turn their large grinding stones. No milling, no flour. At the start of the year, a four-pound loaf could be had for eight *sous*, a price that could extract more than a third of the salary of France's poorest workers. Unskilled laborers took home only twenty or thirty *sous* for a day's work. Even skilled workers like locksmiths and carpenters earned only about fifty *sous* a day, and masons made only forty. Prices at the bakery were inflexible, and recollections of recent shortages spooked shoppers.[13]

By August, the price of bread climbed to twelve *sous*, bakeries ran out of flour, and empty shelves became common. Testy French women and men who believed the harvest of 1789 was better than the awful one of the previous year thought prices should have been lower. The public suspected conspiracy: intentional withholding of grain by merchants trying to drive up prices.

Shouting matches erupted in bread queues. Punches were thrown; men pushed aside women in line. To protect bakers from being harmed or killed, guards were posted to their shops. At Versailles, one baker tried to sell bread at eighteen *sous* to those who could afford it and stale loaves for a lower price to those who could not.[14] A crowd attempted to murder him. It did not go unnoticed that Versailles epitomized the opposite end of the economic continuum. In the kitchens of Versailles, a staff of two thousand served France's King Louis XVI and Queen Marie Antoinette.

On the morning of October 5, 1789, huge crowds of women massed in the central markets east of Paris shouting for bread. Trooping downstream along the banks of the Seine, they forced the bell ringer of the Church of Saint Margaret to ring the tocsin, raising the attention of all within earshot. This bread riot was heading for Versailles.

Leading the march were working women, the kind of tough French street women who could turn a phrase that included more than a few salty adjectives. Within hours they had cajoled, enticed, or forced six thousand allies to join. By nine thirty in the morning, they had overtaken the Hôtel de Ville, Paris's city hall. They disarmed the guards and overran the bell tower, and a handful started a second set of tocsins clanging across the city center. Others tore the place apart searching for arms and gunpowder.

Determined, they headed directly for Versailles, more than a dozen miles away. It was raining. Six hours later, King Louis XVI was faced with six thousand tired, hungry, and very wet women.

They carried a variety of weapons acquired along the route, including a cannon, some muskets, pikes, bludgeons, pitchforks, scythes, crowbars, and other long, heavy implements, which they used to reinforce their request for greater quantities of bread at reasonable prices.

The king, a renowned flip-flopper, debated whether now was the time to flee the country. His ministers' advice was unanimous: scram. The Bastille had been taken by an angry mob just months earlier, and its defenders had not fared well. His odds were not favorable as King Louis surveyed the crowd outside his door. He vacillated. Was he to become France's fugitive king?

While Louis waffled, the opposition's female leadership, who shared none of the king's indecisiveness, burst through the doors of the National Assembly. Protesters, their numbers now swollen by men who had joined their ranks, streamed through the grand doors and directly into the halls of government, carrying with them their pikes, staffs, and scythes. They demanded bread![15]

Women march on Versailles, 1789.

"Order! Order!" shouted the bishop of Langres from the chair of the Assembly. His motion was overruled without debate as women swarmed the platform. "We don't give a fuck for order," they shouted back at him. "We want bread."[16]

Several women leaned across the table, their lips pursed and rain-drenched bosoms heaving, and demanded kisses from the bishop. He obliged. Other women now entered the assembly, having assuaged their march-induced thirst with intoxicants imbibed along the way. Several were now sufficiently *d'ébriété avancé* that they were vomiting across the benches of the Assembly while others sat happily astride the laps of assemblymen.[17]

After lengthy negotiations, the king agreed to meet with six representatives. Pierrette Chabry, an attractive seventeen-year-old flower seller with good diction, polite manners, and nice clothes, was elected as spokeswoman. Upon entering the king's chambers, the nervous Pierrette fought to find her suddenly absent voice. "Sire, we want bread," she said.

King Louis was accommodating. "You know my heart," the king told her. "I will order all the bread in Versailles to be collected and given to you." Whereupon Pierrette fainted. The king rushed smelling salts to the poor girl's nose, which revived her in short order. Grateful, Pierrette asked if she might be honored to kiss the king's hand. King Louis XVI said to all present, "She deserves better than that." He embraced her.

The six representatives to the king, thrilled by their reception, emerged on the courtyard to relay the king's promise. "Bread is on its way to Paris," they announced. The crowd, however, didn't buy it. It's one thing to receive a political promise directly from a king but quite another to be standing in a courtyard in wet clothes after a six-hour hike, invading the National Assembly, and a seemingly interminable wait while a hoity-toity flower girl and five women in nice dresses chitchatted with the king. The crowd shouted, "Bread!

Bread!" until the deputation went back to the king to extract a written promise.[18]

As the night deepened, the king and queen went to bed in their separate chambers. The market women wrung out their skirts and petticoats under what shelter they could obtain, shocking an officer looking upon them. "The scenes which took place amongst them were anything but decent," he told a reporter.[19]

At five thirty in the morning, for reasons not entirely clear, an armed mob entered the palace grounds screaming for the queen's blood: "Where is she? Where is the whore? We'll wring her neck! We'll tear out her heart! We'll fry her liver and . . . have her kidneys in a fricassee!"[20]

In a frenzy, they attacked the Royal Guard. When a guardsman discharged his firearm and killed a rioter, the crowd retaliated by hacking off his head with an axe. Soon, a second guardsman also gave up his head.

The women headed for the queen's bedroom. Marie Antoinette barely had time to throw on a robe before she escaped through a back door, rounded up her two children, found refuge with the king, and hid in his chambers. It was a good thing she fled because the crowd broke through the queen's bedroom door. Upon discovering her absence, they hacked her bed and linens to shreds. Out in the courtyard, throngs of women, men, and men dressed as women marched about with the heads of the slaughtered guardsmen on pikes. Many had the blood of guardsmen smeared on their hands and clothes. They were demanding that the royal family be brought to Paris.

The king attempted to restore order by making an appearance on a balcony above a swarm of disrespectful rioters, to no avail. The mob demanded the queen. France had always had King Louis, at least XVI of them, but Marie Antoinette was another story. Marie Antoinette had been a lightning rod for public discontent for years, and on this October morning, lightning flashed from the courtyard to her balcony.

French peasants did not take well to foreigners, and Marie Antoinette was Austrian: strike one. The queen had been rather young when she was shipped as chattel from Austria to France. Five thousand guests watched the fourteen-year-old girl marry a chubby, indecisive fifteen-year-old monarch who seemed more interested in hunting and eating than in connubial pursuits. Growing up a royal in the public eye, Marie didn't always say the right thing when it mattered. She also had attitude: strike two. And she dressed well: strike three.

Outside the palace, trampling the immaculate gardens of Versailles, was a horde in the throes of hunger and destitution. Whispers passed from person to person until the crowd seethed with hatred for the queen. Probably the most famous quote of the French Revolution, maybe of any revolution, is attributed to Marie Antoinette, who summed up her icy indifference thus: "Let them eat cake!"

The only thing is she never said it. In reality, the quote was not attributed to the queen until half a century after her death, when prorevolutionary historians handed her the line to justify the actions of antimonarchists. To be precise, the quote attributed to Antoinette is "Qu'ils mangent de la brioche!" Or, "Let them eat brioche," a rich, eggy, cupcake-size bread that sports a pronounced bump.

Variations of "Let them eat cake" had been around for more than a century prior to Marie Antoinette's reign. Princess Maria Therese of Spain, wife of King Louis XIV, recommended that if there was no bread, peasants could eat the crust of their pâté. Rousseau spoke the same phrase in 1737. Madame Sophie, aunt of King Louis XVI, was supposed to have made the suggestion to a crowd screaming "Bread! Bread!" in 1751. Another royal aunt, the Comtesse de Boigne, has also been credited with the phrase.

Moreover, it was never in Marie Antoinette's character to brush aside the poor. Unlike anyone else in the royal family, she insisted that royal coaches, for example, avoid running their horses and wheels through peasant fields. She understood how important every stalk of wheat was to the survival of a field hand.[21]

It must have required a deep well of courage for Marie Antoinette to step out on that balcony. She asked her terrified children to join her by her side. With her arms about her children's shoulders, she stared into a crowd of thousands who wished her dead. For two minutes, she stood there as the mood slowly shifted from hatred to respect for her mettle. For the time being, the crowd let her live in exchange for a return trip from Versailles to Paris. The king agreed to the people's demands. "We are going to Paris," he told them.[22]

By afternoon, a most unusual parade left Versailles. The National Guard hauled wagons of wheat and flour toward Paris. The king, queen, their children, attendants, and relatives were ensconced in royal carriages. Trailing them were soldiers and carriages toting deputies of the National Assembly. They were all surrounded by a rather boisterous lot of women bearing loaves of bread on pikes. Market women sang, danced, passed bawdy jokes up and down the line, and drank—some to excess. Victorious women paused their marching to mount cannons, horses, and soldiers. It was still raining, the mud was ankle-deep, and Versailles was abandoned, never again inhabited by royalty. Its next occupants would be tourists.

Having toppled the monarch and his wife from the exalted heights of one of the poshest keeps in Europe to the cobblestone level of fishwives, these women, notorious for their freewheeling abuse of the French language, hurled their vilest epithets at the cowering royals.

"We have captured the Baker!"

"We have captured the Baker's wife!"[23]

S O, WHAT WAS it about French bakers that made them such despised figures that no worse curse could be heaped on a deposed king and queen? To patrons, French bakers were akin to Walmart: oversize, impersonal purveyors of daily necessities. You shopped there because you had to, even though the quality wasn't always what you hoped for, and you spent more than you wanted. A baker was an easy mark to despise, and anyone wishing to win over public opinion made a show of criticizing bakers.

"Local officials—*commissaires* and *judges de police*—in particular found that it was very effective to confront bakers on price issues in front of a crowd. It was grandstanding that might end with a riot, but it communicated as nothing else could that the police were on the 'people's side,'" wrote Judith A. Miller in the *Journal of Modern History*.[24]

Still, maybe because I bake, I find bakers worthy of some sympathy. From a baker's perspective, the cost of fuelwood was exorbitant; government regulators were ignorant baboons; and customers complained about quality, price, and quantity when they thought a baker was short-weighting them. The bakeries were hot and dusty. Sourdough had to be cared for around the clock, and much of the hardest work occurred in the middle of the night. There was ample cause for bakers to be surly and prone to excess consumption of alcohol.[25]

The preindustrial French baker stood in his baking room adjacent to his prized oven. Stacked along the walls were bags of flour. If a baker could afford to buy it or had good credit with a miller, he stored many, many bags. There was also a kneading trough made of hard nonporous wood. Larger, successful establishments sometimes supported two or more troughs. A wooden lid covered each trough when the kneading was complete. A scale was available for weighing loaves cut from a mother dough. In the immediate vicinity were scrapers, spatulas, dough cutters, knives, razors for slashing bread tops, and in some bakeries, wicker baskets to shape loaves. Wicker baskets helped a wet dough hold its shape as it rose. In French, the hemispherical basket is called a *boule*, or "ball," and a French bakery is therefore a *boulangerie*.

Working during the small hours of the morning, each of Paris's more than 1,500 bakers descended to his basement workshop to tend his sourdough starter. Without refrigeration, below-grade spaces were cooler than any other room and the most suitable for storing a starter. The myriad wild yeasts and bacteria thriving in sourdough culture grow more slowly when kept cool; a French baker tucked his sourdough starter away in a corner, behind stone if it could be managed, to guard it against heat radiating from his oven.

Bake rooms were "rarely convenient, always badly situated . . . most often dark and poorly ventilated," wrote Antoine-Augustin Parmentier, a leading bread authority of the day. In the 1780s, he founded France's first school of bread making. Parmentier described basement bake rooms as so stifling that air was hard to breathe and so hot if the oven was fired that dough "melted" during proofing.[26]

French bakers worked with very stiff starters: a lot of flour, not so much water. In what might be called a first refreshing, a baker removed a handful of starter (*levain de chef*) that he had saved from previous batches and added water and then flour. He kneaded and set the dough aside to ripen. The first wait was approximately twelve hours, though in cold months and for some starters or some breads, a few days were required for maturation. Bakers did not rest while their doughs undertook their first rise, however. Yesterday's batch was quickly maturing.

A good baker might refresh, or feed, a dough three or four times during the baking process, adding flour and water to grow the dough. In this way, a baker achieved economies of scale, making more and more bread by feeding a dough infected with a sour-dough starter that was now growing exponentially. As the dough

~~~ **Baker in the sixteenth century.**

grew in size, the swelling population of zealous microbes went to work, leavening newly added flour and water. He had to work more quickly as less and less time was needed for the dough to reach maturity. Each refreshing required a thorough kneading—an act that was increasingly calisthenic as the dough grew in size—and then the dough was covered with cloth to prevent breezes from drying or cooling the rising dough.

The well-trained journeyman—the term for a baker who had trained with a master—knew when to refresh his dough by intelligence and experience. He had to anticipate the *apprêt*, the precise moment of readiness, by matching the leaven to the age and moisture of the flour, the temperature and humidity in the room, and the speed with which the starter was imparting flavor and loft to the kneaded dough. It sounds difficult, but an attentive cook took small pinches to taste and, after making a few thousand loaves a month, rapidly learned to know his *levain*.

Parmentier observed that the traditional leavening method using sourdough imposed "overbearing slavery" on bakers, who were never permitted more than three hours of inactivity.[27] Think, too, for a moment about the labor required to knead the dough following each refreshing. At the start, a handful of starter was mixed with water and flour. Getting water to mix with stiff starter commanded intense finger work. By the third or fourth refreshing, the enlarged dough—now approaching two hundred pounds or more—was ready for "beating." Steven Kaplan, an expert on the history of French breads, said it best: "The baker plunged into the mass, punched, pulled, turned, stretched, pounded, cut, and tossed chunks of ten to twenty pounds of dough around the trough. His cries and groans signaled the enormity and intensity of physical effort. He had barely three-quarters of an hour to knead 200 pounds: if he took any longer, the dough would weaken as the fermentation lost its peak."[28]

Dr. Léon Petit, a contemporary of Parmentier, described the scene with a little more disdain: "There is no species more repugnant than that of the *geindre* [translated as either the "head journeyman" or a "whiner"], naked to the waist, pouring out sweat, gasping in the last throes, spilling and mixing into the dough that you will eat several hours later all the secretions of his overheated body and all the excretions of his lungs, congested by the impure air of the asphyxiating bake room."[29]

After the final kneading, dough was divided, weighed, and shaped. Baking reduces the weight of bread; moisture escapes as steam when dough is heated. Thus, to prepare a four-pound loaf, an experienced French baker added more dough to account for the loss of weight in the oven. The amount lost was a function of the bread's size or, more accurately, its surface-to-volume ratio. Long, skinny breads with lots of surface area lost a lot of weight. A four-pound loaf could lose thirteen or fourteen ounces; a twelve-pounder might lose only a pound and a half.

Bakers in many countries and over many centuries, from the Dark Ages on, were often accused of short-weighting, that is, selling a four-pound loaf that really weighed in at only three and a half, for example. French bakers were not immune to such practices. There were those who undercooked their breads to keep them a little on the moist and heavy side, dampened their loaves before weighing them, or placed a thumb on the scales. However, there were also factors over which a baker had little control that influenced a bread's weight: the heat of the oven was unknowable without a thermometer, scales were not always reliable, flour quality varied, and the experience or level of fatigue of the worker responsible for weighing had an impact.

After rapid shaping, loaves began their final rise. The closer the dough got to baking, the more time sensitive it became. Wait too long and a dough over-proofed. Bacteria and yeast, having exhausted their food supply, excreted unsavory acids, the dough wilted, and the bread was doomed never to rise again. If not enough time had passed, the bacteria and yeast did not have sufficient time to eat, grow, multiply, and dispense flavor-giving acids and leavening carbon dioxide. The resulting loaf was dense and rather bland.

To get the timing right, in most shops one worker divided and weighed dough while a second shaped, rounded, and smoothed it until its surfaces were as flawless as a marble bust. A pair of experienced workers could weigh and shape two hundred to three hundred pounds of bread in half an hour.[30] I have seen this division of labor in modern commercial bakeries, and it may well have been the practice in the bakery I visited in Saint-Rémy-de-Provence. But as my visit occurred during daylight, I cannot be certain which of the two bakers was a divider and weigher and which the shaper or whether they actually employed some other scheme.

Eighteenth-century bread ovens were black ovens, meaning a fire was lit directly on the cooking surface and the roof of the oven was black with soot. Fuelwood—a baker's most precious expense after flour—was loaded directly into the domed fine-clay structure. A baker needed to know how much wood to introduce to his oven, what species of wood he had purchased, and how seasoned it was as he stoked. The objective was to heat the oven walls to sufficiently hot temperatures that enduring heat would continue to radiate after the coals were removed. Because the oven had no flue, the front door was left open to gather air as the wood burned to coals.

After about three-quarters of an hour, the oven temperature was judged by hand. If it was too warm, the loaves burned on the outside before the delicate interior cooked through. The baker and his loaves were forced to wait while the oven cooled. If, on the other hand, it was not warm enough, additional wood was introduced to jack the heat. He wasn't happy in either instance; the rising loaves would have been on the verge of collapse as starving yeast began to perish. At this moment of great anxiety, bakers were known to throw tools, curse at their employees, and hurl invectives by the troughful if invisible currents of warm air caused loaves to rise to their baking point before the oven was ready.

When the oven was the right temperature, it was time to bake. Some bakers brushed out the remaining ashes; others, worrying that brushing would ruin their delicate and expensive oven floors, left them. An oven seven to nine feet in diameter could hold up to three hundred pounds of bread if the loaves were six- to twelve-pounders and only about two hundred pounds if the loaves were petite. The final step was to slash the surface of each loaf, providing room for the bread to make one last leap in the oven. An artfully slashed loaf expanded delicately. A loaf without slashes ripped along unsightly seams.

With a long-handled wooden paddle called a peel, and being careful not to deflate a loaf, the baker quickly placed the large loaves in the oven first. They took the most time to cook and were placed in the back left corner. Working left to right and back to front, he filled the oven as quickly as he could (about half an hour), sprayed water into the oven to create steam, and at last, slammed a door on the front of the oven to keep the heat radiating from the oven's walls from escaping too quickly into the bake room.

If all went well, bread in a steamy, hot oven swelled rapidly. Moisture inside the bread, now exposed to temperatures as high as 800 degrees Fahrenheit, transmuted into steam, which expanded as it warmed. The expanding gas was bound by long chains of bread gluten that had developed with the baker's effortful knead-ing. Unable to escape the loaf, the steam pressed against its con-fining walls, making eyelets, bubbles, and pockets—what bakers refer to as crumb. Behind the closed door of the oven, the breads rose one last time.

A master baker knew when to pull his loaves based on their size, their shape, and his estimation of oven temperature. When his job was done correctly, even the most cantankerous baker must have smiled at the drama. Dough had entered the oven, but behind its sealed entryway, magic happened. It emerged as bread: golden, ochre, or the color of fertile soil. Sometimes it still crackled with heat, strained at its slashes, and bore a dusting of flour or a shiny glaze of an egg or milk wash. When the bottom was rapped with a knuckle, it emitted a sonorous ring and radiated the aroma of rain-fed wheat.

There was one final step: the baker had to sell his product and make enough money to stay in business. His primary expenses were wheat and wood, whose prices and quality varied according to the dictates of supply and demand. In contrast to his fluctuating

⌒⟿ **Eighteenth-century French bakery as depicted in an engraving by Diderot.**

expenses, a neighborhood bureaucrat, entrusted with keeping the cost of bread reasonable, set his prices. When a baker's bottom line threatened to dip into the red, he could purchase inferior flour or wood at a lower price.

There was another way to increase profits, and it was found inside the dough. At no other time in history were industrial efficiency, scientific inquiry, and the worship of technology more prevalent than in western Europe in the eighteenth century. A confluence of bakers wishing to increase efficiency and French commoners insisting upon affordable bread merged to foment a second revolution. More or less running in parallel with the broad arc of history that transformed France's monarchy into its modern democratic government, a scientific upheaval swept Europe. Bread making, a practice largely unchanged for close to six millennia, was about to undergo scientific scrutiny. By the time the nineteenth century ended, elected representatives governed France, and comparatively bland yeast-driven breads were displacing loaves of sourdough.

THE FRENCH CONNECTION 103

UNTIL THE BEGINNING of the nineteenth century, no one really knew what made bread rise, what turned milk to cheese, or what made a mash of grapes become a drink both sublime and intoxicating. Nor did anyone suspect that the same invisible creatures that tailored ingredients into desirable foods were also at play in humans as germs, invading healthy bodies with grippe, tuberculosis, syphilis, and smallpox.

Today, we cower before incorporeal organisms we only imagine we can see. Even before the COVID-19 pandemic, we carried hand sanitizer in our purses and swiped grocery carts with sanitary wipes before touching them. But how did Europeans discover a world that was utterly invisible to the naked eye, and more to the point, once new bits could be seen through microscopes, how did they ever figure out what they were looking at?

As early as 583, stories circulated about "bleeding bread" that oozed a crimson fluid. Since Jesus announced at the Last Supper that his body was bread, bread has been considered holy; thus, in 1169, when a priest in Alsen, Denmark, noticed blood on the host he offered for communion, it meant Christ himself was bleeding.[31] In 1264, a priest in Bolsena, Italy, saw drops of blood fall on his robe from a wafer he offered to a parishioner. The bloody mark transformed into Christ himself. To honor the blessed event, Pope Urban VI declared the Thursday after Trinity Sunday to be the Feast of Corpus Christi.[32] In 1290, on Easter Sunday, a Parisian woman took a holy wafer out of church and sold it to the village's Jews, who according to Christian reports, stabbed it. The piercing drew blood. Christians who observed the bloody injury to Christ's body burned the Jews to death.[33]

The transition from the Dark Ages to an age of science can be observed in the explanation for bleeding bread, which gradually moved from the church to the laboratory. Before scientists' microscopes divulged a world of objects unseen before the 1600s, there was not much need to call into question sanctified explanations of the world. Bread was the body of Christ; if bread secreted a red fluid that looked like blood, it was blood.

In the middle of the seventeenth century, the Age of Exploration expanded from the seas to the heavens and finally to the microscopic. In 1665, Robert Hooke, a British optics enthusiast, published a scientific bestseller, *Micrographia*, which brimmed with pictures of the world beneath his microscope's lenses. Hooke drew a parallel between exploring heaven with a telescope—Galileo's telescopes were expanding the size of the cosmos—and inverting those lenses to see for the first time the invisible world on earth. "Under our feet, shews quite a new thing to us," Hooke wrote, "and in every little particle of its matter, we now behold almost as great a variety of Creatures, as we were able before to reckon up in the whole Universe itself."[34]

But in order to pinpoint the scientific explanation for bread that seemed to bleed, scientists required more than just a microscope to see the imperceptible. Though this seems simple enough in hindsight, they needed to comprehend what all those tiny, wiggly blobs represented. The path to comprehension was long and twisty. The Dutch scientist Antonie van Leeuwenhoek is credited with inventing modern microbiology, mostly because he was an amazing microscope maker. Leeuwenhoek's instruments could enlarge an object 275 times and resolve objects only one micron across. For the record, a human hair is one hundred microns across, and the period at the end of this sentence is around five hundred microns. Suddenly there was a lot to see, and Leeuwenhoek spent the next forty years building microscopes and placing whatever he thought interesting beneath his sight—including red blood cells.

Not to put too fine a point on it, though blood had been studied long before Leeuwenhoek, the fact that it contained discrete objects called cells couldn't be known until it was magnified. And the parsing of human blood into separate particles would prove to be necessary before human blood (or divine blood) could be distinguished from the emanations of consecrated bread. Besides studying his own, Leeuwenhoek examined the blood of tadpoles, bats, eels, and frogs. He magnified feathers, gunpowder (before and after firing), and hair of every color and variety pulled from bears, beavers, elk, and sheep. All of them contained cells—a term invented by Robert Hooke and named for the tiny rooms occupied by monks.

Leeuwenhoek disassembled bees, lice, gnats, beetles, mosquitoes, spiders (and their webs), and mites so that he could detail their brains, eyes, legs, and nerves. Naturally, the scales of fish were worth examining, as were the structures of minerals and salts. He took apart the fibers of several fish species, duck hearts, and whale muscles.

The plant world was full of unexplored terrain: coffee beans, tea leaves, nutmeg, ginger, bark, cork, ebony, lime, and fir all fell beneath his gaze. He examined leaves, seeds, and nuts, which got him to thinking of the reproductive systems of animals, so he magnified spermatozoa. (I'll let you figure out how he got some onto a microscope slide.) Even though Leeuwenhoek found a profusion of very tiny things in semen—he looked at samples from more than thirty different animals—he did not question the dogma of the day, which was that the components of larger organisms, like humans and giant oaks, were present inside the things he could see in his microscope. Spermatozoa and acorns were nothing more than tiny versions of their grown counterparts.

Leeuwenhoek looked at molds on meat and yeast in water. These tiny objects he called *animalcules*, microscopic animals.[35] The yeast he discovered in 1680 in beer wort he called *globules*, the same name he gave to the floating creatures he scraped from the plaque on his teeth. Globules, as far as he could tell, were "formed from the starchy particles of the wheat, barley, oats, etc."[36] What he did not know, and what would take about 150 years to prove, was that he was looking at living cells. The year 1700 was only two decades off; the French Revolution was just a century away, and for the first time in six thousand years, someone had associated something called globules with fermentation.

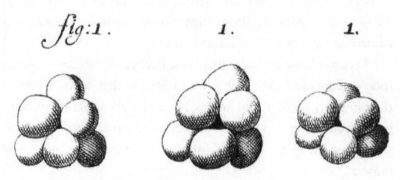

Image of yeast as drawn by Antonie van Leeuwenhoek, 1680.

Many of the scientists who contributed to the emerging discipline of microbiology were from France, the country so renowned for its extraordinary diversity of cheese, wine, and bread—all products of microbial fermentation. The French chemist A. L. Lavoisier added a piece to the puzzle of fermentation nearly one hundred years after Leeuwenhoek described globules, but not long before he lost his head to a guillotine blade in the French Revolution. Lavoisier deduced that yeast globules, when applied to mashed grapes, produced bubbles of carbon dioxide and alcohol. It did not take a scientist to prove what Dionysus knew long before ancient Greeks recorded his myth, that grape juice could be turned into wine. What Lavoisier discovered was that yeast globules were a necessity for completing the chemical transformation: grape must = carbonic acid + alcohol.

Because Lavoisier was a chemist, he balanced his equations the same way high school students are taught today. Lavoisier successfully tracked and accounted for every atom of carbon, hydrogen, and oxygen on both sides of his formula. As a chemist, however, he had no need to change Leeuwenhoek's perception that yeast globules were inanimate. Fermentation, then, at the apex of the French Revolution, was understood as a series of chemical equations activated by some airborne chemical. The late 1700s were tumultuous: French hot air balloons carried men above earth, allowing them direct access to the heavens, a province that during the Dark Ages belonged exclusively to the church; Marie Antoinette and King Louis XVI left Versailles for a Paris prison; Lavoisier was beheaded because many thought his economic views were heretical; yeast could be seen under a microscope; fermentation could be chemically calculated—and still no one knew why aged grape juice became wine or why flour and water, mixed with a cupful of yesterday's starter, rose and became bread.[37]

In the first decade of the 1800s, French chemist J. L. Gay-Lussac took one step closer to understanding yeast. Gay-Lussac filled flasks with grape juice and placed them on ring stands. Beneath each one he lit a Bunsen burner and boiled the liquid until the aroma of Chardonnay permeated his lab. As soon as he turned off the flame, he stoppered each flask and let the liquor sit for a year. He was aware, as all good Frenchmen were, that unboiled grape juice left for a year became wine, or at least vinegar.

Only once he opened his flasks and exposed them to air did his grape juices begin to acquire the aromatic and chemical characteristics of fermentation. His conclusion, dead wrong, was that heat from his Bunsen burner had deactivated his globules and that inrushing air contained the chemicals necessary for fermentation. In truth, once his flasks were unstoppered, bacteria and yeast charged in, landed happily in his sterilized liquids, and began at once to consume grape sugars.

Another piece of the puzzle was placed in August 1819, when so-called blood burst from a batch of polenta in Padua, Italy. The peasant who had cooked it tossed the batch, but the next day it reappeared in his bowl of fresh polenta. A priest was called to pray over the peasant's polenta, to no avail. The following day, the epidemic of bloodstained polenta spread to other households. The press went wild. Soon everyone knew of the terrifying signals appearing in Padua.

The local explanation was that the Almighty was prepping his revenge upon Paduans who had engaged in excessive speculation in the grain trade. Gambling and manipulating prices were renowned sins. Now that the outbreak of discharging polenta had outed the community, doom was sure to follow.

Bartolomeo Bizio, a Venetian chemist, took a scientific approach to unravel the mystery of the bleeding polenta of Padua. Exactly eighteen days after the outbreak, Bizio moistened some bread and some polenta and left them in a warm, damp atmosphere, the kind of environment, incidentally, you might expect inside a medieval church. Twenty-four hours later, they were bleeding. After five years of additional experimentation, he was able to say with confidence that microscopic blobs called bacteria were discharging the red liquid. He named them *Serratia marcescens*. *Serratia* appeared on bread or polenta that was warm and moist. It could be passed from one bowl of polenta—or from one loaf—to another by residue left in a bowl or by the hands of a baker or polenta maker.

In 1827, Jean Baptiste Henri Joseph Desmazières, an editor of scientific journals and amateur mycologist, drew pictures of everything he could see in a magnified sample of brewing beer. He named his microbes *Mycoderma cerevisiae*. *Cerevisiae* is the Latin word for beer. He did the same for wine, drawing *Mycoderma vini*. Desmazières drew figures that sure looked like yeast cells. He even figured out that they were simple living organisms. Regrettably, he failed to recognize them as the creatures causing fermentation.[38]

In the 1830s, a trio of scientists led by Frenchman Charles Cagniard-Latour almost figured it out. Cagniard-Latour possessed an excellent microscope with a magnification of five hundred diameter, with which he observed yeast cells throughout the process of fermentation. At that level of enlargement, he recognized Leeuwenhoek's globules "to be organized beings, which are probably of the vegetable kingdom."[39] As additional proof that these globules were in fact living organisms, he determined that their numbers increased during fermentation. He was able to describe for the first time the act of a yeast cell budding, and he was even able to see two yeast cells parting as they grew older. He pointed out that they broke down sugar only when they were alive, consumed sugar during fermentation, and reproduced like all other living beings. At last, yeast moved from chemistry to biology.[40]

There was still one problem. Spontaneous generation made more sense than infection. Grape must kept in a vat fermented extemporaneously; a slab of meat left unattended generated maggots where none before existed; grain produced weevils even inside closed bags; and a slurry of wheat flour and water began to bubble if left in the open air for three days. How could a scientist prove that living organisms visible only under a microscope were responsible for infecting foods by coming into contact with them? In other words, how does a cupful of today's sourdough starter make tomorrow's bread rise?

In the late 1830s, German physiologist Theodor Schwann filled four flasks with cane sugar and brewer's yeast. Everyone knew that if he left them undisturbed, he'd have a beer-like substance within a month. Following Gay-Lussac's earlier experiment, Schwann boiled all four for about ten minutes. While the flasks cooled, he covered them with mercury, a substance so dense that no air, yeast, or bacterium could penetrate it.

Next, he introduced air to all four flasks, but not the same air. Into two of the four flasks, he introduced air that he had first roasted by passing it through a red-hot glass tube. The heat killed anything floating into his intake. After four to six weeks of incubation, the sugared water in the flasks with heated air was as sterile as the day he sealed them. But the two flasks into which he had poured raw air were covered with a film of living organisms, bubbling away and reeking of fermentation.

Here was proof to counter Lavoisier's earlier analysis, which led him to conclude that his equation depended solely on the correct mixture of chemicals in his substrate and in the air. Schwann demonstrated that whatever was in the air could be killed by heat. When Schwann looked at microscope slides that had been dotted with sterilized laboratory grape juice left open to the air, yeast appeared. It multiplied, and he watched as it produced bubbles of carbon dioxide, the very compound that effervesced beer and raised bread.[41]

Nearly all the pieces were in place. Antonie van Leeuwenhoek had discovered a universe of cells but did not have the tools to understand what a cell really was. Some of Leeuwenhoek's microscopic cells were yeast, and over time, observers concluded that yeast cells were living organisms capable of growth and reproduction.

It took until the 1850s, nearly two centuries after Leeuwenhoek drew a rough picture of a yeast cell, before French biologist Louis Pasteur finally placed the last pieces in the puzzle. Fermentation was possible only in the presence of microorganisms and sugar, he said. The microorganisms consumed sugar, multiplied, and produced alcohol and carbon dioxide. In complete refutation of spontaneous generation and one thousand years of church dogma, Pasteur concluded that yeast, like other microscopic fungi, bacteria, molds, and their ilk, was as omnipresent as God. It floated about us on currents of air, covering every surface in an invisible but unmitigated film.

Science had finally explained what bread bakers had observed but could not explain for six thousand years: to create a fresh sourdough, add water to a mass of flour, and in roughly three days, yeast and bacteria will inoculate the flour and colonize a starter from which a cupful of dough can be saved to infect tomorrow's loaves. Or, and here is the kicker, skip the whole sourdough dance and simply make a trip to the brewery or yeast merchant. Buy yeast rather than wait for it to fly in on the wind or multiply slowly from yesterday's inoculant. Purchased leaven, people realized, could do the work more quickly and efficiently.

B EFORE THE FRENCH Revolution and more than fifty years before Louis Pasteur's discovery, yeast harvested by beer brewers to leaven bread already provided an irresistible economic tug on bakers. Bread leavened with brewer's yeast required far less labor than loaves made with sourdough, and furthermore, yeasted breads rose much more quickly. More bread could be produced at less cost. In the middle and late 1700s, yeast and science were poised to remake the bread-baking industry, and Antoine-Augustin Parmentier wanted to lead the charge in France.

In 1782, to great public fanfare, Parmentier launched the Free Bakery School, L'Ecole Gratuite de Boulangerie, in Paris. Upon its opening, Parmentier said, "My research has no other goal but the progress of the art and general good. The feeding of the people is my concern and my wish to improve the quality and reduce the price of bread."[42] As a young man, Parmentier had fought in France's Seven Years' War (1756–1763) with Prussia. He was wounded in action and captured several times, which meant that he was also released or traded back to the French several times. During his fifth term as prisoner of war, the Prussians fed him only boiled potatoes for two solid weeks, a food at that time considered fit only for animals.[43]

Recalling his diet of potatoes, Parmentier was enamored of the crop's ability to produce plentiful calories even in inadequate agricultural conditions. Parmentier hoped that potato bread could relegate hunger and food riots to history. Under the monitoring eyes, nose, and taste buds of Benjamin Franklin, Parmentier created recipes for potato breads.[44] Propagandize as he might, he nevertheless failed in his efforts to persuade Frenchmen to trade in their love affair with wheat bread. Potato dependence became the responsibility of the Irish.[45]

Undeterred, Parmentier attempted to force science upon bakers "because in doing things better, they would be able to sell more cheaply and earn more at the same time."[46] Louis-Sébastien Mercier, a writer and colleague of Parmentier, lay bare the future of bread for all to see. "Making wheat into bread is a chemical operation that must be enlightened by chemists," he said. "Blind routine denatures the process." Mercier scoffed at every commoner still consuming the same bread, "just as their grandfathers ate it."[47]

I did not find much evidence that the Free Bakery School had significant impact on bread production in France. The oral tradition passed along via apprenticeship and from father to son, often accompanied by a bowlful of *levain de chef*, continued largely unaffected—with one exception. The economic appeal of fast-acting yeast was too tempting, even in France. From the mid-eighteenth century forward, baker after baker gave it a try.

The use of barm, or brewer's yeast, was not a new invention. The technique was around when the Romans made bread, and before them, there is evidence that ancient Egyptians knew to take the foam from the head of top-brewing beer. That foam, rich in yeast, could be mixed with flour, water, and a little bit of salt to improve the taste. As yeast grew, doubled, and quadrupled, it exhaled what all yeasts discharge: carbon dioxide and water vapor.

It is not possible to quantify the number of bakers during any

era who used barm rather than sourdough, as professional recipes have never been widely recorded. Nevertheless, in the 1660s
and 1670s, a proclamation made by the Paris Faculty of Medicine
declared brewer's yeast unfit for human consumption, making it
obvious that in seventeenth-century France some bread must have
been yeasted and at least some French consumers did not mind the
change from sourdough.

One hundred years later, as the eighteenth century was con-
cluding, French bakers were becoming increasingly aware that,
in comparison with sourdough leavens, which required constant attention, brewer's yeast exploded a loaf "like a spark set to
combustible material."[48] A baker could use barm to generate the
same number of loaves with one-third less work. At last, a Parisian baker, enslaved as he was to the constant feeding, refreshing,
and—this is really the term they used—"mounting" of his dough,
had assistance. You can hear the knock of capitalism on the bakery
doorpost. Moreover, nearly everyone who tasted a bread made
from barm recognized that it was lighter and less dense than its
backward sourdough cousin. What baker could resist an opportunity to make more money with less work?

As some bakers let their sourdough cultures expire in favor of
yeasted breads, a bread debate broke out across France's capital. Dr.
Paul Jacques Malouin, King Louis XVI's physician, had mixed feel-
ings about barm. On the one hand, he thought that when it was
properly used "a light and better-tasting bread" emerged from the
oven.[49] On the other, he cautioned that a darkly colored bread leavened by brewer's yeast should be avoided at all costs since it made
dark breads taste too good and feel too light. Traditional sourdough
dark breads, heavy with bran and whole grains, were not only dense
but also generally less desirable and less expensive in the marketplace. Malouin was concerned that if the poor had ready access to
yeasted loaves that were light and tasty, they would eat their fill

too quickly. Their cupboards, stomachs, and purses would all run empty, and everyone in France knew what came next: riots.[50] Malouin ran experiments to determine the right quantity of brewer's yeast to add to a sourdough loaf to reach a reasonable compromise.

In contrast to Malouin's spirit of compromise, and in contradiction to his goal of producing quick, inexpensive loaves, Parmentier went orbital, arguing that barm would cause irrevocable damage to bread, France, and Western civilization. This from the same guy who hoped to produce thousands of loaves from potato starch. According to Parmentier, changing the flour from wheat to potato was a brilliant idea; moving from traditional sourdough to cultivated yeast was heresy.

Parmentier called up statements issued by the Paris Faculty of Medicine in the 1660s and 1670s that argued that brewer's yeast was bad for health. He reissued government pronouncements from 1725 that said, yes, brewer's yeast gave a loaf a pleasant appearance and a certain delicacy in heft, but in truth, bread made from brewer's yeast was "a piece of garbage, very disgusting and capable of harming the human body."[51] Many doctors and moralists joined Parmentier and maintained that brewer's yeast gave bread the same despicable characteristics it imparted to beer. Consumers were warned of nervous system impairment, excitement of their urinary tracts, and flushed complexions.

He was joined by sobrietists looking to expand their war against alcohol with an attempt to stage a blocking action between beer and bread. Dr. Gui Patin, a seventeenth-century dean of the Paris Faculty of Medicine, described brewer's yeast as the "scum" of a "doleful" drink that originated in the disgusting "rot" of barley and water. Any man who consumed such dregs would surely be headed toward ailments most commonly associated with drunkards. Worse, he might contract leprosy.[52]

Defenders of speedy leavening fought back and denounced

sourdough bread as coarse, ponderous, and sour—all of which made traditional loaves difficult to digest. Not scum, they argued, brewer's yeast was in fact the finely extracted remains of a noble product that, upon being incorporated into dough, imparted a "more subtle and more penetrating" flavor to warm bread.[53]

Parmentier didn't buy all that French-speak about brewer's yeast like it was a fine Bordeaux or Chablis. He wanted it banned. Healthy bread, he maintained, depended upon slow, even fermentation, not volatile, unpredictable growth. Bakers, he argued, could never learn to master yeast's explosiveness. The resultant crumb was unstable, and the loaves that followed the fiery bursts of multiplying yeast were less palatable than he thought they should be.[54] He might well have been describing King Louis XVI's management of the fishwives who helped launch the French Revolution.

My realization that yeasted breads challenged sourdoughs in France and the rest of Europe by the late 1700s put a wobble in my sourdough timeline. If a sourdough culture had raised loaves in Cripple Creek, Colorado, in 1893, it needed to get to North America, either as a living culture or as a practice still in use during the nineteenth century, when most Americans and Europeans turned to yeasted breads. If *Western Folklore*'s 1973 article was accurate, then there were Frenchmen in Mexico baking sourdough in 1848, even while Europeans were transitioning from sourdough to purer concoctions of brewer's yeast.

I had to take one more step backward in history if I wanted to ascertain how bread traveled to North America and, ultimately, how sourdough bread climbed the Rocky Mountains. While France had outposts on the northern and central parts of the continent, it was Great Britain's influence that dominated the fledgling states south of Canada and east of the great central wilderness, at the heart of the unexplored mainland. Great Britain exported its style of governance, fashion, and foodways to its colonies. Did the

British eat sourdough like Frenchmen? What happened when the British encountered Indigenous peoples already living in North America? I also had to figure out how sourdough crossed the Atlantic. Did early colonizers carry sourdough cultures aboard ships? Perhaps the natural preservatives imparted by sourdough cultures made them useful on oceangoing vessels—I would soon find out.

PAIN AU LEVAIN: QUINTESSENTIAL FRENCH SOURDOUGH

Yield: 2 loaves

This recipe is adapted with permission from Daniel Leader, founder of the Bread Alone Bakery, author of the exceptional bread book *Local Breads*,[55] and winner of a 2020 James Beard Award for *Living Bread*. I have simplified some of Leader's instructions, but even so, this recipe is labor-intensive. It is not nearly as sour as you might expect, but the crisp crust, chewy crumb, and subtle mix of flavors culminate in a classic. Leader provides measurements in metric weights (grams).

For the *levain de chef*

45 grams stiff *levain de chef* (sourdough starter), refrigerated
50 grams water
95 grams white bread flour
5 grams stone-ground whole wheat flour

For the dough

350 grams water
350 grams white bread flour
120 grams stone-ground whole wheat flour
30 grams rye flour
10 grams salt

Evening, Day 1. Prepare the *levain*. Remove your *levain de chef* from the fridge. Ideally, it should be a stiff *levain*, not a liquid *levain*. Pinch off 45 grams. Add the water, bread flour, and whole wheat flour. Stir with a spatula and then knead with your hands until the stiff dough has absorbed all the flour and water, about 1 to 2 minutes. Place the mass in a clean container and cover.

Let the *levain* grow and ferment for 8 to 12 hours.

Morning, Day 2. Prepare the dough. Pour the water into a new
bowl. Add the bread flour, whole wheat flour, and rye flour. Stir
with a spatula until a raggedy dough forms. Cover with plastic and
let stand 20 minutes while the flour hydrates.

Retrieve your *levain*. To the hydrated dough, add the salt and 125
grams of *levain*. The unused portion of *levain* has been recharged
and can go back in the refrigerator. Turn the dough out onto a
clean, unfloured work surface.

Knead the dough by hand for 12 to 15 minutes. At the outset, this
may be the stickiest dough you have ever worked, but resist the
desire to add more flour. Instead, push the dough back and forth
across the counter, lift it in the air to stretch it, and work it side to
side. Use a dough scraper as necessary. About halfway through the
kneading, the dough should come together, become smooth, and
be only barely tacky. It will stick to itself more than to you or the
countertop.

Place the dough in a lightly oiled dish and let it ferment, covered,
for 1 to 2 hours.

Scrape the dough onto a lightly floured counter. Pat it flat into a
rectangle about 6 by 8 inches. Fold it in thirds, like a letter in an
envelope. Flip it so that the seam is on the bottom.

Place it back in the bowl, cover, and let it ferment another 2 to
3 hours.

Afternoon, Day 2. Cut the dough into two equal halves. They should be about 500 grams apiece.

Pat them flat. Shape into batards, each about 1 foot long, tapered at the ends, and bloated in the center like an American football. (Batard shaping is easier to learn on YouTube than from the printed page.)

Place the batards on a baking sheet lined with parchment paper. Lift the parchment paper between the batards and prop their outsides with rolled towels. Dust the tops with flour.

Cover with plastic and let rise for 1 to 1½ hours.

About 1 hour before baking, heat the oven, with a baking stone on the bottom, to 450°F. Score the batards diagonally three or four times with a single-edge razor or wetted serrated knife. (There is also a unique technique to scoring baguettes that can be gleaned from YouTube.)

Just before baking, introduce a pan of ice cubes into the stove on a rack you will not need for baking. Slide the loaves, still on their parchment paper, onto the stone.

Bake for 15 minutes. Lower the heat to 400°F and bake for another 20 to 25 minutes. If you can stand it, let the loaves cool for 1 hour before slicing and eating.

CHAPTER 4

SOURDOUGH GOES TO AMERICA

T HE TRAIL OF MY SOURDOUGH STARTER WAS steadily making its way from the Fertile Crescent toward Cripple Creek, Colorado. At the same time, my understanding of how Dale Noyd came to be in Cripple Creek to receive a sourdough was becoming clearer. I had learned a great deal about Noyd because his moral confrontation with military superiors and the US court system was featured in the late 1960s in the *New York Times*, the *New Yorker*, *Harper's*, numerous court and military documents, and other magazines and newspapers across America. I also located his son, Erik, who explained that his father had been a man of great vitality and had immersed himself in flying, psychology, philosophy, ethical opposition to the war in Vietnam, sailing, hiking, and throughout it all, eating. The pieces were falling into place. Noyd was a hiker and an eater, and prior to 1970, the year of his confrontation with the US government, he was at the US Air Force Academy, just an hour by car from Cripple Creek.

For the path of sourdough to intersect with Dale Noyd's hikes in the Rockies, the practice of making sourdough bread, if not an actual starter, had to cross the Atlantic. I wondered whether long-haul oceanic explorers ate bread. A quick search of the internet for "sourdough" and "early explorers" hit on reports that Christopher Columbus may have carried a sourdough starter with him to the New World. Was it possible that sourdough came to the Americas as early as 1492?

Unlikely. Sourdough bread continued to serve as the main staple on the European mainland, as it had sustained populations for millennia, but at sea, at least during the first and second centuries of oceanic exploration, neither baking nor storing bread was practical. Warmth and moisture, so conducive to raising a microscopic colony of yeast and bacteria within a sourdough culture, gave equal succor to unwanted and various fungi that floated on air currents and landed upon any damp loaf in a ship's stores.

During the early years of transoceanic exploration, the 1500s to 1700s, sailors invested mightily in food preservation and employed every means possible to thwart the growth of bacteria and yeast. The object, after all, was to carry enough calories and protein for months at a time in forms that could keep so that the human crew might eat before the microbial crew did. It would take centuries before the idea of vitamins, minerals, and fiber—God only knows what early sailors ate to overcome constipation—became standard practice aboard ships. Carbs, preserved meats, and potable liquids were the essentials.

At the end of the Dark Ages, when Columbus was sailing, stews were heated belowdecks in brass cauldrons suspended beneath a tripod. Only on calm days, fires were lit where they could be protected from North Atlantic wind, fog, and rain, above the bilgewater, and either close to or directly on top of the stone ballast. As a journey progressed, the stench that rose from sewage-soaked ballast tended to increase in potency and coated the cooking environs in a distasteful miasma.[1]

None of the references to Columbus's sourdough starter refer to any credible evidence. Yet, just two decades after Columbus's first trip across the Atlantic, in 1512, a sixty-ton ship (about a third smaller than Columbus's *Santa María*) outfitted for the French navy contained a manifest that proved there was bread aboard. The stowed bread consisted of 1,065 dozen *pain biscuits* (also called hardtack or sea biscuit), but there were, in addition, eighteen dozen loaves of fresh bread and a puncheon of flour. A puncheon, depending on the interpretation of various historical measures, is about eighty-five gallons. The ship also carried half a cow, a pair of freshly slaughtered sheep, 211 logs of wood for cooking, forty-four pipes of beer or cider (around 5,550 gallons), two pipes of wine, and twelve pipes of water. Water was drunk only as a last resort, hence the large quantities of beer and fermented cider. Fresh bread and wine were available exclusively for officers. Evidently, even at sea, Frenchmen of stature insisted upon respectable repasts.[2]

At the beginning of the sixteenth century, French breads eaten by French officers were probably sourdough, a great advantage for preservation at sea. One of the salient features of sourdough bread is that its bacteria excrete antibiotics and acids that inhibit the growth of competing bacteria and molds. Even after cooking, these antibiotics and the acidic nature of the bread act as natural preservatives and significantly slow the development of green splotches. At least for the first several days, French officers could have dined upon mold-free sourdough bread. For the crew on a French ship, however, bread was really just *pain biscuit*. There was some sourdough bread, then, on French vessels, but not sourdough starter.

The British, in contrast to the French, loaded their ships with more utilitarian nutriments. Martin Frobisher (ca. 1539–1594) was a professional pirate, which is to say, he was paid by the British government of Queen Elizabeth I to raid French ships as well as set sail for economically viable waterways to connect Britain's colonies. Frobisher made three attempts at the Northwest Passage, so his occupation was additionally listed as explorer. On his second voyage, in 1577, Frobisher listed his foodstuffs, as well as the means by which he calculated his needs:

> *One pound of biscuit and one gallon of beer per man per diem, one pound of salt beef or pork per man on flesh days and one dried codfish for every four men on fast days, with oatmeal and rice if the fish gave out; a quarter-pound of butter and a half a pound of cheese per man per day, honey for sweetening [sugar was an expensive luxury]; a hogshead of "sallet oyle" [salad oil, probably olive oil; a hogshead is sixty-three gallons] and a pipe of vinegar [twice the amount of a hogshead] to last 120 men for three or four months.*[3]

Hardtack, a severely dry form of unleavened bread, was the sailor's main source of calories for both British and French alike from at least 1500 to at least the 1700s. Hardtack was unpleasant. In 1782, Jeffrey Raigersfield, a twelve-year-old seaman serving under Admiral Cornwallis, described his English hardtack, the main staple aboard the forty-four-gun *Mediator*, this way: "So light that when you tapped it upon the table, it

Hardtack (15 × 135 millimeters) from the early nineteenth century, still on display at the National Maritime Museum, London, England.

fell almost into dust, and thereout numerous insects, called weevils, crawled; they were bitter to the taste, and a sure indication the biscuit had lost its nutritious particles; if, instead of these weevils, large white maggots with black heads made their appearance, then the biscuit was considered to be only in its first state of decay; these maggots were fat and cold to the taste, but not bitter."[4]

In the 1790s, the French and the British learned to bake bread at sea. Alexander Brodie, a master blacksmith from Peeblesshire, Scotland, invented a cast-iron oven for ships. Brodie's oven supported two large boilers over an enclosed firebox. In front of the ovens were two open fire grates upon which pots large enough to make stews for a crew could be set to boil. In front of the fire grates was a spit large enough to roast a generously sized carcass. Finally, there was an oven capable of baking eighty pounds of bread at a time, and so at about the same time that Frenchmen were revolting against their monarchy, there was a reason to bring a living sourdough culture aboard ship. Brodie's oven had one additional feature of great import: attached to the stove was a distillery for the purpose of condensing pure water. Capturing steam and condensing it finally solved the problem of months-old water becoming so stale that it could be imbibed only if the alternative was seawater. The British navy was so taken with Brodie's design that it gave him a monopoly for outfitting all British ships for twenty-nine years.[5]

Sir Gilbert Blane, MD, "the father of naval medical science," was particularly taken by the ability of Brodie's oven to bake what was called "soft" bread, "soft" serving as an obvious distinction from the slabs of hardtack. In 1790, Blaine wrote with great joy at the ability of Brodie's oven to finally put Britain's navy in the same culinary ocean as France's: "In the French ships of war there is an oven large enough to supply not only the officers and the sick but part of the crew with soft bread every day; the objection chiefly made to baking on board formerly was the great consumption of wood; but it is now obviated by the general adoption of the fireplaces of cast iron invented by Brodie in which the ovens are heated with the same fire with which the victuals are boiled."[6]

Thus, in 1790, nearly three hundred years after Columbus's first voyage and three years before King Louis and Marie Antoinette lost their thrones and their heads, both British and French ships were able to bake bread at sea. But at sea, as on land, the French remained loyal to their loaves of bread, while the British simply cared less. Their contrasting attitudes toward bread, sourdough, and the preparation of food would play out in North America when immigrants from the two countries established colonies. Take this example, in 1790, from John Cochrane, a Scottish aristocrat in charge of victualing the British navy. Cochrane published a pamphlet with this rather long but very descriptive title (emphasis per the original): *The SEAMAN'S GUIDE; shewing How to Live Comfortably at Sea; containing Among Other Particulars, COMPLETE DIRECTIONS FOR MAKING BREAD, either with yeast or leaven [sourdough], Recommended also to Public Bakers, as well as to Private Housekeepers.*[7]

Nearly halfway through his treatise, Cochrane, having provided what amounted to a twenty-five-page recipe for making bread from sourdough or brewer's yeast, finally arrived at his main lament. All of the large ships of the British navy and its India service, he noted, were equipped with an oven capable of baking bread but in practice did not bake any while a-sea. As sourdough required regular feedings and the ship's crews served systematic shifts, it would be easy to replenish a culture at regular intervals. Ignorance of the care and feeding of sourdough starters, and the inability of most British bakers to make yeast-leavened bread less sour than sourdough, had robbed the British seaman of soft bread, he complained. Because of the dearth of quality bread, the British seaman had lost his vigor. "Nothing conduces more to the health of the crew," he said. About Britain's archenemy, he continued, "All the French ships, whether men of war or merchant ships, regularly bake soft breads for the whole ship's company." Even the British had to admit that the French were the masters of sourdough.

Another publication of the period had something to say about British dislike of sourdough bread. In 1805, Abraham Edlin published *A Treatise on the Art of Breadmaking*. Most of it depicted every conceivable means of leavening bread so that it did not taste sour.[8] Regarding sourdough, Edlin said, "A great deal of nicety is required in conducting this operation [fermentation], for if it is conducted too long the bread will be sour, and if too short a time has been allowed for the dough to ferment and rise, the bread will certainly be heavy."[9] Edlin recommended Schweppes carbonation, yeast generated by potatoes, barm taken from beer brewers, water that had fermented in the bottom of oceangoing casks, toddy (fermented coconut water), and dunder (the sludge at the bottom of the rum barrel). Add potash to the dough, he wrote, to remove some of the sour. In short, Edlin was promoting any viable means available to leaven bread that avoided the use of sourdough.

At the beginning of the nineteenth century, typical British bread on land and at sea, according to Edlin, went through the same transformations as bread in France, only more so. "The bread used principally in this country is fermented with yeast or the froth which rises on the surface of beer in the first stages of fermentation," he wrote. The benefit to the British way of leavening bread with brewer's yeast was that "when it is mixed with the dough, [there is] a much more speedy fermentation than that obtained from leaven [sourdough], and the bread is accordingly much lighter, and unless it is improperly prepared it is never sour."[10]

The answer to the question, then, of how and when sourdough arrived in America is lost in a North Atlantic fog, I'm afraid. There is no evidence that Christopher Columbus shipped a starter, and even if he had, he left no bakers behind. It is probable that British colonists along the eastern seaboard of North America used sourdough if they had to but preferred quicker, less tangy approaches to leavening, if they could acquire them. Meanwhile, Frenchmen colonizing their portion of Canada and the central part of the continent, which would eventually be sold to Thomas Jefferson as the

Louisiana Purchase in 1803, were probably preparing bread that was sourdough or leavened with purer colonies of yeast.

I could find no evidence that anyone, not even a ship's primary baker, disembarked in the New World with a sourdough starter. The absence of evidence doesn't guarantee that an event never occurred, but because new sourdough starters are not difficult to make, it is reasonable to presume that the practice of making sourdough bread in North America arrived by ship as a skill, rather than as a lump of living dough. I dispensed with the notion that my Cripple Creek sourdough was so old and well loved that it had somehow arrived from Europe packed by an itinerant baker or ship hand. I suppose it is possible, but it does not feel very likely.

T O FIND CRIPPLE Creek's antecedents, I set my focus on food production and preparation in North America as it was practiced by its early colonizers. One path to Cripple Creek was the circuitous route from France to Mexico to California and then to Colorado, but it seemed equally plausible that sourdough simply inched its way westward as expanding populations moved from North America's eastern seaboard toward Cripple Creek. I decided to investigate the British and then the French to see what I could learn about how they made their bread as they moved from coastal toeholds toward more central towns and cities. For the British, I decided to go back to 1620, when Pilgrims who sought liberty from the Church of England first set up camp in Massachusetts.

The archetypal story of the Pilgrims typically ends with the holiday of Thanksgiving: a savory meal of celebration buried beneath an onslaught of pumpkin pies, sweet potato casseroles, cranberry sauces, and roast turkeys. Even today, four centuries after a meal commemorating the willingness of Wampanoags to save the starving Pilgrims, the foods Americans heap upon their Thanksgiving tables are largely native to North America, though what was actually served was probably very different. The Wampanoags probably did not serve marshmallow-covered sweet potato casserole, for example. Likewise, bread was not present in 1621, and if it is found at all at a contemporary Thanksgiving dinner, it is usually an afterthought or stuffed inside the bird. Bread, the basic staple of Europeans, would take some time before it became American.

Pilgrims were not farmers before they embarked for America, which explains some of their ineptitude in Massachusetts. Rather, they were religious fundamentalists whose differences with King James I and the Church of England had turned decidedly nasty. The Puritans, as they were also known, fled to the Netherlands. They lasted barely more than a decade in Holland before they became repulsed by what they perceived as the country's unbearable permissiveness. William Bradford, the spiritual, military, and political leader of the Pilgrims, complained that "the great licentiousness of [Dutch] youth . . . and the manifold temptations of the place" tempted English children "into extravagant and dangerous courses."[11] Apparently, even in the early seventeenth century, Dutch youth were hard partiers.

On Saturday, September 5, 1620, William Bradford and his followers boarded the *Mayflower* for the New World, a land so far away they could practice their strain of Christianity without interference. On most days, stormy conditions in the North Atlantic prevented the preparation of hot meals. For those who could eat, meals were hardtack dipped in beer or served with butter or cheese. Sometimes they gnawed at dried pork, salted cod, and dried tongues, and on rare days when the Atlantic was calm enough that fires could be set beneath tripod ovens in the ballast, they soaked their hardtack in stews made with rehydrated meats and fish.[12]

Early-onset scurvy was already afflicting the *Mayflower's* passengers—according to Bradford, 50 of the 102 passengers died of the disease in the first winter. One of the first symptoms of scurvy is teeth that loosen in their sockets; unsoaked, unforgivingly compact hardtack would have been very difficult to eat.[13]

The Pilgrims landed on November 9, 1620, after sixty-six days at sea. Bradford sent a fully armed exploratory party ashore. The small group of men climbed the beach, peered over the seagrass-covered dune, and found a cleared field. They homed in on a recently abandoned village, within which was a constructed mound. Native Americans farmed the coast in the summer and moved inland to hunt during the winter. The mound served as food storage awaiting their springtime return. The Pilgrims could still discern handprints in the sand.

When they dug into it, they discovered "a little old Basket, full of faire *Indian* corn, and digged further & found a fine great new Basket of very faire corn of this year . . . some yellow, and some red, and others mixt with blew, which was a very goodly sight."[14] Bradford's armed explorers hoisted the bushel baskets of Indian corn from the ground. What spilled over the tops they slipped into their pockets. Then they wobbled across the sand, their swords and muskets interfering with their booty, clamored into their dinghy, and rowed back to the *Mayflower* to top its stores.[15]

The majority of the Pilgrims hailed from the southern end of the British Isles, where wheat grew well. In the north of Great Britain, where it is too cold and damp for wheat to be grown reliably, Scottish oatmeal and Irish oatcakes were more common fare. To class-conscious Englishmen, oats bore a stigma; they were eaten by lower castes, namely, Scots and Irishmen. Even lower in the British caste system than oats, Scots, and Irishmen were corn and Native Americans. Previous explorers had alerted the Pilgrims that the Indigenous peoples of North America, called Indians by the new settlers, were godless heathens, and Indian corn was their food.[16] Indian corn—what Americans today simply call corn and

Europeans refer to as maize—was not exactly manna, but the Pilgrims were hungry, and their preferred grain, wheat, which is not indigenous to North America, was obviously not around.

John Gerard (1545–1612), a famous Elizabethan herbalist of the immediate pre-Pilgrim era, castigated corn in his report on plants. His account was printed in 1597, again in 1633, and one more time in 1636. "[Maize] doth nourish far lesse than either wheat, rie, barly, or otes," he began. It is hard and dry as a biscuit, "hath no clamminess at all,"[17] yields little or no nourishment, and causes constipation. Gerard made it clear that only barbarous natives of North America thought that maize was food. In reality, he said, maize was food for swine, not men. To the Pilgrims, the basic staple of the New World not only tasted bad but also held the added humiliation of being food meant for philistines and pigs. It must have been very disheartening for the people of New England, religious zealots who found old England insufficiently observant and Holland intolerably lax, to have to survive on the food of people they considered uncivilized and subhuman.[18]

As new English colonists followed the Pilgrims to New England, they too found corn to be a significant stumbling block. Edward Johnson, an early member of the Massachusetts Bay Colony (1628–1630), reported that his fellow colonists longed for their English grains—wheat, barley, and rye—and found that bread that incorporated corn made them sick to their stomachs.[19] Many a colonist must have poked at a bowl of mushy corn porridge and wondered if she would ever again taste her mom's roast swan, comforting ale, and freshly baked sourdough bread made of kneaded wheat flour.

The multihued kernels hauled back to the *Mayflower* by William Bradford's soldiers actually indicated advances in maize breeding performed by Native Americans over the years. At roughly the same period in history when protocivilizations were domesticating wheat in the Fertile Crescent, Indigenous peoples of North America were selecting varieties of corn suited to each region's rainfall, soil, season length, and preferred tastes. Corn grown by Hopis in the American Southwest, for example, is blue and white and holds, to this day, both religious and curative properties, while corn raised by Wampanoags in Cape Cod is typically red, yellow, and orange.[20]

For Native Americans, corn supplied abundant carbohydrates, could be dried and stored through cold winters, and provided perfect nutritional balance when eaten with beans. Contrary to the perceptions of newcomers from Europe, who perceived only savages and wilderness, the Indigenous communities they encountered in the New World were, in fact, clever land managers and skilled cooks. Corn does not contain gluten, however, and so is best suited to making flat, unleavened bread.

However, it was not long before Europeans schlepped over bags of wheat seeds. Through the sixteenth and seventeenth centuries, fields of wheat were slowly established in New England. What remained an obstacle until the eighteenth century, when Pennsylvania became the breadbasket of the Americas, was that the climate of the New England colonies was not much more suited to the production of wheat than the climate of Scotland or Ireland. Rain, damp, and cold were more favorable to wheat diseases than to wheat. Some wheat could be harvested, but not enough to satisfy demand. In the fields of Massachusetts, Rhode Island, and Connecticut, where English colonists prevailed, corn outproduced wheat fivefold.[21] Englishwomen had to find a way to cook with both corn and wheat if they wanted to make bread.

The best description for how Englishmen came to terms with so-called Indian corn was written by John Winthrop, Jr., who became governor of the Connecticut Colony in 1657, a position he held until his death in 1676. The father of John Winthrop, Jr., John Winthrop, Sr., was a Puritan who fled England to found the

Massachusetts Bay Colony. Like earlier colonists, the elder Winthrop considered Indigenous peoples, and presumably their food, beneath him. He took hold of Pequot land,[22] then captured and shipped Indigenous warriors to the West Indies in exchange for "salt, cotton, tobacco, and negroes," keeping one man and two women for himself.[23]

And yet the son, John Winthrop, Jr., praised corn. In 1662, during a trip to London, he was asked to write a treatise about corn for England's Royal Society. Winthrop obliged and, in so doing, described a rather remarkable change in English attitudes toward corn, if not toward Native Americans. In the opening paragraph of "Indian Corne,"[24] Winthrop took aim at John Gerard, the Elizabethan herbalist. To Gerard's claim that corn was neither nutritious nor fit for human consumption, Winthrop insisted that corn was wholesome, able to be used in a wide variety of tasty dishes, and downright "pleasant."[25] In just two generations, corn had worked its way onto British tables and into English hearts. Englishmen were becoming American.

About half of the essay was dedicated to bread made with corn. Some batters were thin and baked for twelve hours or more in a very hot oven, he wrote. Others were poured like pancakes onto the swept floor of a stone oven. When the first layer was partly cooked, a second layer of thick batter was poured on top. A well-baked double-layer corn cake, Winthrop raved, radiated deep yellow.[26]

Other recipes called for mixing cornmeal with rye or wheat flour or both and then—wait for it—sourdough or yeast to make it rise. This bread was kneaded and shaped into loaves and baked like bread from the old country. Even the double-layer flat cakes, he said, benefited from leavening.

The British had brought with them rye and wheat from home. Even if they had not carried sourdough starters across the Atlantic, they had brought with them the practice of setting up a starter and allowed the microscopic beasts in American air to fall in. They had experimented with combinations of corn, which grew readily, and Old World grains, which were still quite finicky in New England's variable climate and rocky soils. They shaped loaves that reminded them of home and invented a new kind of bread that was fundamentally American. It was made with varying quantities of cornmeal, rye, and wheat, in proportion to their availability, and sourdough or brewer's yeast. They called it Rye and Indian, Rye and Injun, or sometimes Ryaninjun.[27] Adding sourdough made sense for Rye and Indian because rye flour has a little bit of gluten, and if a New England farmer had managed to harvest a decent enough crop of wheat for wheat flour to enter the dough, even more gluten might have been present.[28] An almighty leavened loaf was possible.

According to Winthrop, the English made one more important addition to New World cuisine. "The English," he reported, regarding their growing familiarity with corn, "have found a way to make very good Beere of this Graine."[29] Had his father, who once introduced temperance legislation to England's Parliament, still been alive, he would have spit in frustration.[30]

In addition to Rye and Indian and corn beer, the English adapted a third mainstay to the American table. This, too, was a kind of bread compromise derived of thrift and necessity. Many early Americans ate boiled bag puddings, which received their name from the manner in which they were prepared. A wide array of otherwise difficult to work with ingredients were sewn inside a bag to be boiled or baked. In the Old World, puddings were a means of making use of every part of a slaughtered animal, including its blood, which gave black pudding its designation. Animal innards, which could not be readily turned into roasts or stews, were supplemented with grains, currants, bread crumbs, eggs, or cream. The contents were baked or boiled and then served as a slice, in a pie, or as a lump. The key feature, if you look closely at the ingredients, is that every calorie of cow (or pig or sheep) and every crumb of stale bread had been put to use.

In the New World, housewives contrived a new cooking invention: cloth. Formerly, puddings were prepared inside a sack made from an animal's gut, which was hard to fill and harder still to clean. A sheet of broadcloth, however, was a key to fast food. Laid upon a table, it could first be lined with ground Indian corn, from which no decent bread could be raised, and then filled with whatever bits of meat were at hand. The flavor could be enhanced, depending on the season, with huckleberries, wild currants, molasses, maple syrup, eggs, butter, and spices. It was, if you reduced the amount of meat and increased the proportion of sweets, an early iteration of a dessert pie.[31]

Boiled bag puddings did not require a great deal of attention. If a cow had to be milked, or if a child's scraped knee required undivided attention, and a distracted mother failed to notice that the fire beneath the pot of boiling water had gone out, not much harm came to the final product. Boiled bag puddings simmered for three hours or five. They were served hot or cold and eaten with a spoon or a knife. Boiled bag puddings remained a staple of New England cooking into the twentieth century, and they were nearly always referred to as Indian puddings to indicate the presence of cornmeal.

When published recipes started to appear at the beginning of the nineteenth century, Rye and Indian was usually included.[32] Sarah Josepha Hale (1788–1879) prepared one of America's first cookbooks in 1839. Her Rye and Indian bread was made from four quarts of sifted cornmeal (she called it Indian meal) to which were added two quarts of rye meal, a tablespoon of salt, and two quarts of boiling water. One fascinating fact about old recipes that required leavening is that they insisted that before a sourdough starter could be added, the dough to which it would be joined needed first to come to "milk temperature." Milk temperature was well-known to all housewives who milked cows, as milk squeezed from a teat emerges at the internal temperature of a cow: 101.5 degrees Fahrenheit. Milk temperature is a perfect temperature for growing yeast and bacteria, both good and bad. When Hale's dough cooled to milk temperature, a fistful of sourdough starter was mixed in.

The dough was kneaded, but the recipe made clear that the mixture would not hang together the way dough made from wheat held its own. After mixing and kneading, the batter was left to rise—by the fire in wintertime and definitely away from fire in the summer to prevent over-proofing. About an hour to an hour and a half after a properly raised Rye and Indian was put together, its top began to crack. The dough was placed in a buttered deep pan, probably cast-iron, that was then placed into a well-heated oven (no precise temperature was knowable, prescriptible, or necessary) and cooked for three to four hours. It was best to cook Rye and Indian inside a Dutch oven to help it hold its shape. If there was enough time, a good Rye and Indian bread could be heated overnight because cornmeal, Hale pointed out, needed to be well cooked. The final loaf weighed between seven and eight pounds, and if the weight of its iron cooking pot was added, we can surmise something about the ability of colonial women to perform bicep curls with hot pots.[33]

To counteract the sourdough flavor—which the British did not care for—imparted by cultures used in Rye and Indian, cookbooks in the mid-nineteenth century recommended the addition of molasses, which soon became a standard practice. Boston brown bread is today's descendant of Rye and Indian. Modern recipes use baking soda and baking powder for leaven, a mixture of rye, wheat, and cornmeal, and a hefty dose of molasses. For a time, it was cooked in a coffee can, but the principle is the same: the dense bread is steamed, just as in the days when Dutch ovens were a primary means of cooking over an open flame.

Rye and Indian was part of the creation of a New World fare that married foods of Native Americans with Old World traditions to create new dishes. Because historical records from the middle of the seventeenth century showed the practice of adding sourdough cultures to Rye and Indian breads repeated in Sarah Josepha Hale's cookbook in 1839, I know that in America in the middle of the nineteenth century, sourdough was still in use. So, a descendant of a British colonist or a British baker who headed West in search of gold could have taken an East Coast starter with him. On the other hand, by the time rushes for gold were underway in the Rocky Mountains in 1893, an Englishman's tastes might have veered more toward bread leavened with brewer's yeast, the bread of choice in Great Britain at the time and increasingly the bread of choice for Americans. Perhaps a Frenchman brought it West.

B Y 1750, GREAT Britain controlled the Atlantic Seaboard, yet it was France that maintained control over Quebec, parts of central Canada, and most of the Mississippi watershed south to New Orleans, a combined territory often referred to as New France. French families, traders, trappers, and explorers in New France, just like their relatives back in Europe, had to have bread to survive. According to one New World account from 1636, "Each labourer eats two six- or seven-pound loaves a week."[34] Another, in 1716, said, "The colonist consumes two pounds of bread and six ounces of lard per day."[35] The French, like the British on the coasts, did what they could to raise wheat, but in some years hunger surely drove some Frenchmen to lower themselves to eating bread adulterated with rye flour, then rye and barley, and if things were really bad, then oats and even pea flour had to do.[36] But bread was what a Frenchman had to have.

New France, ca. 1750.

Much of what I learned about French sourdough bread in early North America was the result of a Canadian research project carried out in the late 1970s. Lise Boily and Jean-François Blanchette, two employees of the National Museum of Man and the national museums of Canada, set out to document the clay bread ovens of Quebec. Boily and Blanchette were able to do so because there were still French Canadians alive who could recall baking bread using the same methods employed by France's first colonists in the New World.[37]

They discovered that the French method for constructing a bread oven described in Diderot and d'Alembert's *Encyclopedia of Science* (1782) was the same method used by rural farmers in Canada well into the twentieth century.[38] Unlike in France, the abundance of wood in the New World meant that every family had enough fuel for a personal oven. Communal ovens and ovens managed by a lord of the manor were unnecessary on a continent covered in forest. Abundant woodlands thus augured a kind of democracy not available in Old France.

Because early Canadian bureaucrats listed every oven in New France, Boily and Blanchette were able to confirm that some ovens in the New World dated to the middle of the eighteenth century. Atop a stone foundation, a clay dome was raised above firebricks or a hearthstone. Builders packed clay around a lattice of bent alder saplings until the oven walls were at least eight inches thick. Clay was readily available across New France; not only was it inexpensive, but it also retained and radiated an enormous amount of heat and, consequently, made great bread. "In these [clay] ovens," wrote Diderot and d'Alembert, "the bread bakes easily, perfectly, and for little cost, especially when the dome is not too high, when care has been taken to make the sides of the dome sufficiently thick, and when the cracks have been adequately repaired."[39]

As clay dried, it contracted. The fresh alder saplings bent with the shrinking clay, and a patient oven builder filled cracks as they formed. Many an old-timer interviewed by Boily and Blanchette reported that the rounded clay dome held the same silhouette as a crouching beaver. When the oven had finally air-dried and all its cracks were filled, the interior clay was vitrified with a serious inferno, thus completing construction. To protect the clay from rain and snow, the final step was the construction of a roof over the oven. Newly constructed ovens were baptized by local priests and celebrated with parties thrown for all the neighbors.[40]

❧ **A Quebecois bread oven.**

With these bread ovens, French life could begin in earnest, and Boily and Blanchette suggested that sourdough cultures were at work in French settlements from the early days, cared for and cultivated exactly the way they were back in France. The day before major baking was to occur, the household culture was expanded with fresh flour and water. On baking day, it was added to dough headed for the ovens. Of course, a handful was removed before baking to be saved for the next batch, and if it was forgotten or lost, neighbors shared with one another.[41] Several older Canadians interviewed by Boily and Blanchette reminisced about the largely forgotten technique of raising, expanding, saving, and storing sourdoughs. Not a single interviewee thought that commercial yeast or store-purchased Canadian bread was an improvement.

Baking bread in the newly settled lands of northern North America was done much the same way as it was in the bakeries of pre-revolution Paris. Cedar, if it was available, was burned on the hearthstone until the clay dome was thoroughly heated. Black smoke poured from the single opening. To determine if the oven was the correct temperature for baking, each housewife had her own counting method. She inserted her arm into the center of the oven and began, "One, two, three, four . . ." If she could keep her arm inside until her own personal number—four, ten, twenty, twenty-five, or thirty-two—it was bread-making time. If she had to withdraw before her number came up, she waited while the oven cooled.[42] If the oven took too long to cool, her breads rose, her cultures consumed all their food, and the breads collapsed before baking. The taste would be too sour, the cooked breads too dense, and the family pigs would be having a feast.

On a successful day, at the moment the oven reached the right temperature, ashes were swept from the hearth while a parade of children carefully brought loaves to the oven door. The family matriarch used her long-handled peel with speed and precision to place the largest loaves in the back and near the walls. She left space at the front for tiny practice breads prepared by the household's youngest. When all were loaded, she placed a door over the opening, sealing it shut.

As dispassionate as Boily and Blanchette attempted to be in their formal museum document, it was impossible to miss the degree to which Boily and Blanchette were influenced by the fond nostalgia of their informants. "As she waits patiently," they reported, "the cook spends the last few minutes imagining a beautiful batch of golden-brown well-shaped loaves. . . . Everyone is on hand for the magic moment when the loaves are taken out of the oven."[43]

For a French family living the country life in Canada, according to Boily and Blanchette and the old-timers they interviewed, freshly baked sourdough bread was the star of the meal, from its earliest days in the seventeenth century right through the beginning of the twentieth. The main loaf was placed before the head of the family to be blessed. With a knife, he made a fine cross in the end of the loaf as a religious symbol of thanks, cut it, passed slices to the most senior family members first, and finally handed slices of warm bread to what must have been some very fidgety children.

A S SOURDOUGH STARTERS moved closer in time and distance to Cripple Creek, Colorado, I observed a recurring theme with respect to American culture that reached a peak in legends about gold miners. Literature of the era celebrated the fortitude, self-sufficiency, and mighty independence of early Americans. Hale colonial farmers were often described as raising all their own staples, while hardworking wives made all their food, including sourdough bread. Interestingly, I discovered that this characteristically American attribute of self-sufficiency was largely based on a fraudulent manuscript.

In 1787, just more than a century before gold was discovered in Cripple Creek, the misleading document was first published as a series of letters from an early American farmer to a Philadelphia magazine called *American Museum*. "Nothing to wear, eat, or drink was purchased," wrote the farmer, demonstrating the virtues of frugality and self-reliance.[44] The farmer said that he was so poor as a child that his parents had to give him up to another farmer until he was twenty-one and able to become a self-made man.[45] The writer's humble beginnings and rags to riches journey have been cited and republished in history textbooks and political essays ever since.

Alas, when professional historians subjected the letter to close scrutiny, they discovered not only that the exploits of "A Farmer" were illusorybut also that the farmer-writer himself was probably fictitious, invented for political reasons. Moreover, the farmer's wife, "a very good working woman," could not have existed either.

She was supposed to be the mother of seven, and as all imaginary farmwives were, she was responsible for bread baking, meal preparation, clothing production, grain processing, and supervision of children and livestock.

While our frugal Yankee farmer was outside plowing fields, trimming apple trees (did he really manufacture his own saw blades?), and shoeing horses, consider the expectations for "the housewife that made everything from scratch." As Carole Shammas, a historian of medieval England and colonial America, put it, "She had to possess the knowledge of the flax spinster, wool spinster, weaver, dyer, fuller, tailor, knitter, miller, baker, gardener, dairy maid, chandler, and soap maker." She had to be good at these things lest her family become filthy, raggedy, and hungry. Moreover, she had to complete these tasks betwixt the corralling, dressing, washing, and feeding of many small children.[46]

Deconstruct any single task, like making clothing from wool, and it is hard to conceive that a single housewife excelled at so many different duties. After it was sheared from the sheep, wool had to be cleaned, degreased, carded, spun twice before weaving, woven, and dyed with the petals gathered from Jerusalem artichokes, irises, cedar berries, and so forth. Then, and only then, could a housewife begin sewing. If any further proof were needed of the improbability of a housewife mastering cloth production on top of her other chores, an inventory from the Virginia settlement taken during the years 1660 through 1676 found that only 1 percent of households made any reference to a spinning wheel.[47]

Where statistics proved that it was nearly impossible for Americans to have had lives devoid of trade, sale, or purchase,[48] basic economics confirmed the illogic of self-sufficiency even for farmers ringing Boston's growing metropolis. By 1710, the city was home to nearly ten thousand people; between 1735 and 1744, it grew to seventeen thousand. In the countryside, some housewives were excellent spinners and surely would have sold a frock or two to a city lady. The revenue generated by the sale of a shawl could have been applied to the purchase of soap, candles, or bread from a commercial baker. And all those people in the city? Instead of making it all themselves, many of them walked to the neighborhood baker to buy bread, too.

Even as I learned that bakeries sold bread to many Americans as early as the 1700s, still I pondered the claim of grain independence written up in *American Museum*. I wanted to know how difficult it would have been for a farm family to make bread from start to finish, so I tried my hand at turning wheat from sown seed into bread made from Cripple Creek sourdough.

Early in 2015, I planted a small patch, twenty-four feet long by four feet wide, of Glenn hardy spring wheat in a raised bed outside my office in Meadville, Pennsylvania. Three months later, it was a muggy mid-July day when I pulled a small army of summer interns from other professors' labs and offices for a couple of hours of reaping. The first thing I noticed when we began harvesting was how beautiful the wheat was. The small sheaf of gold I held bunched in my hand splayed like fireworks, each tiny seed bundled in a husk peaked by a single spiky awn.

Being eye to eye with a stalk of wheat made it easy to comprehend the challenges of preindustrial farming. A colonial rhyme captured my observations:

One for the bug
One for the crow
One to rot
And two to grow.[49]

There were bare patches in my small field where birds had eaten my seeds right after planting. Many of the plants had lodged, which is to say that they had fallen over and failed to mature, or were just plain hard to grab before cutting. A few seed heads had molded during incessant June rains, and intertwined everywhere were weeds. Bennett, a college junior clipping plants at their base by hand, turned to me and said, "Wow, this is a lot of work!" I made certain Bennett understood how grateful he should be that someone else had invested the energy of adding compost as our fertilizer source.

As the heat of the afternoon bore down and my appreciation of the beauty of the wheat was replaced by the effort involved in clipping and binding, I focused more closely on the seeds from which we would make bread. Compared with the bundles of wheat I was trying to tie into sheaves, the seeds themselves suddenly appeared to be very, very tiny. How much bread could I make from this field? How many calories and how much additional energy would I expend in doing so? We still had threshing, winnowing, and grinding to go before we could even contemplate kneading.

It took only a week from the time my students and I harvested our wheat, bound it into sheaves, and left it upright until the heads, cut off as they were from their roots, had completely dried. It was time to disconnect the seeds from their shafts. We spread a large tarp on a patio, and when our homemade flailing stick disassembled on the third whack, we danced our way toward loaves.

To coax seeds from their bundles, we lay stalks of wheat on the tarp and then trampled them with our feet in much the same manner that ancient inhabitants of the Fertile Crescent used mules to break free the seeds of their subsistence. The shuffling thresh was about 85 percent effective, and not one of us could resist the urge to hand rub recalcitrant seeds from resistant clusters.

If a seed rolled off the tarp, my first instinct was to pick it up from the concrete and return it to the pile. Students were crawling everywhere like a hive of disturbed ants, tweezing tiny seeds from the ground. Everyone knew at some primal level that our ancestors would have depended on such diligence for their survival.

Winnowing was more frustrating than threshing. This is where the phrase "separating the wheat from the chaff" arises. The wind has to be strong enough to blow off inedible bits of straw and seed husks but not so powerful as to blow out seeds dropping into the catchment.

Alas, sultry summer days are also windless ones. I tried making a breeze by waving a huge piece of cardboard up and down while Sarah, my research assistant, poured wheat from one bowl to another. My intention was to raise a strong enough gust at just the instant chaff was falling eighteen inches into the catchment. The air I generated moved hardly anything. We tried a fan and then a larger fan before the chaff blew off across the patio. Slowly, the number of ruddy seeds grew, and the remaining contamination of stalks, spiky awns, unopened pods, and yellow heads of unhusked grain dwindled.

Although an early farmer would have used a hand-cranked mill if he wasn't going to pay a professional miller for the service, I departed from traditional practice. A good friend supplied an aged, deafeningly loud electric mill, and we milled our grain into beautiful flour, nine and a half cups of it. After mixing half a cup of water into my Cripple Creek starter, I added nearly a cup of freshly ground wheat and waited. I admit I was not confident that wheat I grew, harvested, threshed, winnowed, and milled would really work, but I was pleasantly mistaken. My sourdough culture behaved as it always had when given fresh flour and water.

I mixed my starter with most of the remaining flour, another cup of water, and some salt. I kneaded and let the dough sit for a couple of hours, and fermentation began—a process practiced in Pompeii before Vesuvius, pre-revolution France, Quebec, and near Boston in the eighteenth century, and now, in Meadville,

Pennsylvania. I folded the dough over itself after an hour and again after two hours and then realized I was not going to be able to stay awake late enough to bake it. I put the whole thing in the fridge and went to sleep.

Ordinarily, when I place a dough in the refrigerator, my sourdough takes the night off, and the dough comes from the fridge in the morning approximately the same size it was the night before. But something in the fresh wheat really appealed to Cripple Creek; my microbes continued working through the wee hours. By morning my dough had *doubled* in size. I folded it one more time and preheated a cast-iron Dutch oven to 500 degrees Fahrenheit. At eleven in the morning, I turned my dough into the pot, covered it, baked it for thirty minutes, removed the lid, and baked it another twenty minutes, and it was done. Going into the oven, the bread looked no different than any others, but coming out, it was darker and more deeply hued than any bread I had ever made. It was also stuck to the bottom of the pot.

Knowing a dozen people were waiting for me, I went to work trying to extract it, but—as anyone who has wrestled a nearly cylindrical pot that is 500 degrees Fahrenheit can attest—there was no simple way. I tried—and bent—spatulas of varying design, a letter opener, a couple of different kinds of knives, a cheese slicer, and a pie server. I burned myself and cursed up a storm. The beautiful crackling crust developed a seismic fault. I dented the edges of the bread and turned the twelve-pound pot upside down, banging it against a cutting board with increasing passion.

All breads continue to cook for quite a while after they come out of the oven, and a large bread like the one I had just made needed to cool for more than an hour. During all that time, it would continue to release water vapor, and if I did not get it out of the pot, that beautiful crust was going to turn soggy, the crumb was going to be gummy, and twelve anxiously waiting recipients were going to have to be polite and encouraging about how next year would surely be better. Finally, the seismic fault provided enough pliability; although I sacrificed some of the bread's surface integrity, I was able to get a spatula beneath it and lifted it to a cooling rack. The bottom was charred.

It turns out fresh flour does make a difference. This loaf was not like any I had ever made. The Glenn hardy wheat must have produced extra sugar because the bread tasted of molasses. The brittle crust and caramelized bottom were indicators of sugar that appealed to my century-old sourdough culture. The combination of smoky-sweet overtones, dark, almost pumpernickel-like color, and sourdough flavors overcame the dozen bread eaters. Not even politeness could keep the last slice from disappearing. In fifteen minutes, only crumbs remained. In my experiment, from a hundred square feet of well-fertilized, stone-free land and with the assistance of a small band of students, an electric fan, an electric mill, a refrigerated sourdough culture, and a gas oven, I made two loaves of bread.

What I learned from growing my own wheat would have been obvious to early American farmers: it required a lot of labor and land to be self-sufficient. Even the addition of horsepower would have come with a requirement for acreage with which to fuel the horse. Consequently, as colonists filled in the Eastern Seaboard, economic exigency won out over the myth of American self-sufficiency. Big wheat farms in Pennsylvania were able to produce more wheat at lower costs than farmers in New England tilling its rocky slopes.[50] Planting, harvesting, threshing, winnowing, and milling were too much work and economically inefficient for a small farmer to take on by himself.

Except for those who lived far out in the country, the effort required to bake bread at home could not compete with the ease and efficiency of a professional baker. Just as urban Frenchmen began to purchase bread from neighborhood bakeries in the middle of the eighteenth century, American city dwellers went to bakeries with increasing regularity. Interestingly, the price of a loaf of bread purchased from an American baker was subject to the same economic forces that dictated the price of bread in pre-revolution France. Food riots in the New World followed the same pattern as those in the old. Between 1776 and 1779, cities in Pennsylvania, New York, Massachusetts, Rhode Island, and Connecticut were subjected to the rage of buyers demanding bread. Women led many of the protests because of what they perceived as unfairly high prices. They hounded shopkeepers and merchants, took home loaves they needed, and on most occasions, in the middle of a riot, left a payment considered reasonable on the counter.[51]

To reduce costs, keep prices down, and avoid food riots, commercial bakers in America adopted the same solutions as their French counterparts. With yeast purchased from a beer brewer or a middleman, a baker was able to make a whole lot more bread in a lot less time and with much less effort than it took to make the same number of loaves using a sourdough starter. Moreover, bakers used more white flour, which is made from only wheat's starchy white part, the endosperm. White flour had more gluten per ounce, from which a lighter loaf could be made, especially when leavened with yeast. American consumers liked yeast-raised white breads, and as cities grew, so too did the gradual displacement of the old five-pound sourdough round. America and Europe were on parallel paths.

At the turn of the nineteenth century, the question of who made America's bread and what went into it became quite politicized. Fighting in support of homemade sourdough bread was Sylvester Graham (1794–1851), a Presbyterian minister and dietary crusader. There is scant evidence that Sylvester Graham invented his eponymous cracker. He would have positively flailed at the pulpit at the very notion of a s'more, one of today's most perfect foods, combining as it does a toasted marshmallow and slowly melting chocolate sandwiched between two crackers. Graham crackers, like Graham bread—which Sylvester promoted but probably did not invent, either—were designed to snuff out pleasure, not induce it. But to understand Sylvester, it is important to first consider the geography and sociology of the newly created country.

The American economy matured in the closing decades of the eighteenth century: the middle states produced the bulk of America's bread wheat; southerners grew tobacco and cotton; and towns in the Northeast joined Europe's Industrial Revolution. Cities filled with lawyers, barbers, cobblers, policemen, teachers, and other professionals who, not unlike modern Americans, took to dining out. Because men worked outside the home, it was mostly men who frequented eateries. Drinking out and its accompanying debauchery were also male-only pastimes, and drinking became disturbingly popular.

Domesticity became a moral battleground as girls and women were urged to entice American men to accede to home cooking, forsaking alcohol and its attendant iniquities. Armed for a war against hedonism of all stripes was Sylvester Graham, a Puritan in all but name. Ordained as an evangelical minister, Graham rose to public prominence in 1830, when he accepted a post with the Pennsylvania Temperance Society.[52] In 1834, he published *A Lecture to Young Men on Chastity: Intended Also for the Serious Consideration of Parents and Guardians*. In the preface to the second edition, published in 1838, Graham wrote, "Self pollution is actually a very great and rapidly increasing evil in our country, far more than I dare describe, lest I should do harm; for there are some things that may not even be named."[53]

Graham was a cofounder of the American Vegetarian Society (along with Amos Bronson Alcott, Louisa May's father, among others). But vegetarianism was only the beginning of Graham's remedy for what he perceived to be increasing American impiety.

His prescription for the righting of America was something he called farinaceousness, a diet of sourdough bread baked with a generous proportion of germ and coarsely cut bran.[54] Prior to consumption, he said, bread should be set out for at least twelve hours. He also advocated frequent cold-water baths with vigorous scrubbing by brushes. Loose clothing and hard mattresses were important tools in battling sexual corruption. He disparaged alcohol and tobacco. And he drew a connection between sourdough and the prevention of masturbation.

Bran-filled bread was important, according to Graham, because it counterbalanced the sensory appeal of food. Sourdough bread, bran filled or not, made bread less appealing because of its inherent acidity. In his speeches, he addressed young men and their parents and guardians, "If, therefore, you are very much reduced, and afflicted with involuntary nocturnal emissions, and distressed with pains and impaired senses, and enfeebled mind, and cheerless melancholy, tending to despair and madness," then the solution was to monitor what you ate and when you ate it. Stimulation of any organs, especially alimentary ones, could invariably excite nearby organs, which, according to the reverend's interpretation of scripture, had to be discouraged: "An over-fullness, or late supper will almost invariably cause this evil . . . and while these emissions continue, it is impossible for the system to recover strength and vitality."[55]

Graham told his crowds that "costiveness [constipation] of the bowels is sure to keep up the nightly discharges." Constipation was indeed a widespread problem for people whose diets relied heavily on meat and yeasted breads made with white flour. In the next sentence, however, Graham announced with equal assuredness that any medications taken to relieve constipation could also stimulate the alimentary canal because "it is sure to perpetuate the mischief."[56] Graham also acknowledged that women of a similar age were not immune to sexual impulses and should, of course, avoid self-pollution at all costs.

The cure for frequent emissions could be obtained by following Graham's intricate dietary regimen: no meat, milk, alcohol, coffee, tea, pepper, ginger, peppermint, mustard, horseradish, or food that was still hot from the oven. In short, avoid anything that could rouse a taste bud or any other part of the body located lower down than a taste bud. Graham boasted that he had treated many young men "who were exceedingly reduced and afflicted by venereal errors" by placing them on his special diet. Beware the backslide, he warned: "A single glass of brandy and water, or a glass of wine or porter, or a cigar or a cup of coffee, or a full meal of flesh, would cause emissions in the following night."[57]

There was another important piece of Graham's solution: he recommended that wives and mothers bake whole grain sourdough bread at home. In 1837, between his two editions of *Lecture on Chastity*, Graham published *A Treatise on Bread and Bread Making*.[58] Wives and mothers must, he wrote, "fully comprehend the importance of good bread in relation to all the bodily and intellectual and moral interests of their husbands and children." He implored women to recognize that resting solely in the palms of their hands and upon their responsible shoulders lay the "domestic and social and civil welfare of mankind, and to their religious prosperity, both for time and eternity."[59]

The flour that bears his name was yet one additional method to prevent stimulation. Not at all like the cracker named for him, graham breads were ruthlessly wholemeal. His flour was roughly akin to whole wheat, but it was prepared somewhat differently. Dark, grainy specks of germ and bran ordinarily removed from white flour were returned in bountiful quantities to graham flour. His conclusion was that such a mix of germ, endosperm, and bran could pass from a person's mouth to his terminal orifice in complete stealth.

As for the leavening agent, Graham recognized that by the third decade of the nineteenth century, yeast had already replaced sourdough. Graham disdained yeast purchased from the brewer. That the initial purpose of brewer's yeast was to produce alcohol stuck in his craw, though Graham conceded that brewer's yeasts raised very light breads. Still, he insisted that he could always detect a disagreeable taste if brewer's yeasts were used instead of homegrown yeasts or sourdough leavens.[60]

Graham was fighting a losing battle on behalf of sourdough. Bakers and recipe books were advocating baking powder, alkali, molasses, and baking soda to neutralize or mask the acidity of bread. Graham's retort? "Bread free from acidity [imparted by sourdough] . . . is also destitute of the best and most delicious properties of good bread." Graham wrote that "by the time it is twenty-four hours old—and this is particularly true of bakers' bread [leavened with yeast]—it is as dry and tasteless and unsavory as if it were made of Plaster of Paris."[61] You would think that bread related to plaster of Paris might inhibit carnal inspirations, but evidently that was not the case. The proper antidote to lasciviousness, according to Graham, was actually acidity.

Enough Americans cottoned to Graham's austere diet of vegetarianism and wholemeal breads—think about the modern-day appeal of gluten-free to get a potential sense of the impact on sales—that bread sales dropped. In the late 1830s in Boston, a mob of frustrated bakers attacked his lectures. Another mob went after him in Portland, Maine.[62] Ultimately, the baking industry came out on top: Grahamism was in full play for only about a decade, his followers never grew large in number, and home baking was but a passing fad. Persuading Americans to forego soft and chewy in favor of sour, rough, homemade, wholesome, and chaste was—and remains to this day—a difficult argument to maintain.

Still, Graham was not a lone voice in the culture wars aimed at keeping women in the kitchen—and by virtue of their labors, keeping men on the up and up. Sarah Josepha Hale, a contemporary of Sylvester Graham, also believed in the value to society of women who stayed at home cooking. In 1839, Hale authored one of America's first cookbooks, the one with the recipe for Rye and Indian, called *The Good Housekeeper: Or, the Way to Live Well and to Be Well While We Live: Containing Directions for Choosing and Preparing Food in Regard to Health, Economy, and Taste.* Hale was widely recognized for her extraordinary literary and political accomplishments in an era when women were relegated to the private side of life. Widowed at the age of thirty-four, mother to five children, and an autodidact, she was among America's first published women. In addition to her cookbook, she wrote poems, including "Mary Had a Little Lamb," novels, and opinion pieces and edited influential magazines well into her nineties. She is widely credited with being the creator of the American holiday we know today as Thanksgiving.[63]

Hale began *The Good Housekeeper* with bread. "The art of making *good bread* [emphasis Hale's] I consider the most important one in cookery, and shall therefore give it the first place in the 'Good Housekeeper.'"[64] Immediately, and without actually naming him, Hale put forth a diatribe aimed at what she perceived as Sylvester Graham's crazy notions on vegetarianism.

Part of Graham's rationale for vegetarianism was that the teeth and stomachs of humans closely resembled those of monkeys. Hale countered that eating meat distinguished human from ape. "Those who should live as the monkeys do would most closely resemble them," she wrote. Following two pages of biblical bolstering for meat came Hale's unpalatable proof (unpalatable, that is, by any modern standard of humanity) of the essential requirement for carnivorism. Among those who consume the greatest amount of meat, she wrote in her cookbook, is where "the greatest improvement in the race is to be found, and the greatest energy of character.... Forty thousand of the beef-fed British govern and control ninety million of the rice-eating natives of India."[65]

Finally, after four and a half pages of rant, Hale pulled back on the reins to introduce flour. Hale insisted—and in this case, I agree with her completely—that fresh flour made the best and sweetest bread. Her recommendation was to take only one or two bushels at a time to the miller. A bushel of wheat berries yielded fifty-six pounds of flour, enough to last a large family through the week. Small families of four or five persons, according to Hale, needed to begin with only twenty-seven pounds.

Hale's bread recipe was decidedly not sourdough. It included half a pint of brewer's yeast, or the thick sediment taken from the bottom of home brew, which was one more indication that the early 1800s were witness to yeast's gains against sourdough's historical entrenchment in the battle for leaven supremacy. In France, the United States, and Great Britain, while prominent authorities busily advocated for one over the other, both bread producers and bread eaters were moving steadily toward yeast.

Hale advised home bakers to pour a slurry of yeast into a well in the center of the flour so that they could prove to themselves that their yeast was alive before making a full commitment. Her basic bread recipe called for a gallon of water, two tablespoons of salt, and kneading. It sounds so simple, but it is hard to imagine anyone doing a decent job of kneading thirty-five pounds of dough. Actually, I wonder for whom exactly *The Good Housekeeper* was intended. To make this much bread, in addition to strong shoulders, a baker would have needed an enormous kitchen and enough room to store bushels of wheat berries. The housewife needed access to a brewer selling yeast or had to make her own home brew in large quantities. She also needed a book on cookery because though she was likely literate, she must have failed to learn to cook from her mother as pre-cookbook generations must have. If I could have afforded it back in 1839, I would have gone to the bakery.

The rest of Hale's bread recipe was not any different from recipes used by bakers since antiquity: fire up the oven, remove the coals, insert the loaves at the peak of their rise, seal the oven tight, bake, and let cool before eating. Repeat weekly. Like Graham, Hale was hoping to persuade Americans to forego the convenience provided by commercial bakeries. Bread purchased from a professional baker "is not as healthy or nutritious as bread made from the flour of good, sound wheat, baked at home, without any mixtures of drugs and correctives." She decried additives employed by professional bakers of her era "and the use of certain ingredients—Alum, ammonia, sulphate [sic] of zinc, and even sulphate [sic] of copper."[66] Hale probably had a point. The Industrial Revolution, then operating at full throttle, was reaching into bakeries in England, France, and America, and bakers were adopting new techniques and ingredients in pursuit of lower costs and increased revenue.

Their publications and speeches in support of home-baked bread notwithstanding, the efforts of Hale and Graham were about to disperse like flour in the wind. The additives Hale mentioned were a harbinger of nineteenth-century bread made for quick sale to workers confined to urban dwellings without time, space, or energy to make all their own food. The beginning of the eighteenth century marked the beginning of the Industrial Revolution, an era during which mechanization changed the way Europeans and Americans went about their daily lives. The clothes they wore, the jobs they held, and the bread they ate were all about to be reconfigured. The Industrial Revolution was my next stop.

EXCELLENT HOUSEHOLD BREAD

This recipe is from Sarah Josepha Hale's 1857 cookbook *Mrs. Hale's New Cook Book: A Practical System for Private Families in Town and Country*.[67] It is reprinted verbatim. No yield or method is provided.

Take 4 quarts of the best flour, a tea-spoonful of salt, three table-spoonsful of yeast, a pint and a half of warm water.

ANOTHER EXCELLENT BREAD

This recipe is also reprinted verbatim from *Mrs. Hale's New Cook Book*.[68] This one includes a bit more detail than the recipe for Excellent Household Bread.

Sift half a peck of the finest flour into a kneading-trough; make a hole in the middle, and put in half a pint of warm milk, and half a pint of good yeast; work it with a little of the flour; cover it well up in a warm place an hour to rise; add 1½ pint of milk and half a pint of water, of a proper warmth, with a quarter of a pound of fresh butter, and 2 spoonsful of sugar [a nineteenth-century spoon of your choice]; knead it well, and set it again before the fire; put in a little fine pounded salt; knead it well; form it, and put it again before the fire to rise; bake in a quick oven.

SOURDOUGH BOSTON BROWN BREAD
Yield: 1 loaf

Among old cookbooks and across the internet one can find many recipes for Rye and Indian bread, Boston brown bread, or as it is sometimes called, thirded bread (because equal quantities of rye, wheat, and cornmeal are used). The final ratio of flours and quantities of ingredients depended upon what was available in the marketplace, the cost of each grain, the size of your covered cooker, and the number of people you wished to feed. The coarseness of the flour did not vary much; whole grains went to the miller, and unless you were exceptionally wealthy, unsieved, coarsely ground rye, wheat, and corn, with their bran and germ included, were what you took home. This is my variation. This bread is delicious with baked beans or a cup of dark coffee.

> 1 cup buttermilk, room temperature
> ⅔ cup whole milk, room temperature or warm
> 2 tablespoons active rye or wheat sourdough starter
> ½ cup molasses
> 3 tablespoons unsalted butter, melted
> ¾ cup whole rye flour
> ¾ cup whole wheat flour
> ¾ cup cornmeal
> 1 teaspoon kosher salt
> 1 cup raisins

In a large bowl, mix the buttermilk, milk, and sourdough starter together. Add the molasses and butter. Mix well to combine.

Add the rye flour, wheat flour, cornmeal, and salt, stirring until a smooth dough forms, then fold in the raisins.

Cover the bowl with a wet towel or plastic wrap, and let the dough rest at room temperature for 8 to 12 hours, or overnight.

Preheat the oven to 375°F. Grease a 10-inch Dutch oven well with butter or spray. You can also use a similar-size baking dish with a tight lid or a heavy cast-iron pot with a lid. The lid is important, as this bread is steamed.

Pour the dough into the prepared Dutch oven and cover with the lid. Bake for about 90 minutes, or until a cake tester inserted into the middle of the bread comes out clean and the top of the bread shows cracks.

Let the bread rest in the Dutch oven for 5 minutes, then transfer it to a wire rack to cool slightly. Serve warm.

CHAPTER 5

A REIGN OF YEAST

MY FINAL STEP BEFORE MOVING WEST TO AT last search for Cripple Creek sourdough in, well, Cripple Creek, Colorado, was to explore the impact the Industrial Revolution had on both the production and consumption of food. Hoping to gain a front row view of the birth of manufacturing, I submitted a proposal to the US Fulbright Scholar Program to study the relationship between the rise of industrialization in England and the fall of sourdough as the main leavening agent of bread consumed in Western civilizations. I think I was probably the first professor to suggest an academic study of sourdough, but reviewers on both sides of the Atlantic liked the idea, and in 2016, I was awarded a grant as a Fulbright scholar. Within days of my arrival on New Year's Day 2017 in Lancashire in North West England, still bleary with jet lag, I had to make my way to a gathering of Britain's Fulbright scholars in Newcastle. While I was doing my best to meet my fellow researchers and teachers, the UK program director came flying out of the crowd of fifty American professors and graduate students to meet me. "My sourdough guy has arrived!" she said, beaming with delight.

For six months in 2017, I toured stream-powered grain mills and bobbin mills, museums of science and industry, restored factories from the earliest days of industrialization, deafening textile contraptions, microbakeries, ports that once received cotton picked by enslaved American labor to be sent to textile mills in Great Britain's interior, and canals that bustled coal from mines to factories that belched enough soot to turn the trunks of trees black. Half a year later, I understood how innovation in the manufacturing methods of cotton textiles led to a transformation in the way our food was produced, what we ate, and how yeast came to nearly finish its usurpation of sourdough.

First, I set out to establish how bread was made in Britain in 1760, at the approximate onset of the Industrial Revolution. As was true in France and the United States in the middle of the eighteenth century, a considerable number of British bakers had already transitioned from yeast to sourdough. It was not pure yeast, however, as there was still not a better way to capture yeast than to take it from the brewer, and the yeast used by brewers likely contained bacteria, which gave their product a wild, sour taste.[1] Nevertheless, the ratio of yeast to bacteria was very much skewed toward yeast, causing doughs, according to Antoine-Augustin Parmentier and his colleagues in France, to rise at explosive, almost uncontrollable speeds. This undemanding leaven would have been as appreciated by British bakers as it was by French and American bakers working in the same decade.

To begin, a professional baker mixed five imperial gallons of yeast with water prewarmed to milk temperature. He dissolved three and a half pounds of salt and poured the slurry onto the top of 112 pounds of flour resting in a wooden trough. He mixed wet and dry until the mixture was smooth, leveled the surface, dusted the top with flour, covered the trough, and waited twelve hours for the sponge to ferment.

When fermentation was complete, he added another three and a half pounds of salt dissolved in warm water and an additional 336 pounds of flour. Next, diving in with both hands and sometimes his bare feet, grunting and perspiring, he grappled more than five hundred pounds of dough. He would have had to make adjustments to the quantity of water and his rising times, as the strength of his yeast was not consistent between batches. He let it proof for ninety minutes before dividing, weighing, and shaping.[2] A sharp-eyed baker also checked the skies before lighting the fire in his oven; on a clear, cool night, dough rose slowly. During the small hours of the morning, he shaped loaves from his rising dough while the brick dome of his oven absorbed heat from the blaze within. You know the drill: rake out the coals, slash the loaves, place the loaves back to front, largest to smallest, seal the oven's front, and wait.

Here, I must make two observations. The first is that the wood-fired beehive oven and the process of mixing, kneading, and baking would have been completely recognizable to ancient Romans. Second, in 1760, if there was ever an industry in need of modernization, it was bread making. The Industrial Revolution, about to ignite in Great Britain, was going to begin with the transformation of textiles, but in short order it would spread to manufacturing of every stripe and hue. The preparation of food, including the baking of bread, would undergo a change that rivaled the discovery of agriculture in its magnitude.

Cotton is like wheat. Both are nurtured in the field, harvested, processed by human hands, and reconfigured. Inside a living cotton boll, every strand of fiber is of a slightly different length and thickness, entangled with its neighbors, and headed in a direction all its own. To turn those tiny strings of cellulose, each only a few microns thick, into a thread that can be woven with other threads, whose combined surface will keep someone warm and clothed, is a trick nearly as magical as the transubstantiation of wheat flour, water, and sourdough starter into a loaf of bread.

The oldest method of spinning relied upon a barbed spindle to engage the fiber and a whorl to act like a flywheel on the rotating spindle. The skill was applied with the fingers of the left hand, which released a steady line of filaments from the disordered mass of cotton to create a thread of unwavering diameter. Meanwhile, the right hand pulled on the growing thread to lengthen it, turning the spindle at a constant speed. After a length of yarn had been coaxed from a raised left hand, a distance of perhaps two feet, the spinner stopped, unhooked the turning spindle from her newly wound thread, poked her barbed stick once more into her chaos of fibers, and repeated. Beginning roughly in the same period—very approximately, around the dawn of agricultural domestication in 10,000 BCE—thread and bread were both made by hand.[3]

By 1769, Richard Arkwright possessed the business acumen to invent, borrow, co-opt, and steal all the necessary components to transfer the manufacture of fabric—but also the very nature of fabrication (note that the origin of that word, fabrication, is *fabric*)—from human hand to the arms of a contraption. Arkwright patented his invention under the name water frame because the mount that held all the gears, turners, and winders was powered by a waterwheel. His yarns were consistently tight and smooth, absent the hairy projections typical of hand-spun yarn. An unlimited number of bobbins could reap yarn simultaneously, as long as an operator was available to supply feedstock, piece together broken ends, and replace full bobbins with empties. No skill was necessary. Arkwright hired women and children because they were cheap, and he worked them through the night since the machine had no need of rest.

In a stroke of entrepreneurial genius, Arkwright's patent dictated that licenses could be purchased only for units with one thousand spindles. The machine would work as well on half a dozen spindles as it did on one thousand, but his patent prevented all of England's women from trading their spinning wheels for tiny pedal-driven machines placed in their parlors. Small contraptions were illegal. By thinking big—huge buildings, enormous machines, hundreds of workers toiling around the clock—Arkwright constructed the set upon which the Industrial Revolution was about to be played.[4]

Arkwright opened his first mill in 1771 in Cromford, England. Since he hired whole families to work, his town boomed like a gold rush village. Within a decade, he employed more than one thousand laborers. He made so much money that wealthy capitalists from Manchester, England, to Manchester, New Hampshire, took notice. Thousands of large mills spread across Great Britain and New England. America's first textile mill was built in 1790 in Pawtucket, Rhode Island, by Samuel Slater, a British cotton worker who skirted Britain's prohibition against sharing technological secrets by emigrating to the United States with the inner workings of a British mill fully memorized. Sixty years later, in 1860, there were more than one thousand cotton mills in the United States operating more than five million spindles. Back in Great Britain, there were six times as many spindles in operation.[5] In 1860, in Lancashire County—the rural backdrop of sheep pastures and forests during my 2017 Fulbright residency—nearly five hundred thousand people worked in a textile factory; 10 percent were children.[6]

In Great Britain, children began their days at five thirty in the morning with a piece of bread and were at their machines by six. Because they were undernourished, factory children were small in comparison with children today—perfectly sized for darting beneath moving spinners and looms to reattach broken threads. They swept cotton dust from gears to keep machines lint-free and the factory running without pause. During three short breaks, they received some oatmeal. At eight thirty at night, their day ended with another piece of bread and sometimes broth.[7]

Certainly, children who worked in factories did not bake their own bread, and neither did their parents, if the children had parents, or other adults who worked long and tiring days and nights. Just as important as a waterwheel (or, later, coal) was for spinning and weaving machines, a great number of bakeries were necessary to fuel workers. In the 1780s and 1790s, workers in England were moving to factory towns, just as French workers were moving toward Versailles and the French Revolution. Cheap bread was needed in both countries, and yeast was rapidly becoming the leavening agent of choice. Bread did not have to be good so much as it had to be inexpensive, filling, and readily available.

To meet the rapidly rising demand for bread to feed hungry factory workers, bakeries were in desperate need of large quantities of pure yeast. Just as scientists, businessmen, and engineers set their sights on profits to be made in textiles, a similar rush took off in the search for new means of turning out yeast for professional bakers. The growth in the number of methods for cultivating yeast is evidence that there was no foolproof, easier, or more consistent substitute for sourdough. Even if it was comparatively slow and labor-intensive, sourdough in the hands of a professional baker was reliable. The nineteenth century offered a hodgepodge of bread leavens, described in myriad books.

The following example of a yeast recipe from 1864 comes from *The Complete Confectioner, Pastry-Cook, and Baker: Plain and Practical Directions for Making Confectionary and Pastry, and for Baking; With Upwards of Five Hundred Recipes.* The book, available in both Britain and the United States, claimed that sourdough bread was more digestible, "but it is not so pleasant to the taste. Leaven [their word for sourdough] is now only used at sea."[8] Imagine that. Alexander Brodie's shipboard oven eventually succeeded in moving sourdough from shore to ship.

The requirements for good bread, according to *The Complete*

Confectioner, remain as true today as they have for all of recorded history. "The goodness of bread," wrote the authors, "whether baked at home or abroad, will depend, firstly, upon the quality of the flour employed; secondly, upon the quality of the yeast; and, thirdly, upon the skill and care of the baker. . . . In making pure wheaten loaf bread, no other ingredients should be employed but flour, water, yeast or some other innocent fermentation."[9]

The question of the century was how to make fast-acting yeast, keep it alive, and prevent it from being infected by bacteria, which released sour flavors. It was important to acquire fresh table ale, as ale yeasts made bread that was considerably less bitter than breads made from yeast in stronger beers. Table ale, also known as small beer, had an alcohol content under 3 percent and frequently contained even less than 1 percent.[10]

If table ale was not available, another option was to acquire an excellent sample of brewer's yeast, raise a large batch, and preserve it via dehydration. Laying brewer's yeast to rest was like painting a wall, with the added proviso that care had to be taken to prevent bacteria from landing on the surface. Using a soft brush and a wooden bowl, the homemaker swept beer foam across her bowl, covered it to keep out unwanted contaminants (in 1864, the notion of contamination was not yet fully understood), and let it dry. She then repeated this process with a new layer of brushed-on beer foam. She did this over and over until she had a block of yeast a couple of inches thick.[11]

In the absence of ale, baking yeast could be made in the home from a mash of potatoes, according to *The Complete Confectioner.* One pound of warmed potatoes was cooled and treated with treacle for the yeast to consume and—here is the difficult part to understand—"two large spoonfuls of yeast." That recipe could produce a quart of yeast just by itself, and it was supposed to be every bit as good as brewer's yeast. No explanation was offered for the origin of the large spoonfuls of yeast.

The Complete Confectioner contained another yeast recipe
attributed to a Dr. Lettsom. The doctor's concoction began with
two quarts of water, four ounces of flour, three ounces of brown
sugar—and here it comes—four spoonfuls of baker's yeast. The
baker was advised to always keep some on hand to start the next
batch. I suppose the advantage over sourdough was the higher ratio
of yeast to bacteria, which meant that there was a lower likelihood
the final bread would turn out sour, a characteristic tang that must
have fallen out of favor rather precipitously by the 1870s.

A recipe from the "late Mr. Henry" required four ounces of
flour, some powdered marble (yes, the metamorphic stone used
by sculptors), sulfuric acid (which somehow must have been easier
to acquire than brewer's yeast), and an airtight machine. The late
Mr. Henry's "flour jelly" could be impregnated with gas generated
by the acid and marble. Unlike other formulae, this one must have
been useful for the housewife who could not acquire brewer's yeast,
was an able baker, and did not make home brew, but had access to
sulfuric acid and a machine with which she could capture and then
release pressurized gas.[12]

Other cookbooks provided recipes for something called
Connecticut yeast from hops, potatoes, and—I just don't get it—
yeast.[13] By 1885, even an American cookbook with French origins,
La Creole Cuisine, began its unit on bread as follows: "Without
good yeast to start with it is impossible to make good bread." It
went on to describe something called "turnpike yeast," which was
made from hops, cornmeal, and ... yeast. There is a recipe for liquid
yeast that did not turn sour and was made with parched corn, hops,
vinegar, sugar, salt, mashed potatoes, and yeast. It took two days.
Miss Beecher's potato yeast was grown on mashed potatoes without hops. *La Creole Cuisine* had a recipe for salt-rising yeast prepared with fresh milk still warm from the cow. There is even a yeast
recipe that began with a strong tea concocted from fig leaves.[14]

The White House Cookbook, one of the most widely distributed cookbooks in American history, was published in 1887. Author Fanny Lemira Gillette cleverly dedicated her new cookbook to the wives of US presidents. As far as anyone can ascertain, Gillette never met a president's wife or ever visited the White House. Still, *The White House Cookbook* became the book given to newly married women in America's growing middle class. New editions were printed for decades.

Before Gillette's bread recipes were even presented, she proposed that soured dough could be recovered before baking by the addition of what she referred to as super-carbon of soda (baking soda). "All bread is better, if naturally sweet, without the soda; but *sour bread* [emphasis Gillette's] you should never eat, if you desire good health." In 1887, when the first edition was published, Sylvester Graham had been dead for just thirty-six years and Sara Josepha Hale only eight, but already their appeal to authentic bread of basic ingredients had given way to bread containing additives.

It was time for me to undertake another test. I wanted to understand why nineteenth-century bread makers went to such extraordinary lengths to acquire yeast. In order to taste a bread made from fresh brewer's yeast and to gain a feel for its appealing quickness, I asked my friend the master brewer John Mangine to prepare some for me. John brewed an amber ale, and as his yeast multiplied, he siphoned some into a mason jar. With time, the yeast cells settled toward the bottom, and he poured off the extra liquid. He added fresh water and then repeated the process several times to increase the concentration of active yeast in the remaining liquid. The process is called yeast washing, and having a higher concentration of harvested yeast certainly seemed like something a nineteenth-century baker would have wanted. Without any sugars to consume, however, Mangine's yeast would have died if the washing went on too long. In other words, John had to rush his jar of yeast from his house to mine, where I had a bowl of flour waiting.

Because the number of yeast cells still alive was incalculable, neither he nor I knew how much of the jar to add to my flour. I poured in everything he had given me: about a cup and a half of slurry, the top three-quarters of which was pretty clear. The bottom inch or so was an opaque cloud of ochre yeast cells.

I kneaded. John's yeast cells did their thing. Our bread rose in an hour to a height that would have taken Cripple Creek five times as long, if it could even have pushed a dough that high, and I baked it. As whenever I make bread, I was surprised that it worked. It all feels somehow out of my control: a wondrous biology at work in a bowl and the supernatural action of a magic liquid on a mass of flour.

The finished bread looked just like all of the sourdough breads I had ever made, but its essence was something else entirely. Two features set it apart. The first was that the final bread tasted, to my surprise, a lot like beer. After all those washings, the absence of strong hops—actually, hardly any hops at all—and the small quantity of yeast-infused water compared with the final volume of bread, I was taken aback by a loaf that definitely tasted like ale. If I could taste beer, that meant antialcohol activists in England, France, and America could, too. For four centuries, guys like Sylvester Graham, Antoine-Augustin Parmentier, and Dr. Gui Patin could certainly have pointed out the permeating taste of beer in bread leavened with brewer's yeast—and easily suggested that the bread carried the same ills as beer. On the other hand, bread eaters evidently did not care. Moreover, temperance supporters would have been incorrect about the presence of alcohol in the bread. The heat of the oven would have vaporized any alcohol produced by yeast, whether the yeast was originally from the brewer or from a sourdough culture.

My second observation was that the bread was plain. Aside from the flavor of beer, and it was not an exceptionally interesting beer,

there was not much else going on. In sourdough bread, various species and strains of bacteria and yeast jostling inside a sourdough culture each impart flavors of their own. A good sourdough, depending
on the skill of the baker, might or might not be sour, but it will certainly have multiple rich and complex layers of flavor that can range
from creamy to tangy. Yeasted breads, in comparison—and this one
was no exception—tend toward the quick and utilitarian.

The number of methods for growing household yeast published in the late 1800s in both Britain and the United States confirmed that sour breads were rapidly falling from fashion, but all
those recipes also shed light on a hidden problem, especially for
professionals: yeast did not last. It needed to be coddled with cool
temperatures, protected from souring by errant bacteria, prepared
anew on a regular basis, and added to recipes by the pint. Depending on its origins, it could even impart an unwanted flavor of its
own. Leavening with yeast took less skill and worked more quickly
than sourdough, and in that regard bread production increased
alongside the output of the day's textile mills. Efficiency, larger production runs, and less artisanship were gaining traction in both the
factory and the bakery. To further increase the speed and number
of breads being baked, bakers needed purer, more consistently reliable yeast, mass-produced in much the same way as clothing.

DURING THE LATE 1850s, coal-fired trains roamed the American countryside, British inventors introduced coal-powered
pistons to drive textile machines, and Louis Pasteur's careful
experiments began to explain what yeast was and how it worked.
Scientists in the new field of microbiology now understood that
the diversity of microscopic organisms that fermented mashes of
various ingredients—such as stomped grapes, malted barley and
hops, or wheat flour and water—was responsible for very different

products: wine, beer, and bread. Also, in an age before sterilization, most pulps and purees had a nasty tendency to include bacteria, single-celled organisms from an altogether different kingdom than yeast. Today, scientists know that bacterial exudates are sour, and sour isn't good for wine or beer or for bread being sold to Americans and Brits.

The goal for inventors in the years following Pasteur's discoveries, then, was to culture pure strains of yeast, free of bacterial infections. In the 1870s, Emil Christian Hansen, a Danish microbiologist, used an updated version of Antonie van Leeuwenhoek's microscope to look closely at his Old Carlsberg beer. What he found was that when wild yeast infected his brew, his beer tasted rather wild. By the end of the 1880s, he was able to isolate a single cell of yeast and then get it to multiply into an untainted and abundant throng. If his beer was fermented with hand-selected, unadulterated beer yeasts, Hansen had a reliable mug he could drink one after the other from without complaint.[15] Hansen refused to patent either his process, which he published, or his yeast, *Saccharomyces carlsbergensis*. Instead, he gave it away, which probably says something about Danish culture.

Not everyone liked Carlsberg's species of yeast. Old-timers who preferred wild beers thought purebred beers tasted unappealingly simple. Breweries, on the other hand, liked the predictability of standardized yeasts but still had a devil of a time keeping wild yeasts and bacteria from sneaking into their vats. It was one thing to make a pedigreed beer under laboratory conditions like Hansen's but something else entirely to try to scale up to production levels.

Hundreds of European and American scientists began inventing new methods for growing yeast in volumes large enough and pure enough to commercialize. It took several decades before yeast making solidified into an industry of its own, and between 1850 and the 1920s, bakers yeasted their doughs with yeast prepared with a dizzying array of methodologies. Home bakers made yeast from family recipes or from cookbooks, and professional bakers probably purchased yeast from a local producer using whatever method he was most comfortable with.

In 1914, both the panoply and uncertainty around leavening a loaf of bread were described by an American named Richard Newell Hart, who authored *Leavening Agents: Yeast, Leaven, Salt-Rising Fermentation, Baking Powder, Aerated Bread, Milk Powder*. The book was published by the Chemical Publishing Company for professional bakers. Judging by the large volume of ingredients used to raise colonies of yeast, he was probably also writing for a new class of yeast merchants. As Hart made clear in his preface, American bakers of the period knew a great deal about flour but almost nothing about aerating agents and yeasts.

Hart provided a recipe for growing bread yeast, *Saccharomyces cerevisiae* (the same species employed in brewing beer), using something called the "Vienna process," presumably named for the city that popularized the practice of skimming yeast foam from the top of beer vats.[16] To make yeast, Hart wrote, a manufacturer needed a suitable growth medium; an unalloyed source of yeast cells; a means to raise and multiply his brood; a technique to harvest his crop; the ability to separate living yeasts from any extraneous jetsam that had made its way through the system; a press for removing water used during the growth and washing process; and finally, a package. At each step, he had to keep out microbial invaders that, in the absence of sterilization, waited patiently in everything from the corn mash used to feed the yeast to the wrapping paper bearing the seller's proud logo.

Hart's recipe began with eight hundred pounds of kiln-dried malted barley (barley seeds that have been germinated but dried before they grow too large), eight hundred pounds of rye, and eight hundred pounds of corn. This was mashed with water (the recipe

doesn't specify the amount) and heated to 145 degrees Fahrenheit to kill bacteria. At roughly the same time the main mash was
being prepared, the operator had to raise an inoculant of pure yeast,
known as seed yeast or mother yeast, from which any living bacteria
had been eliminated. Then uncontaminated seed yeast was added to
the 2,400 pounds of combined grain and water.

To grow a colony of mother yeast required 150 pounds of rye
and 150 pounds of malt, also ground and mashed. But here is the
confusing part: first, the grower had to actually introduce bacteria. As counterintuitive as that seems, the addition of bacteria
that produce lactic acid was necessary to kill all the other bacteria
that produce rotten flavors. You might think of it as adding one
kind of insect to eliminate another, like importing ladybugs to
demolish aphids.

Hart's *good* bacteria were *Lactobacillus*, the genus found in—
hang on—nearly all sourdough cultures. Hart's *Lactobacilli* produced acids that were deadly to varieties of bacteria that should
never be found in food. Hart's preferred method of gathering a
really healthy colony of lactic acid bacteria was to use a kind of
sourdough starter "by adding a little soured yeast mash taken
from a previous yeasting."[17] In order to prepare yeast capable of
leavening bread and fermenting beer that was without sour notes,
Hart turned to sourdough cultures to generate the good bacteria
that defended his yeast from unwelcome bacteria. Remarkable
use of biology.

Purified of undesirable bacteria, the giant tub of mash was now
intentionally infected with mother yeast and left to ferment. The
action of so many respiring yeast cells raised the temperature in the
mash. Bubbles of carbon dioxide started to accumulate on the surface. As a rich cream developed on top, an experienced yeast man
harvested the foam, then doused it in cold water. Chilling halted
the process of fermentation in much the same way that placing a

sourdough starter in a refrigerator will put your microbes to sleep until you are ready to wake them for their next bake.

The foam was then passed through silk or a superfine mesh of fabric. Water passed through the tiny holes, albeit slowly, while yeast gathered on top of the cloth. Workmen shoveled yeast into molds, where it was pressed to release more water and then wrapped. From the moment the yeast was packaged until it was unpackaged and dispensed upon a kneadable dough, it had to be kept chilled.[18]

By no means was Richard Newell Hart's the only means of producing yeast for bread. Advancements in yeast production, ever freer from sour flavors imparted from unwanted bacteria, could be seen as an explosion in the number of home recipes and scores of patents. Between 1875 and 1900, German entrepreneurs filed forty-four patents for the manufacture of yeast. Englishmen invented forty methods of their own, and Americans in the same period developed thirty-four patents. Add in the other bread and beer countries of Europe, and the total number of methods for isolating baker's yeast reached 178 by the beginning of the twentieth century.[19] And yet, even with all the end-of-century innovation and experimentation, in high Colorado's Rocky Mountains, bakers or gold miners were making bread the old-fashioned way, with sourdough.

In the last two decades of the nineteenth century, roughly one hundred years after Richard Arkwright's invention of a water frame for the mass production of fabric, the assembly of bread was about to undergo its own mechanization. In 1879, a German firm produced a double-bladed dough mixer that bakers adopted, giving up the arduous task of hand kneading. Over the next two decades, as affordable steam engines were installed outside individual bakeries, mixing machines came into their own. A series of pulleys, belts, and gears turned the cranks. Mechanized dough mixing and kneading finally started to displace hand kneading.[20] In 1880 in Hungary, rollers replaced millstones inside grain mills. Wheat berries were rolled flat rather than being crushed between stones, readying their bran and germ for easy sieving. The resultant flour was dazzling white.

Together, the inventions of roller mills, mechanical dough mixers, and pure cakes of living yeast were about to transform bread. After six thousand years of very little change, the production and taste of bread in western Europe and the United States were about to mimic the manufacture and flavor of cotton.

Human-powered kneading machine, 1877.

The star example of the era was Vienna bread, not unlike a pillowy kaiser roll you might find in a supermarket today in a clear plastic bag of four or six on a shelf near the deli counter. Back in the late 1800s, Vienna bread was formed into a variety of shapes, and there were many recipes. What they all had in common was yeast, not sourdough, and exceptionally white flour. Vienna bread was first popularized in its namesake city, but the expansion of Hungarian roller mill technology to other countries meant that Vienna bread became a thing in much of Europe.

Bakers added equal parts milk and water to a batch of cotton-white flour to create a pearly white dough. They leavened the mass with yeast that had been collected on fabric after water had been pressed out of it. It was known as press yeast, which was more concentrated and easier to use than the older method of pouring yeast washed from beer, as I had done with Mangine's ale yeast. By the late 1800s, there were enough yeast makers and vendors that it was no longer necessary to purchase it from a brewer.

Vienna bread wasn't completely free of acidity, a flavor associated with sourdough bread, as it was nearly impossible to remove all the lactic acid–making bacteria from press yeast. Nevertheless, a Vienna roll must have been heavenly for European workers and high-end consumers alike: a welcome change from large, dark, whole grain, sour-tasting loaves that were still remembered by grandparents from back in the day and still eaten by rural folks and the poor.

Vienna bread was such a marketing novelty that the Scientific Commission of the United States dispatched scientists to the Vienna International Exhibition of 1873.[21] Two years later, in 1875, Eben Norton Horsford published the exhaustively detailed *Report on Vienna Bread.* "*Kaisersemmel*," Horsford wrote, "presents a rich reddish-brown crust and delicately shaded yellowish, almost white interior. It is always light, evenly porous, free from acidity in taste or aroma, faintly sweet without addition of saccharine matter to the flour or dough, slightly and pleasantly fragrant, palatable without butter or any form of condiment, and never cloying upon the appetite."[22]

Horsford cited an example that demonstrated just how popular press yeast had become and, by implication, how quickly sourdough was disappearing. A Viennese yeast-making company called A. I. Mautner and Son sold some 72,400 pounds of yeast in 1846. Less than thirty years later, in 1872, Mautner and Son earned the Grand Diploma of Honor for sales. They sold more than three million pounds.[23] In the third paragraph of Horsford's report, the lead sentence declared that "the uniformity of the product demonstrates that the making of good bread has been solved." Take that, sourdough!

Horsford was probably overstating the case, for even as the 1800s were nearing their end, mass-produced yeast was still a work in progress, and in some locations in England, France, the United States, and elsewhere, sourdough must have been hanging on. The gassing power of yeast, for example, was not wholly predictable. Nor, it turned out, was the degree of sour—imparted by those lactic acid–making bacteria omnipresent in sourdough—fully knowable until the final loaf was tasted. The shelf life of yeast was still limited. Even the color of yeast and the shading it imparted to bread were not the same from package to package.[24]

Which is why it is not totally wild that the next big craze would be aerated bread. If the purpose of yeast was to impart bubbles of carbon dioxide into tiny envelopes of dough, why not just introduce carbon dioxide directly to wet dough and make leavening instantaneous?

John Dauglish, an anxiety-ridden physician, gets the credit for marrying engineering and sanitary nutrition into a single machine that could aerate bread without the use of biology. After four years of studying medicine in Edinburgh, Scotland, he concluded that Scottish bread was "insipid." It aggravated his dyspepsia.[25] Using mechanical skills he learned from his mother, he created a device that could inject carbonated water into a hermetically sealed container of flour. His first patent was taken in 1856.[26]

Dauglish's device was a cast-iron sphere a yard in diameter and three-fourths of an inch thick. It could easily have passed for a sea mine. It was mounted upon a wooden frame five feet above the ground. Gears and pulleys projecting from its bulging midline turned internal kneaders. An adjacent torpedo was filled with

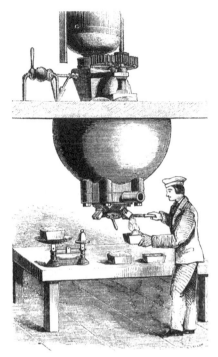

⌐══ **John Dauglish's aerated bread machine, 1866.**

carbon dioxide; the gas had been previously generated by dissolving chalk in sulfuric acid and capturing the emergent bubbles in an India rubber bag.

To make bread, the operator loaded flour, water, lard, and salt into the enamel-lined globe and bolted the top shut. He threw an electrical switch that powered internal arms that blended and turned the dough for half an hour. Once he had determined that the dough had reached the right consistency, he resealed the vessel, set the dough mixers back in motion, and piped in gas, building the pressure until his gauge read two hundred pounds per square inch.

After twenty minutes of gassing, the machinist flipped a lever and opened the carefully designed "dough cock" at the bottom. The machine expelled a squirt of pressurized dough with a "cough" into a waiting tin. Instantly, now that the pressure had been released, the dough expanded. A pair of men could dispense two sacks of flour, weighing a combined 560 pounds, in forty minutes. An hour later, four hundred tins of two-pound unfermented loaves came out of the oven.[27]

Two hours from flour sack to marketable loaves was fantastically quick compared with the six or eight hours necessary for yeasted breads and the two days required for sourdough. Moreover, there was no need to purchase yeast. Instead, leavening was as reliable as a chemical equation. Great Britain's Industrial Revolution had climbed a new peak.

Most people who consumed early loaves, however, said that they tasted a lot like raw wheat. Human beings missed the flavor of bread that had been fermented, that is, predigested by microorganisms. To overcome the bread's unappealing nature, chefs added malted extract, a sweet syrup isolated from barley. The new recipe worked. Bread aerators spread to Germany, France, and the United States, but they were most successful in Britain.

In the early 1860s, when John Dauglish assembled his first machines, he also incorporated and sold shares in Great Britain's Aerated Bread Company. ABC, as the company was affectionately called, opened tearooms in London that artfully combined the sale of nutritious, sanitary white bread, delicately arranged slices of meat, and Britain's love for tea. ABC doubled its clientele by marketing to women. In the 1870s and 1880s, Victorian women began to demand new rights. They wanted to vote. They also wanted to be able to eat in public without chaperones and without stigma. ABC happily obliged them.[28] Scores of ABC tearooms served tea and sandwiches to small gatherings of unaccompanied women. By 1886, in London, ABC was running through one thousand sacks of wheat per week.[29]

Citizens of Great Britain ate a considerable number of aerated loaves in large measure due to the efforts of Sir Benjamin Ward Richardson, MD, an antialcohol activist cut from the same cloth as Sylvester Graham. Richardson was the author of multiple publications, including *Total Abstinence, Dialogues on Drink, Public School Temperance* (all from 1878), *Ten Lectures on Alcohol* (1880), and other antialcohol tracts interspersed with medical treatises. Because fermentation drives the production of alcohol and bread, the association of the two remained intimately tied one to the other in the minds of antialcohol activists.

Richardson was vice president of the Bread Reform League, later to become the London Vegetarian Society. The Bread Reform League promoted what they called wholemeal bread, also known at the time as brown bread. The League condemned white bread but did admit that sour flavors affiliated with brown bread, which may have been leavened with sourdough, made their wholemeal bread less palatable. Richardson said, "Brown bread is, as a rule, very much *over fermented*, and the public is scarcely to be blamed for preferring well-made *white* to badly made *brown* [emphasis Richardson's]."[30]

Among his writings, Richardson reasoned that the act of allowing yeast to grow meant that some of the flour waiting to be eaten by humans was first being consumed by yeast before it could be cooked, thereby decreasing profits. Aerated bread, absent the need for any fermentation, saved money, argued Richardson. According to Richardson's computations, the baking industry lost some five million British pounds sterling every year as vaporous gases.[31]

Richardson's claim that weight loss in a baked loaf was dramatic and profit sapping was disputed rather forcefully in the scientific journal *Nature*. In 1878, printed adjacent to an article describing the invention of a new electric lamp and immediately beneath "The Reproduction of the Eel," a challenge came in 1878 from one A. H. Church, a British chemist and botanist:

> *As to the small loss of nutrient materials involved in the ordi-*
> *nary fermentation of dough, it hardly merits consideration.*
> *Perhaps Dr. Richardson alluded to it because it gave him an*
> *opportunity to have a fling at his old enemy, alcohol, of which*
> *it has been found that a newly baked loaf made of yeast con-*
> *tains about 0.25 percent.*

A man would have to consume twenty loaves, each weighing 3.5 pounds, to match the volume of alcohol in a bottle of port, Mr. Church claimed. The conversion of starch to alcohol by the voracious appetite of yeast was a red herring.[32]

In 1884, Richardson tried again to advance aerated bread. He summarized the already burgeoning storehouse of sanitary, economical, and socially beneficial arguments in favor of bread made by ABC machines in his booklet *On the Healthy Manufacture of Bread: A Memoir on the System of Dr. Dauglish*. Because an aerated batch of dough could be prepared in thirty minutes, Richardson pointed out, no longer would bakers be required to begin their tasks before midnight, haul large sacks of flour, inhale dust, hand knead in overheated bake rooms, and go without sleep until late the next day. (The average life span of a nineteenth-century baker in England was only forty-two.) Richardson went on to contradict himself by making it clear that Dauglish's aerated bread machine was equally productive in daylight and in darkness. Just like Arkwright's water frame for textiles, a bread aerator could work continuous shifts, so long as a parade of workers kept it stocked night and day.[33]

Having hyped the benefits of the cost and efficiency of aerated bread to bakers, Dr. Richardson offered a distinct case to consumers. Aerated bread was free from all remnants of human contact. No hair, nails, sweat, flannel, cloth, or splinters from kneading troughs and shaping boards. The dough was never touched by human hand or foot, exposed neither to the noxious fumes of the bake house "nor to the emanations escaping from the skin and breath of the workmen."[34] Even Church, in his rebuttal in *Nature*, conceded the point. The mechanical process of manufacturing aerated bread was perfectly clean and "immeasurably superior to the barbarous and old . . . system of kneading dough by hands and feet of workmen."[35] The absence of flavors reminiscent of sourdough was another big selling point. "It does not undergo the sour or acid change that is sometimes met with in fermented breads," Richardson said.[36]

In 1895, the *New York Times* crowed at the introduction of aerated bread to New York City. "The New Aerated Bread Company has fired up its ovens to 420 degrees Fahrenheit at 449 West Fifty-third Street," read the headline. The "excellence" of the loaves was "inspired by the knowledge that in the whole course of its manufacture there was no manipulation of it, and that the absence of yeast rendered unclean and unsanitary decomposition impossible." Twenty delivery wagons worked full-time to deliver aerated loaves across the city. An amply sized loaf cost a very reasonable five cents. The same article continued, "The system is so admirable that the bread is recommended as pure and healthful by physicians." Is it meaningful that a large print advertisement immediately beneath the article in the *New York Times* was for "Beecham's Pills for Constipation 10¢ and 25¢"?[37]

The last ABC tearoom in England closed in 1982, just eleven years before London's streets were introduced to the Seattle Coffee Company, the chain that was purchased by Starbucks in 1998.[38] In Great Britain today, a cold foam cascara nitro has supplanted Earl Grey for many Londoners on the go; coffee is now more popular than tea.[39] Yet, to this day, afternoon tea accompanied by small triangular sandwiches on yeasted white bread sheared of their crusts remains a British tradition.

THE FINAL BURST of yeast, which together with white flour pushed whole wheat and sourdough bread to the distant margins of society, is often attributed to Charles Fleischmann. Fleischmann did not invent anything; his primary contribution to the evolution of bread making was in selling. He sold yeast to Americans as if it were a product that could transform their lives. Kind of like Steve Jobs and Apple. When he died in 1897, Charles's wealth, in today's dollars, would have made him a billionaire.[40]

Born in 1835 in Moravian-Silesia, then part of the Austro-Hungarian Empire, Charles was the son of a yeast maker. Being under Austro-Hungarian rule and interested in yeast, Charles received some of his education in Vienna, where he also managed a distillery. While he oversaw the manufacture of spirits, he was also living at the epicenter of bread innovation. Hungarian roller mills were, after all, spinning out calcite-white flour; Viennese bakers were kneading that flour into loaves of such delectability that the exhibition of the Vienna Model Bakery created quite a stir at the Paris Exposition in 1867. The Vienna Model Bakery won all the bread awards that year in France, formerly home to the best bread in the world.[41]

The 1860s, however, were not great years to be living in Vienna. Otto von Bismarck was enlarging his influence across central Europe, and not all of Prussia's expansion was peaceful. In 1866, Austria was invaded by Prussia. Looking across the ocean, Fleischmann's parents saw that America's Civil War had finally ended and sent Charles in 1867 to the United States. According to Fleischmann biographer P. Christiaan Klieger, "The great founder boldly strutted down the gangplank in New York City, humming the new popular march from 'The Tannhauser,' with a tiny vial of yeast [probably dried] secreted in his waistcoat pocket, thus beginning the fabulous food and beverage industry."[42] By the middle of the nineteenth century, it was at last possible to carry a prized culture of yeast, or yeast and bacteria in the case of a sour-dough starter, across the ocean with the intention of using it upon landing on the other side.

Figuring out that there were many Americans willing to pay for better-quality bread was Charles Fleischmann's particular stroke of genius. In the late 1860s in America, when Charles was settling in, yeast was available, but there was not yet a clear process for moving yeast from producer to consumer. Thousands of home bakers, many now embarking on westward journeys into a rural continent with few bakeries, had to rely upon sourdoughs or one of those rec-ipes for making home yeast that all too often listed yeast among its ingredients.[43] Was one of those westward-traveling families carry-ing a sourdough culture on its way to Cripple Creek, Colorado? It is possible.

In 1867, Charles and his brother Max, also recently arrived, worked in New York City at a distillery that used a Hungarian pro-cess for manufacturing yeast. According to a 1909 report of the USDA's Bureau of Chemistry, the Hungarian process cultivated yeast on a mash of rye and malted barley. The aromatic mixture fermented into a very thick paste. Growing yeast for the produc-tion of beer or spirits is very much the same as it is for bread—sometimes the species or variety varies, but the cultivation does not change much, if at all. The yeast thriving on Hungarian mash could be used to make an exceptionally decent rye whiskey, for example.[44] Charles must have concocted a personal variation because he pat-ented his own method for making Hungarian yeast.

A year later, in 1868, Charles, Max, and a third partner, James Gaff, moved to Cincinnati, Ohio, to open a yeast factory. In 1868, Cincinnati was the third-largest manufacturing hub in the United States. It was located on the Ohio River; railroads connected the city to the rest of the rapidly growing, newly reunified country. Moreover, there were well-established populations of Germans and eastern Europeans anxious to consume decent breads that reminded them of their motherlands.

The Fleischmanns grew yeast in copper vats filled with a brew of malted barley, corn, rye, and sugar. Their vats foamed, and the air filled with the robust piquancy of fermentation. Carefully, they skimmed their crop, rinsed it many times over with fresh water, and pressed their vibrant yeasts onto cleaned cloths, squeezing as much water as they could into the shop drains. Their product was formed into cakes, wrapped in shiny tinfoil, and sent out for immediate sale. Their yeast was viable for only a few days without refrigeration.

Charles went door-to-door hawking yeast to the city's population of Jewish and German immigrants. When he attempted to expand his sales to gentiles, blue bloods, and Cincinnati's bakeries, prospective buyers were skeptical of the young entrepreneur with the European accent. The early going was difficult. Gaff and the Fleischmann brothers hunted for a better market and homed in on the flood of European immigrants settling in New York City.

They purchased a distillery in Blissful, Long Island, where they set their copper vats to double duty. From the top, they harvested yeast to sell to bakers and brewers and then created a second product from the remaining liquid. Boiling the surplus liquid vaporized unwanted water. What remained behind was condensed into some very fine grain alcohol. The Fleischmann Distilling Company produced America's first gin. Selling both gin and yeast helped the bottom line, but not a lot. Profits were still skinny.

The breakthrough for the Fleischmanns took place in 1876 during America's centennial, which the country celebrated with a world's fair. Prior to 1876, world's fairs were Eurocentric. That is why America had to send Eben Norton Horsford to the Vienna International Exhibition of 1873 to learn all about Vienna bread and pressed yeast. Evidently, Horsford's government-sponsored report did not bring high-speed change to the bread of America. That task would be accomplished by the Fleischmanns.

World's fairs and international exhibitions were modeled in some respects on an ancient Roman approach to categorizing, listing, and judging everything that was known about the world. Think of them as three-dimensional encyclopedias analogous to Pliny the Elder's ten-volume *Naturalis Historia*. European exhibitions endeavored to display a representative of every country, vegetable, handmade or contraption-woven carpet, hat-felting machine, suit coat, locomotive, dining room table, meteorite, stuffed polar bear, wallpaper printing press, photograph, pie, and piglet.

Between 1798 and 1849, the French hosted eleven such fairs. By 1834, national exhibitions had been held in Spain, Austria, Portugal, Russia, Denmark, Sweden, Bavaria, Prussia, Holland, the Netherlands, and both Sicilies. In the 1860s and 1870s, London, Paris, and Vienna hosted fairs, in a serial competition of extravagance.

Beginning in 1871, the United States started planning for its debutante ball. The US government established the Centennial Commission. Befitting the character of the country, the Centennial Exhibition of 1876 was expansive, less refined than its European predecessors, with their Austrian attention to order and taxonomy, French focus on aesthetics, or British porcelain appeal to fine taste. The US World's Fair was housed in more than 200 buildings sprawled across 450 acres in Philadelphia. The Main Hall ran more than a third of a mile. Machinery Hall covered about 500,000 square feet and housed more than 1,900 exhibitors.

Approximately ten million people trekked through Philadelphia's fairgrounds, and most of them were overwhelmed by its immensity. Few Americans had ever been to a museum or even a department store; to see so much on display in one location must have been immobilizing. Dazed men, women, and children walked by dozens of taxidermied animals, scores of ripe pumpkins, Swedish steel, railway axles, French lace shawls, Brazilian textbooks, live camels shuffling in their stalls, the Indian Bureau's display of living families of Comanche, Apache, Kiowa, and Piute, buttons, a glass case of false teeth, corsets, thousands of cold-punched screws, artfully displayed plastering trowels, and mannequins of a Scandinavian family mourning a baby's death.[45]

The incessant din of trundling spectators reverberated from walls and ceilings. Somewhere in the distance a piano or an organ was playing—there were more than six hundred performances during the Centennial's six-month run—and yet ears and eyes were not the only senses under assault. Lubricating oils easing the work of thousands of machines evaporated into the air of the buildings in which they were enclosed. Horses, mules, asses, horned cattle, sheep, swine, goats, dogs, and poultry all did their business. Chemical displays and mounds of wool sent olfactory tip-offs before they were ever visible. Cigar vendors hawked from wooden stands, and next to you were the tired bodies of cranky children, increasingly impatient parents, and shambling seniors, all sweating in Philadelphia's summer heat.

Near the Art Gallery stood a small but undoubtedly welcome building just 142 feet long and 105 feet wide. Its sign read "Vienna Bakery and Coffee-House." Inside, a weary visitor much in need of fortification could enjoy a tiny taste of European refinement and an escape from the exterior commotion. Gaff, Fleischmann and Company, of Cincinnati, Ohio, had erected the booth. Its sign read, "Here can be obtained tea, coffee, and all kinds of pastry, etc."[46]

It is easy for me to envision the US World's Fair of 1876 and imagine the degree of emotional investment put forth by the Fleischmanns. My hometown of Meadville, Pennsylvania, hosts an annual county fair that is a descendant of the European tradition. The Crawford County Fair is not just the largest of its kind in the commonwealth; it is the largest agricultural fair east of the

Mississippi River. Among the hundreds upon hundreds of items entered into the fair are homemade breads. In 2010, I entered a loaf of bread made from my Cripple Creek sourdough.

The day before the fair opened, I baked two loaves of bread. I made one loaf I was sure would be a winner in the "Other" category: a four-pound artisanal loaf. I used the white flour sourdough starter my wife made in 1990 with yeasts she captured from wild Meadville grapes. The recipe I chose for the fair produced a round bread with a stunning crackly crust of fine concentric rings imparted by a French wicker boule. I used 90 percent white flour and a half cup of rye to give it body and a full tablespoon of salt for flavor. Instead of kneading, I let it rise untouched for eighteen hours. The sourdough did the work. I've seen loaves like it in boulangeries sell for a pocketful of euros.

Then I had a dilemma. Because I converted Cripple Creek to whole wheat when I first received it and had never used white flour to grow it up (I add white and other flours only *after* I've removed my cup of whole wheat starter to return to the refrigerator), I thought I'd try to enter Cripple Creek under the whole wheat category. When I phoned Jeanne, the self-described white-haired lady who made competitive peanut brittle every year, to ask if I could use a sourdough bread in the whole wheat yeasted division, she was insistent about two things. First, because there is no sub-sub-sub-subdivision for sourdough, my bread had to be entered in the "Other" category. Second, only one entry per category.

I defied Jeanne, stretched the truth, and entered my Cripple Creek in the whole wheat yeasted division anyway. The yeast in my loaf just happened to be a wild one captured, perhaps, in some Rocky Mountain mining town more than one hundred years ago.

Adding to my disquiet over being caught trying to scam the system, I was frustrated by the plastic bag rule. Fresh bread should be kept in the open air or paper bags for the first twenty-four hours so that excess moisture can escape. Really, they should be eaten within twenty-four hours because they just don't taste as good when they are a day old. But for the Crawford County Fair, all the breads had to be entered inside plastic bags. My loaves were being handed over on Friday afternoon. Judging wasn't going to begin until Saturday at noon. My breads were going to be a day old and coming out of plastic bags. "OK, Pallant," I told myself. "It's only the Crawford County Fair. It's not a job interview."

The exhibit hall where all the home products were concentrated was sealed at noon on Saturday so that the judges could discuss their evaluations in private. The doors remained shuttered to everyone until five thirty in the evening, when the auction of all the baked items began.

An hour into the auction, I won a Hawaiian coconut-pineapple cake, orange on the inside with white coconut-flake icing: eight dollars for the "Best of Show" cake. I was so excited by my purchase, I didn't notice that my artisan white bread was up next, buried beneath three kinds of cookies. The cookies were a big hit, and my bread was obviously tossed in to get rid of it. The whole bundle sold for seven dollars to the family on the bench in front of me. My hubris was self-evident. The huge loaf with the beautiful spiral-imprinted crust I was certain would win bore no ribbon. When I told the family in front that I had made the bread and that it was likely very good, they smiled benignly and asked me what kind it was.

"Sourdough," I told them.

"Oh, we were wondering what it was," they responded politely.

As the auction continued, it became clear that pies were selling for nearly double the price of cakes and that all the breads were being hidden behind cookie platters and muffins. My Cripple Creek loaf went up for sale concealed behind cinnamon rolls and chocolate chip cookies. Two elderly women behind me purchased the group. Cripple Creek was wearing a brown third-place sticker on the plastic bag. I asked if I could borrow the bread so that my wife could take my picture. My grin was one hundred acres wide. As a third-place finisher, I had just won $2.75. Once, at an industrial exhibition in Cincinnati, the Fleischmanns had won a bronze medal for their yeast.[47] The Fleischmanns and I had something in common.

To hear the Fleischmanns tell it, the summer of 1876 marked the inflection point of the company's earning potential. Pale and soft Vienna breads were as much a success in Philadelphia as they had been in Europe. It was one thing to read Horsford's report on Viennese rolls and another thing entirely to taste one. As thousands of weary sightseers drank hearty cups of coffee or steaming mugs of tea and restored their flagging blood sugar with "all kinds of pastry, etc.," Fleischmann's servers made certain that every customer learned that the secret was in Fleischmann's packaged yeast.

Americans and immigrants about to become Americans raced westward across the continent's grasslands, prairies, and Rocky Mountains. Ranchers, farmers, farriers, teachers, dentists, barbers, teamsters, grocers, hoteliers, and mayors needed to eat. Some among them made their own bread and therefore had to have live active yeast if they did not possess an heirloom sourdough or the willingness to grow their own yeast each time they wished to bake their daily bread. Professional bakers in emerging towns and cities learned to bake Vienna breads, and naturally, they, too, needed consistently dependable yeast. Aerated bread, it seems, never really took off in most of the United States. Railroads laid tracks to cover America's great distances, and in the 1880s, refrigerated railcars were finally capable of carrying live packaged yeast anywhere a freight train could haul it.

The Fleischmanns did not invent yeast, but their packaged stock was more steadfast and a heck of a lot more convenient than following a recipe that began with a boiled mash of grain and molasses, acquisition of living yeast, and then a prayer that not too many air-borne bacteria had swan dived into your porridge. Moreover, the Fleischmanns were heirs to the practices of the itinerant Jewish vendor. They could deliver. By the time of the Centennial Exhibition, they knew how to market. Fleischmann's Yeast was a brand.[48]

"By 1881, Fleischmann and Company had over 1,000 bakeries as clients, and untold individual customers," according to P. Christiaan Klieger. One company slogan proclaimed without exaggeration, "In storm, in sunshine, rain or sleet, you see our wagons on the street." The "Fleischmann Man" became a common sight in America, his horse-drawn carriage parked in front of the bakery, delivering fresh packaged yeast. The combination of dependable production, constant refrigeration, and speedy delivery meant that customers anywhere could count on receiving Fleischmann's Yeast that was 100 percent alive.[49]

By the 1890s, Charles Fleischmann was operating four production plants. He had become so wealthy, he owned a mansion in Cincinnati, vacation homes, a yacht, and a stable of racehorses managed by a famous jockey of the era, James Forman "Tod" Sloane. He was elected to the Ohio state senate and was a renowned patron of the opera, stage, ballet, and symphony.

In the second decade of the twentieth century, Fleischmann's Yeast erupted. The Fleischmann School for bakers opened in the Bronx, New York, in 1911. More than three thousand bakers learned to use their yeast. To serve bakers outside New York, the company created a traveling school: two canvas-covered wagons equipped with ranges, hoods, and mixers traveled to cities and towns. Instructors rented vacant lots and taught bakers "modern" techniques. Fleischmann's Yeast sponsored home economics classes in high schools and colleges and underwrote baking contests.

To bolster demand, Fleischmann's launched the "Eat More Bread" campaign. In one ad, a cartoon figure of a bread man was standing upon legs of joined loaves of bread. The smiling puppet had a chest of bread and jointed loaves for arms. He wore an apron embroidered with the words "John Dough, raised on Fleischmann's Yeast."[50] The copy read: "Good properly fermented bread is 'light' on the stomach."

New Americans would have recognized this not-so-subtle reference to heavy sourdough breads eaten by their parents and grandparents back in the old country. The half-page ad continued, "It is quickly absorbed by the system. More than this—it is richer in nutriment than meat, potatoes and other foods which are harder to digest. **Eat more light bread.** You'll *feel* better for it and *do* better for it—for a light stomach makes a clear head. Try it!" There's more, but you get the drift.

From 1917 to 1924, sales of yeast tripled, and four years later, Fleischmann's controlled 93.4 percent of all yeast sales. In the 1920s, Fleischmann's rose into the top ten advertisers in US magazines. The company had twelve plants and 2,500 sales representatives. It sold yeast as an animal supplement and as a product an industrious homemaker could use to prepare root beer. As this was also the period of America's experiment with Prohibition, an attentive homemaker or home-wrecker could use the same yeast to make beer (or wine or moonshine). Sales were sales, after all. To further increase demand now that they had virtually monopolized the sale of yeast for the bakery business, Fleischmann's entered the health food market.[51]

Fleischmann's "Yeast for Health" campaign accurately matched the burgeoning desire of Americans, even one hundred years ago, to use food as a pharmaceutical. An advertisement in *Popular Mechanics* from 1938 asked, "Embarrassed by horrid pimples?" Acne's cause, it seemed, was intestinal poisons, and the affliction could be cured by Fleischmann's Yeast. "Start eating Fleischmann's Yeast now—three cakes daily—one cake a half hour before each meal. Begin now!"[52]

A 1932 advertisement in the magazine *Good Housekeeping* featured Dr. Maliwa, head of the "noted Sanatorium Esplanade" at Baden near Vienna. In his right hand he held an X-ray of a large intestine glowing white with discomfort. The lead paragraph? "In cases of constipation and intestinal sluggishness... I prescribe fresh yeast." Looking directly into the camera was the vaguely relieved Mrs. Diane Craddock of Tulsa, Oklahoma. The swollen large intestine was obviously hers. "The least little thing would wear me out. My whole system was sluggish," said Mrs. Craddock. After acceding to the advice of her doctors to increase her consumption of yeast, her fatigue dissipated, her complexion cleared, and her appetite returned. Just in case you missed the point, a manuscript that looked an awful lot like a scientific report was on display. Its prescription was presented in block print: "Eat, or drink, three cakes of Fleischmann's Yeast every day."[53]

Promoting "Yeast for Health" was such a success that revenue jumped from $1 million in the 1920s to $10 million by the late 1930s. Though the company encouraged patience because results might not be seen for months, yeast cures extended beyond constipation and acne. Eating chalky blocks of yeast paste thrice daily was also touted for its ability to cure bad breath, boils, furry tongue, colds, "fallen stomach," depression, headaches, obesity, and tooth decay. It could give you added energy, eliminate crying spells, sharpen intellect, and strengthen intestinal muscles. One 1937 ad even claimed that Fleischmann's Yeast had "restored a woman's ability to walk."[54] Additional yeast sales to Americans anxious to reclaim both their pep and their poop were welcome revenue to a company that had lost so much of its income when the production of alcohol was prohibited in America.

Alas, the Federal Trade Commission finally intervened. The FTC battled the company through the 1930s until Fleischmann's finally cut back on its ubiquitous health claims. Before we laugh too heartily at claims that compressed yeast in an iconic foil package could provide an intestinal cleansing—recommended every spring!—or make pimples vanish, today, one can find similar claims about juice cleanses and chia cures all over the internet or the vitamin aisle of a modern grocery store.

Eat Yeast. Look Swell, a 1941 advertisement for Fleischmann's Yeast.

As I surveyed the advancement of readily available yeast, so effective in its leavening power that less and less skill was needed to produce a loaf of bread, I was increasingly bewildered by my exploration for Cripple Creek's origins. My question was no longer why and how yeast replaced sourdough or why store-bought bread replaced the home loaf but rather the opposite: how did sourdough ever survive the twentieth century?

A last redoubt of sourdough appears to have been hidden in tiny leather pouches protected by weather-beaten gold miners. Personified in an unconstrained miner, now called a Sourdough, slogging his way into the wilderness in search of gold was the American ideal of beginning in rags and finishing with riches. Living only on essentials he could carry and relying on nothing more than the labor of his own two hands and bread or pancakes he made himself, he embodied the American exemplar of self-sufficiency. An American miner was a westernized version of an American farmer, introduced as an icon in 1787 by *American Museum*, a magazine published in Philadelphia.

That image of a gold rush miner exists among no shortage of nostalgic books, and why not? The essence of one view of American history is here: strong-willed independence. A man battles the harshest elements the new continent can throw at him. He has a gun. He is capable of cooking a few things, and one of them is sourdough hotcakes baked on nothing more than a fry pan and an open fire.

I used to tell people stories about my sourdough starter that came from the Cripple Creek Gold Rush of 1893. As I sliced Cripple Creek loaves to share with newcomers, I rendered ballads right from the American songbook of lonesome miners who once baked with my starter. And then I did the research. Almost no part of the miner myth was true.

A DOZEN SMALL VIENNA BREADS
Yield: 1 dozen small breads

Vienna bread was a revolution in bread making; roller-milled white flour, high-quality yeast, and an astounding tradition of Viennese baking all came together at the end of the nineteenth century. This recipe is inspired by *Vienna Bread: Instructions and Recipes*, published in London in 1909 by Charles and James Scott.[55]

> 1 cup whole milk
> 2 teaspoons active dry yeast
> 5 cups all-purpose flour
> 5 tablespoons granulated sugar
> 2 teaspoons salt
> 1 large egg
> 3 tablespoons unsalted butter, at room temperature
> 1 egg yolk beaten with 1 tablespoon whole milk, for glazing

In a small bowl, warm the milk for 30 seconds in the microwave, until it is about 100°F—warm enough to activate but not kill the yeast. Dissolve the yeast in the milk and let stand, covered, for 5 minutes. Lightly oil a large bowl.

In the bowl of a stand mixer, combine the flour, sugar, and salt. Make a well and add the egg and milk-yeast mixture. Run the mixer for a few minutes on low speed until the dough starts to come together. Add the butter in pieces, and continue mixing until the dough becomes homogeneous.

Continue running the mixer on low speed until it becomes smooth and elastic. Place in the large oiled bowl. Cover with a damp cloth or plastic wrap, set in a warm place, and let the dough rise for 1½ hours, or until it has roughly doubled in size.

Cover a baking sheet in parchment paper dusted with semolina or cornmeal.

Punch down the dough. Turn it out onto a floured work surface and knead a few minutes to soften it. Divide the dough into 12 equal pieces (about 70 grams each). Let the pieces rest, covered, for 15 to 20 minutes.

Shape each piece of dough into 6-inch oblong rolls, then place them on the prepared baking sheet, spacing them at least 1 inch apart, as they will swell a lot. Cover with a damp cloth or plastic, and let them rise again for 45 to 60 minutes, until they are a little less than doubled in size.

Preheat your oven to 450°F.

Brush the bread rolls with the yolk-milk mixture, then score the rolls down the center with a wetted serrated knife. Spray the walls of the oven with water before sliding in the bread (or add 1 cup of water to a steam pan). Turn the temperature down to 400°F and bake for about 10 to 15 minutes, or until the rolls are golden brown and the internal temperature is 200°F.

CHAPTER 6

HOW MUCH BREAD CAN YOU BUY WITH GOLD?

I N THE LATE 1840S, JOHN SUTTER, A GERMAN IMMI-
grant to North America, constructed a mill in Brighton, California. Sutter planned to harvest lumber for fences and hoped
to sell sawn wood to squatters in the tiny village of San Francisco.
Some longer-term inhabitants of the Bay Area were ready to move
out of their tents and into wooden structures. Sutter calculated
that he could make a profit bringing lumber from California's rain-
ier mountains to its drier coast. In the end, however, Sutter's profits
appeared in the form of tiny golden nuggets that sat on the bottom
of his sawmill's sluiceway.[1]

Peering toward the sun rising beyond snowcapped mountains
in the Sierra Nevada, Sutter scouted the foothills for a river surrounded by forest and enough current to power a sawmill. He
settled upon the north branch of the American River and hired
thirty-three-year-old James Wilson Marshall, a native of New
Jersey, as foreman to oversee its construction.

On Monday morning, January 24, 1848, Marshall opened
the millrace on Sutter's watermill. Water ran through the channel
recently hand dug by some of California's Indigenous inhabitants,

whom Marshall called "simple, awkward savages."[2] When the flow equilibrated and the water finally cleared, Marshall regarded a shiny golden fleck among the newly dug sediments.

The discovery of gold was not an easily held secret, and by late spring 1848, both of San Francisco's weekly newspapers had published news of the discovery at Sutter's sawmill. Historian Hubert Howe Bancroft described what happened next: "The strongest human appetite was aroused—the sum of appetites—this yellow dirt embodying the means for gratifying love, hate, lust, and domination. If Satan from Diablo's peak had sounded the knell of time; if a heavenly angel from the Sierra's height had heralded the millennial day; if the blessed Christ himself had arisen from that ditch and proclaimed to all mankind amnesty—their greedy hearts had never half so thrilled."[3]

By the middle of June, three-fourths of the male inhabitants of San Francisco had abandoned their homes and businesses, leaving the city shuttered and largely abandoned. Fields were left half-planted. Homes under construction were vacated. Wagon trains by the scores headed east.[4] Departing miners were quickly followed by an inrush of hopeful new prospectors. San Francisco boiled over. In 1848, there might have been one thousand poor settlers. Two years later, there were twenty-five thousand.

California gold fever infected people around the world. Tens of thousands arrived from Hawaii, New Zealand, and Australia. They came to "Gold Mountain" from China and the Philippines. Mexicans and Latin Americans made their way north. Black men escaping slavery in the American South, Brazil, and the Caribbean sought their fortunes. Britons, Italians, and Germans crossed an ocean and a continent. By 1855, there were some three hundred thousand new Californians searching for gold or starting businesses to serve the prospectors.[5]

Among those masses were Frenchmen. News of gold in

California arrived at an opportune moment in France. From 1846 to 1847, the price of French wheat and the bread upon which all Frenchmen, both rural and urban, depended doubled. Frenchmen responded as they always had; protests and riots spread across the country. The combination of domestic turmoil, a foundering economy, and empty stomachs increased French susceptibility to infection by the global spread of gold fever. Among the hordes disembarking in San Francisco were thirty thousand people from France,[6] and a few arrived from a settlement in Mexico.

As it turned out, at least a few Frenchmen found their fortune in bread, not gold, which makes sense. In most respects, French immigrants in California were much like others newly arrived from the eastern United States, Europe, South America, and Asia. The trip was long and arduous. A French traveler in 1848 complained, as only a Frenchman could, that even at the captain's table "the menu consists of bad bread, detestable wine from the Midi, undrinkable water, worthless coffee, and good tea."[7]

Consider the choices faced upon arrival in California, especially for those latecomers who arrived after all the easy gold had already been scooped. Landing in California after more than half a year's journey, having invested all his hopes in finding riches, the average man with a pan faced the following monotony: soggy feet, pruned fingers, and eyes crossed by the hour-upon-hour search for lustrous flakes of gold. A few among them had the wisdom to perceive that real money could be made by resuming a job they had once done back home. A newly arrived Frenchman could earn 1,000 francs a month as a baker (or a butcher, carpenter, or cook). Frequently, the costs of lodging and laundry for tradesmen were covered, too.[8] The real money was to be made mining the miners.[9]

It's likely that at least some of these French bakers were using sourdough. Yes, by the middle of the nineteenth century, yeast was already replacing sourdough as the preferred method for leavening

in many parts of Britain, France, and the United States, but remember that yeast did not travel well over long distances or without
refrigeration, and in remote locations, it had not yet completely
eradicated sourdough. In gold-mining hotspots like California in
1849, the elevated peaks of the Rocky Mountains in 1893, and outposts near Klondike, Alaska, in 1896, sourdough was more readily
available and easier to provide than yeast.

Between April 1 and November 10, 1849, 1,113 ships unloaded
food in San Francisco's hectic harbor.[10] Where miners settled, small
villages sprang up about them, with the truly steady business accru-
ing to merchants furnishing miners with bread, meat, potatoes,
onions, sex, and alcohol in all its varieties.[11] Teamster traffic grew to
huge proportions as harnessed trains of forty or fifty mules at a time
left the ports of Stockton, Sacramento, and San Francisco, heading
for stores, restaurants, and saloons in the Sierras. Thousands of men
drove many thousands of mules carrying food, clothing, towels,
combs, stationery, and well, the kinds of things you buy in a store.[12]

By 1854, the city of San Francisco listed in its directory sixty-
three bakeries. Many suggested the bread of home: Ohio Bakery,
Georgia Bakery, Boston Bakery, New York Bakery (two), German
Bakery (two), New England Bakery, and Philadelphia Bakery.
Two bakeries were called French Bakery, one was named the
Franco-American bakery, and three were named for French owners:
LaFitte, Larege, and Jourdan. The total came to nine if the New
Orleans Bakery, the New Orleans Fancy Bakery and the Louisiana
Bakery, were included.[13] By 1856, three additional French bakeries
had arrived: Beraud Freres, Mme. Lantheaume, and Longraies &
Co.[14] What I don't know is how many of those sixty-three baker-
ies were using sourdough and how many were using newfangled
leavens like baking soda and brewer's yeast. What I do have is the
article from *Western Folklore* that declared that Frenchmen from
Mexico came to San Francisco in 1848 and brought with them

their sourdough starters.[15] Another historian suggested that San Francisco's sourdoughs arrived with Basque immigrants.[16]

Unfortunately, neither author offers much in the way of verification. Perhaps there is none to be had beyond the circumstantial evidence of plentiful French breads in San Francisco and a proclivity among Frenchmen for a taste of sourdough from their mother country. I don't know whether those beautiful French starters traveled by ship from Paris, Brest, or Bayonne or whether they were created anew in the New World.

What is certain is that sourdough bakers were doing business in San Francisco during the gold rush era. In fact, one French sourdough culture from the gold rush era is still in use today at Boudin Bakery on San Francisco's wharf. It was established as the Boudin French Bakery in 1849 and has been keeping a record of its sourdough starter ever since. Boudin Bakery remains a major tourist attraction today and holds a great deal of responsibility for the entanglement of sourdough, the Gold Rush of 1849, and the city of San Francisco.

Sourdough bread and San Francisco are as synonymous as Maine and lobster, Wisconsin and cheese, New York City and bagels, or Boston and baked beans. One answer to the question of where in America sourdough survived the nineteenth century was inside the French bakeries of San Francisco. And consequently, it is feasible that a starter at a gold rush town in Colorado in 1893, at a time when many Americans were eating yeasted bread, came from California. And if the starter itself wasn't brought there, then at least the knowledge of how to make a starter and turn it into bread could have originated near San Francisco.

I N 2013, I traveled to San Francisco to learn what I could about Boudin's famous starter and to see for myself how America's original gold seekers acquired their sourdough bread. There was a tiny museum, a much larger gift shop, a bakery, and a restaurant all housed at Boudin at the Wharf in San Francisco. In the museum, the Boudin family tree was proudly pictured on one wall as proof that the family had begotten a long line of master bakers, a distinction earned by extensive training and guild certification. The tree's foundation was anchored by François, who was soon overtaken in fame by his son Isidore, who arrived from Burgundy as a sixteen-year-old. Isidore was the first Boudin to work as a master baker in America, and he was the progenitor of a long line of master bakers at Boudin.

A bust of Isidore sat atop a prominent pedestal. Circling the pedestal in glassed cabinets were tapered French rolling pins, wooden kneading troughs, bowls to hold rising doughs, metal scoops, brass and copper ladles, proofing boards, scrapers, and long-handled baking peels. An antique bakery wagon sat in the middle of the gallery, the centerpiece in a space about the size of a middle-class living room. In the early days, horse-drawn wagons carried fresh bread across the city. Filling out the room, audio of clopping horse hooves descended from overhead speakers.

A fog generator blew mist across a sign describing the bacteria and yeast dwelling within Boudin's sourdough culture. According to the sign, microflora found within the Bay Area's unique combination of clouds, humidity, temperature, and rainfall have enabled unique combinations of life-forms found only in sourdough cultures in San Francisco. Is there any premium worth more than an exotic flavor that cannot be reproduced in any other location?

The tiny museum paid special tribute to Louise Boudin, wife of Isidore. In 1906, when an earthquake leveled the city and a massive fire burned much of it to the ground, Louise raced to the bakery and filled a bucket with starter, saving what would become Boudin's most famous marketing contrivance: a sourdough culture whose origin is forty-four years older than mine. Today, there are fourteen Boudin bakeries in California, a stand at the San Francisco airport, and a demonstration bakery at the Disney California Adventure Park. To ensure the authenticity of Boudin's bread, every twenty-eight days, each branch receives a fresh batch of starter from the mother.

One wall of the museum had been displaced by glass. Interested viewers could peer down on three stories of gleaming metal machines. I watched white-suited bakers scurrying about industrial mixers, kneaders, and mechanical shapers. Loaves rose in bread pans arrayed for a military parade, and strikingly uniform boules emerged from ovens on their way to becoming hundreds of hollowed bread bowls for creamy clam chowders. Pallets groaned beneath chest-high piles of flour from Conagra mills. There were also hundreds of pounds of white sugar, the mold inhibitor calcium propionate, five-gallon jugs of canola oil, jars of caramel color, and dough conditioner. To attend to the 2.5 million visitors to its facility on the wharf and all of its outlets,[17] Boudin has done its best to match sourdough with industrial production. Boudin's shop floor, seen from above, was a brightly lit, antiseptic beehive of activity that Arkwright and his cofounders of the Industrial Revolution would have understood. What I could see from the museum catwalk was not at all like what I saw at the tiny bakery I visited in Saint-Rémy-de-Provence, France.

Boudin's sourdough, when I tasted it, was uniquely theirs—very sour, almost like bread dosed with white vinegar. To my taste, a Boudin sourdough is bread in the same way a Budweiser is definitely beer. Like a can of chilled Budweiser on a sweltering summer day, Boudin's bread is incredibly satisfying. Boudin's sourdough prickles your tongue, and it can be an especially fine accompaniment served warm alongside fresh seafood and a smooth red wine, but it isn't terribly complex or interesting.

A renaissance of sourdough bread making has been going on in San Francisco since around 2000, and I was not going to waste a trip to the city without sampling as many of the new bakeries as I could. I also wanted to test for myself the hypothesis that sourdough cultures in San Francisco are fundamentally indigenous. Was it true, as Boudin claimed, that San Francisco's unique climate fostered cultures of bacteria and yeast that could be created only on location?

Accompanied by my wife and her brother Marty, an exceptional cook, I started at Arizmendi Bakery, a co-op. The day I arrived was its thirteenth birthday, and a big handmade sign celebrated its survival. The storefront was small, like something you would find in Paris. There was barely room for a counter and a few baskets of bread and sweets. Flour-dusted work tops were right behind the counter, and the ovens were within arm's reach of the shaping tables. A banner read, "Make Loaves, Not War!"

It was Saturday, and the staff were making pizza before closing for Sunday and Monday, their rest days. A lead baker with piercings and tattoos sported a short, spiky haircut and arms like Hercules. On her black T-shirt in bold white lettering was "Body by Pastrami."

While I agonized over how many items I could feasibly sample, a twenty-something woman wearing a bicycle jersey stepped to the counter. The server asked, "Did you ride your bicycle here?"

"Yes," she said.

"You get a 10 percent discount, then."

Arizmendi's sourdough baguette was quite different from Boudin's. It was speckled with a mix of seeds—I'd say 40 percent hulled sesame, 40 percent poppy, and 20 percent fennel, just the right ratio to give a delightful pop every couple of bites. The bread was mild, nowhere near the powerful sting of Boudin's. The loaf was firm, the crust was a beautiful rust color—almost too tough at its tapered ends to bite through—and the crumb was a textbook display of open holes. What struck me most was that it wasn't intensely sour. There were a hundred subtle flavors that neither yeasted bread nor Boudin's contained. I liked it a lot. Perhaps if early Americans had had Arizmendi's on every corner, they would not have been so quick to give up on sourdough. My first non-Boudin sample was so distinctively different in flavor and character, I had to question Boudin's claim that San Francisco's microbes were the unifying basis of the city's sourdough bread. I also started to question whether the age of a starter had any bearing on the taste of the breads it made.

Arizmendi's sourdough croissants were seraphic. I purchased an almond and a chocolate, both of which were rectangular in deference to their fillings, and my wife, Marty, and I retired to a sidewalk bench to sample them. The flavors were symphonic, and on the spot, Marty and I committed to an annual tradition of preparing sourdough croissants. As we ate, the croissants scattered a meteor shower of flakes to the sidewalk. I didn't taste sourness, but I knew right away I wasn't dealing with a commercial yeasted white flour bread with its monotonic flavor and dripping-in-butter feel. These sourdough croissants were as light as cherry petals on the wind. I still dream of Arizmendi's delicately sweet pecan sticky bun, the very opposite of the clobber-you-over-the-head stickiness that comes from corn syrup lathered onto mass-produced varieties. Arizmendi's pecans were fresh from California orchards; caramelized sugar infused delicate sweetness and toasted almond coloring. The bakery was hiring, and I am still thinking I should move to San Francisco.

After Arizmendi's we went to Semifreddi's, Acme, and Firebrand before we found our way to Panorama, where we watched a shaper turn an enormous mass of sourdough rye into loaves, just as bread shapers have for millennia. The loaves would rise overnight, and the Panorama's journeyman handed us a leftover loaf from yesterday as we headed out. But the best bread I had in San Francisco came at the end of the day, at Tartine. Tartine's master baker is Chad Robertson, who is the author of several award-winning cookbooks about bread. He is a rock star in the baking world and has been featured in *Vogue, Martha Stewart Living,* the *New Yorker,* and the *New York Times.* He creates new breads from ancient grains by handling dough with the exquisite attention of someone fluent in wheat, emmer, kamut, spelt, oat, and rye. He bakes only 240 loaves a day, the opposite approach to Boudin. Lines form outside his bakery; weary though we were from covering so much of Berkeley, Oakland, and San Francisco, I insisted we wait our turn.

Panorama's tools of the trade. About the same as in sixteenth-century France.

I purchased a large round of emmer bread. Four thousand years after Egyptians made sourdough bread from emmer, one of America's best bakers was doing the same. I pulled off a hunk and, with the first mouthful, concluded that I had never eaten another bread as sublimely good. I chewed with my eyes closed to the busy San Francisco street corner.

Robertson is a strong proponent of sourdough, but he does not think that the age of the culture has much bearing on the final product. Robertson's conclusion was echoed by other bakers in San Francisco, as well as by their counterparts I spoke with on my trip to France. Great bread is made by bakers using great care. Sourdough's wild yeasts and companionable bacteria are essential to making bread with complex, multilayered flavors, but more than these things, to make great bread, a committed baker needs to throw body, soul, and occasional emanations into the work.

I was reaching the conclusion that sourdough starters were not like fine wines; there was not much evidence that they improve with age. If 1893 was the earliest I could push back the origins of my Cripple Creek starter, its value would lie in something more than a genetic legacy that could be traced across generations. The value of Cripple Creek sourdough lay in its callback to bakers in Egypt, Rome, the Dark Ages, pre-revolution France, and San Francisco during the Gold Rush of 1849. I remained resolute in my search for a gold miner who had Cripple Creek in his kitchen.

THE MINERAL CALLED telluride, common to Cripple Creek, Colorado, contains the element gold, only its color is brassy yellow, gray, purple, or silver white, but never really golden.[18] Nowhere in Cripple Creek, "The World's Greatest Gold Camp," does telluride break into shiny nuggets that float about in streams to be picked out by squatting miners with wok-shaped pans. Instead, to extract gold—and there are very few mines anywhere in the world that have been producing as long as the mines have at Cripple Creek—mining had to wait for the right person to make it possible.

Bob Womack was that guy. In 1874, "Crazy Bob" heard from a geologist working for the US Geologic and Geographical Survey that there was probably gold in the area. Womack joined nearly one hundred prospectors on an expedition into the Cripple Creek region. They blasted a tunnel one hundred feet into the side of Eclipse Gulch, but when they found nothing of value, everyone but Womack went home. For the next fifteen years, Womack rode a horse through the semibarren mountaintops, pushing along cattle, his eyes glued to the ground.

Womack had a good enough eye when he was sober. In 1878, he brought a chunk of gray rock down to a gold assayer who told him it was worth $200 per ton of gold ore. He crowed about his find to his mates drinking whiskey on neighboring barstools. The trick for Womack was to discover the source of the float, a term referring to chunks of rock hanging out on the earth's surface. It took him twelve more years.

In 1890, Bob Womack persuaded his dentist, Dr. John Grannis, to lend him $500 at 7 percent interest. The first thing Womack did was spend twelve dollars on a pair of new boots. Then he headed off to Colorado City to get drunk. In September of that year, Womack isolated a gravel wash that was dense with pieces of gray and purple stone that did, in fact, contain marketable quantities of gold. He spent a week in October blasting away at a submerged vein of rock he was certain was the parent of the gold-filled rocks in the outwash plain. He staked out a perimeter 1,500 feet in length and 300 feet across, an area roughly ten acres in total, and posted in large letters, "EL PASO LODE. Located October 20, 1890, by R. M. Womack and John Grannis. Unknown Mining District."[19]

Not one to keep his mouth shut, especially while nursing a drink (or three) at a bar, Womack spread the word. Over the next year or two, additional prospectors recognized several things. First, they were looking for telluride ores, not glittering gold nuggets. Second, the rock they needed to acquire in hopes of becoming fabulously wealthy was underground. And third, ore-bearing minerals were scattered about like a crazy quilt of threads and veins running alongside granite cracks. Hundreds of mines, therefore, were possible, and beginning in 1893, a rush was underway. Prospectors came by the thousands. The Teller County census from 1900 listed the birthplaces of adults residing in the Cripple Creek District: 17,193 of them. Slightly more than a quarter of the population were first- or second-generation Americans of European origin, many from countries where workers had expertise excavating coal. Only forty-four came from France, or just 0.2%. The rest came from fourteen states.[20] Cripple Creek, Colorado, became the largest gold strike in the history of the United States. It still produces gold today, making it one of the world's top ten producers, according to one source.[21]

When Douglas Steeples first told me that my starter came from the Cripple Creek Gold Rush, I fell into the trap of believing my starter had been harbored by a lonely miner. NPR, *Smithsonian Magazine*, and San Francisco Travel all reported that gold miners in California and Alaska kept their sourdough starters alive by cuddling them.[22] Gold rush stories usually go like this: as the sun rose, an isolated prospector started his campfire or lit his portable cast-iron stove. Atop a skillet, he fried up a slew of sourdough flapjacks. You can find recipes with accompanying stories in many Alaskan cookbooks. After a day of squatting over a pan in a river of glacial meltwater, the miner retreated to his streamside tent before tucking into a hearty loaf of sourdough bread or freshly fried sourdough pancakes, a tin of baked beans, and a slab of barely torched moose. When I went digging for authentic stories of gold rush miners, the truth lay a long way away from an isolated campfire and well-guarded pouch of sourdough starter. In reality, most miners worked as wage earners in someone else's mine, lived in a boardinghouse, and ate bread baked by someone else.

The fusion of sourdough bread and gold miners, along with the exaggerated degree of self-sufficiency miners were supposed to possess, lies in tall tales penned by author Jack London and a contemporaneous poet named Robert Service. Service was the nineteenth century's most successful poet, netting $100,000 from the sales of his book of poems *Songs of a Sourdough*.[23] The Sourdoughs of his title referred to Alaskan gold miners—remember, the ones who were called Sourdoughs because they ostensibly took on the aroma of their personal starters. Read a few stanzas from "The Heart of the Sourdough" and imagine how they must have appealed to a working stiff constrained to an office job in summertime Philadelphia:

> *There where the rapids churn and roar, and the ice-floes*
> > *bellowing run;*
> *Where the tortured, twisted rivers of blood rush to the*
> > *setting sun—*
> *I've packed my kit and I'm going, boys, ere another day*
> > *is done.*
>
> *I knew it would call, or soon or late, as it calls the*
> > *whirring wings;*
> *It's the olden lure, it's the golden lure, it's the lure of the*
> > *timeless things;*
> *And to-night, O God of the trails untrod, how it whines in*
> > *my heart-strings!*
>
> *I'm sick to death of your well-groomed gods, your make-believe*
> > *and your show;*
> *I long for a whiff of bacon and beans, a snug shake-down in*
> > *the snow,*
> *A trail to break, and a life at stake, and another bout with*
> > *the foe.*[24]

Jack London authored scores of short stories, dozens of poems, and more than twenty novels. Take this passage from Jack London's "A Klondike Christmas":

Mouth of the Stuart River,
North West Territory,
December 25, 1897.
My Dearest Mother: —

Here we are, all safe and sound, and snugly settled down in winter quarters.

Have received no letters, so you can imagine how we long to hear from home. We are in the shortest days of the year, and the sun no longer rises even at twelve o'clock.

Uncle Hiram and Mr. Carter have gone to Dawson to record some placer claims and to get the mail, if there is any. They took the dogs and sled with them, as they had to travel on the ice. We did expect them home for Christmas dinner, but I guess George and I will have to eat alone.

I am to be cook, so you can be sure that we'll have a jolly dinner. We will begin with the staples first. There will be fried bacon, baked beans, bread raised from sourdough.

London's treacle continued for several pages before two strangers, not unlike angels from the frozen mist, arrived at the forlorn cabin. "Their heads were huge balls of ice," wrote London, "with little holes where their mouths should have been, through which they breathed." Their mountainous beards were so encrusted with ice, the pair was on the verge of starvation. The newly arrived men thawed slowly by the central stove: Christmas dinner would not be so desperately lonesome after all. A small Christmas Eucharist ensued as the defrosted strangers received their sourdough bread. "The poor boys handled the bread reverently, and went into ecstasies of delight over it," wrote London.[25]

In the writings of London and Service, Alaska's mountains grew more majestic, the snow deeper, the solitude more isolating, the bears larger; the wind howled with unbridled ferocity. Miners' beards grew longer in tune with their dance hall unruliness. The men of the Klondike Gold Rush of 1897 were personified as Sourdoughs: acidic and vinegary on the outside, but deep within, soft, pliable, and bubbling with life that could not be contained by civilization.

Life on the ground, however, was a lot more complex than appeared in a short story, and one poem buried near the end of *Songs of a Sourdough* gave away the game. Called "The Song of the Wage-Slave," the first line read, "When the long, long day is over, and the Big Boss gives me my pay, I hope that it won't be hell-fire as some of the parsons say." The wage-slave complains of "masters, big-bellied they be, and rich; I've done their desire for a daily hire, and I die like a dog in a ditch."[26]

In short, especially in a location like Cripple Creek, Colorado, where gold lay hidden inside multihued tellurides buried deep within the earth, mining operations shifted quickly to wealthy mine owners. In 1890, three years before Bob Womack's discovery, the population of Cripple Creek was approximately five hundred. By 1894, a year after the world learned there was gold, the city's population had grown to more than ten thousand. By 1900, when the district population had nearly doubled again, one in ten people owned a business, while one in one thousand owned a mine. The wealthiest 1 percent were more like the wealthiest one-tenth of 1 percent. More than fifteen thousand people wore blue collars and earned a salary.[27]

A Cripple Creek miner earned three dollars for each eight-hour day spent working underground. If a man was single, he might have enough left at the end of a week to blow on a drink at a tavern, take in a show of so-called dancing girls, and purchase a quick romp in a willing woman's bed. If he was frugal with his other expenses, he could purchase girls who were pretty and liquor that did not hurt when he drank it. If, on the other hand, he had a wife, children, and maybe even dependent relatives with him, three dollars didn't go very far. An unfurnished house cost $1.75 per week; a boarding-house, with meals included, was $2.50 per week.[28]

In 1894, colluding mine owners lengthened the workday to ten hours from eight without raising wages. Workers went on strike and formed their own militias. In response, former police and firefighters were deputized as soldiers while national labor unions funneled food and supplies to hungry miners. Owners imported African Americans, desperate for work, as strikebreakers. On May 25, 1894, more than three months into the shutdown of the area mines, and with tensions escalating, angry strikers laced the Strong Mine with TNT. They blew the mine's shaft house three hundred feet into the sky.

It took until June 10, after 130 days of hostility, for owners and miners to sign a peace treaty. The miners agreed to surrender their arms to authorities of the United States. Mine owners agreed to reduce the workday to eight hours with payment of three dollars. Though it may not seem like a victory, the workers succeeded in avoiding ten-hour days with no pay increase, or eight-hour days at a reduced rate of $2.50. The National Guard stayed in place until all the mines were operating once again.[29]

Until the Cripple Creek strike of 1894, no labor dispute had been longer or more acrimonious in US history. It cost the regional economy $3 million in lost wages, production, and the provisioning of three armies—the strikers', the miners', and the US Army. As soon as the strike ended, however, Cripple Creek's economy resumed its torrent. By 1895, the district had produced more than $8 million in gold, surpassing the California Gold Rush of 1849. Buildings, businesses, and even railroads were tumbling over one another. In 1900, the Cripple Creek Mining District produced more than $18 million in gold. The region was now home to twenty-seven millionaires; hundreds of prospecting holes and mines peppered the landscape. The district's population had grown to 50,111, half of whom now resided in Cripple Creek, the fourth-largest city in Colorado.[30]

By the end of the century, so much money flowed through Cripple Creek that 170 commercial buildings, built of brick and sandstone, were standing, nothing short of remarkable, as a pair of fires during the last week of April 1896 had essentially leveled the town. Offices had steam heat, telephones, modern telegraph machines (more direct than telephones at the time), electric lights, elegant carpets, and even elevators.[31] Eight thousand miners had their choice of five daily newspapers, sixteen churches, and nineteen schools. They hosted tourists arriving by the trainload from Colorado Springs and Denver. Each day, nine long passenger trains chugged up the mountain over a trestle above the shacks of Poverty Gulch into one of the town's two depots. Upper-class citizens stayed in the five-story National Hotel, hopped on one of the ever-present streetcars, browsed Bennett Avenue's resplendent department stores, and applauded shows at one of the city's opera houses. Like modern-day Las Vegas, scores of gambling houses and more than seventy saloons drew customers around the clock.[32]

And like Las Vegas, female entertainment in Cripple Creek ran the gamut from stage dancers to sex workers. Pearl de Vere was Cripple Creek's wealthiest madame and charged $250 a night for her company. Her house on Myers Avenue, now the Old Homestead House Museum, has been preserved as an icon of high-class prostitution; her grave on the edge of town is a regular recipient of fresh flowers and gifts; and in 2019, the city celebrated its first Pearl de Vere Day in the center of town. Pearl's sex workers occupied the top of the prostitution ladder, and many have received the same kind of historical recognition as the handful of millionaires they entertained. Pearl's women were expected to service five men a night at fifty dollars a pop. Pearl kept 60 percent.[33]

But the story of Cripple Creek's high-class madame is as relevant to the lived experience of working women as the story of a millionaire mine owner is to the men who spent their lives in underground darkness. In 1896, there were 350 prostitutes in Cripple Creek, one for every hundred residents. A miner who received three dollars a day walked downslope toward entertainment he could afford. There was a lot to choose from. Among Cripple Creek's boomtown business endeavors were eleven parlor houses, four dance halls, and twenty-six cribs, tiny abodes rented by sex workers.[34] Under the railroad trestle, where trains wheezed into town after climbing through the Ute Pass, in the aptly named Poverty Gulch, were the dwellings of the low-pay prostitutes, in order from most to least expensive: French, Japanese, Chinese, Mexican, Native American, and African American. It should be noted that Pearl de Vere kept a few African American women in a separate accommodation in back of the big house.[35]

On payday, a skilled prostitute could service as many as eighty miners. A pimp posted up outside her door to hawk nighttime pleasures. Men stood in line, cash in one hand, their hats in the other. To move that many customers, a woman wore next to nothing because a man who had waited impatiently, and likely drunkenly, did not want to pause for the painfully slow process of disrobing. He was in and out in a matter of minutes. After work, a prostitute received her earnings from her pimp. She took her salary and went in search of emollients, alcohol, or laudanum to dull pain, fatigue, and public humiliation. Before collapsing for a day of sleep, she staggered toward a restaurant or bakery in search of some coffee, a couple of scrambled eggs, and some toasted bread.[36]

Miners and the women whose income derived from providing a grueling service turned to the same staples: bread purchased from a bakery. Bread, as it has done for Western society since the days of the pyramids, supplied the caloric fuel to keep the worker bees buzzing another day. The city had eight bakeries; eleven more bakeries were baking bread within an area of only ten square miles.[37]

It is hard to know to what extent sourdough was used in Cripple Creek's bakeries, however. Unlike San Francisco's bakeries of the 1849 Gold Rush, whose names reflected their national origins, the clientele they were hoping to attract, or simply panache, the gold rush bakeries of Cripple Creek offered few clues. Cripple Creek's bakeries bore no readily discernible last names with French spellings, only Archibald, Burchart, Gourley, Frazier, Harm, Lang, Munroe, Peterson, Taylor, and Ray. Down on Myers Avenue, in the Red Light District, were the Gold Dust Bakery, Harder, and Miller Brothers.[38]

I N 2010, I traveled to Cripple Creek to ask as many people as I could if they knew anything about a sourdough starter affiliated with the city and its Gold Rush of 1893—and Dale Noyd, the man in the center of my mystery. I had pieced together that Noyd grew up in Wenatchee, Washington, entered ROTC in the early 1950s, and was the only member of the Washington State ROTC class of 1955 to receive a regular commission. After several years of training and outstanding grades, he was given his first-choice military assignment: three years of duty as a tactical fighter pilot in Woodbridge, England, two hours northeast of London on the Channel coastline. During his tour of duty in Europe, Noyd earned a medal and official commendation. Dale's son, Erik, sent me a photo of the plaque: WELL DONE: FOR AN OUTSTANDING FEAT OF AIR-MANSHIP. 1ST LT. DALE E. NOYD. 10 JULY 1959.

The commendation came because he landed a badly crippled F-100D, also known as a Super Sabre, that news reports claimed was carrying nuclear weapons.[39] There was no way of knowing whether his particular plane was loaded since the Air Force does not typically point out which planes are carrying nukes, only which ones are "nuclear delivery capable."

By the mid-1960s, the Super Sabre was the go-to fighter-bomber in Vietnam. Zooming just above Vietnam's farms and jungles at 350 to 550 miles per hour, F-100s were assigned the task of attacking bridges, river barges, road junctions, and rural villages. During a one-year period beginning in May 1968, Air Guard Super Sabres flew more than 24,000 sorties, launched 423,000 rockets, dropped 14 million pounds of bombs plus a quarter million pounds of cluster bombs, fired 1.8 million rounds of 20-millimeter ammunition, and sprayed more than 5 million pounds of napalm.[40]

As the war escalated, the Air Force needed new pilots, and Captain Noyd was asked to train them. With his hundreds of hours of flight time in the right kind of plane and a hero's plaque, he was the right man for the job. In advance of the expected order, he told the Air Force, however, that he was going to refuse, saying that he would not participate in "a war that I believe to be unjust, immoral, and which makes a mockery of both our Constitution and the Charter of the United Nations—and the human values which they represent."[41]

On December 4, 1967, Dale Noyd's squadron commander, Colonel Homer K. Hansen, handed him an order to train a young lieutenant to fly F-100s. Colonel Hansen, knowing that Noyd would defy his order, accompanied his command with the military equivalent of Noyd's Miranda rights. Noyd refused the order.

He was convicted in a military court with a sentence of hard labor but lived under house arrest at the Air Force Academy in Colorado Springs, about an hour from Cripple Creek. Noyd's case was heading to the US Supreme Court. His son, Erik, who was seven years old at the time, recalled being able to visit his father once a week.

Six months later, on June 16, 1969, a majority of Supreme Court justices refused to overrule the military, and rather than impose its initial sentence of hard labor, the military's highest court of appeals dismissed Noyd from the military.[42] Within months, Earlham College in Indiana, a small Quaker school, hired him to teach psychology and anthropology. It was a perfect match: a college established by one of the few groups with a congressionally approved mandate to avoid warfare and a professor with an aversion to fighting in unjust wars.

Neither Douglas Steeples nor Erik Noyd could recall the precise timing, but sometime between his release from house arrest and around the time he started his new job, Dale Noyd immersed himself in wilderness backpacking. He headed to the Rockies and Tetons, the Southwest and Northwest. Hiking was like bread baking. Both were incontrovertibly deliberate and unhurried, the precise opposite of flying a Super Sabre. Noyd hiked with such infectious earnestness that, by 1971, he and a handful of fellow faculty members had created a wilderness program at Earlham that continues today: a twenty-four-day August expedition. Its core mission: education by experience. The establishment of Earlham's wilderness program in 1971 suggested that Noyd was hiking in the Rockies between 1969 and 1970, and I focused on those years when I went to Cripple Creek forty years later to see if there were any locals who could remember a lone hiker or a sourdough starter.

I started with the Cripple Creek District Museum. The museum held three floors of dusty exhibits. Faded newspaper clippings announcing things like FDR raising the price of gold in the 1930s were stuck on the walls. Scores of grim-faced miners had posed for black-and-white photographs that filled the remaining wall space.

The highlight of the museum was the fellow behind the desk who took my admission fee. He was new to the place, busy reading a history of Cripple Creek when I walked in. Early thirties, I guessed, with a goatee, close-cropped hair, broad shoulders, a hoarse voice, a pair of high-top Doc Martens, an above-the-knee kelly green skirt, and a real willingness to figure out who in town might know someone who baked sourdough bread in the late '60s or early '70s. But there was nothing in the archives or anyone among the people he called that could tell me anything about sourdough bread.

I was lucky that my visit to Cripple Creek coincided with the one day a year when the Gold Camp Victorian Society was in town dressed in their period costumes to have tea. The society president, Steve Smith, after hearing my story, graciously reserved a seat for me. There were seventy people in attendance, and I was the only one not garbed in nineteenth-century regalia and one of maybe only a handful who wasn't retired.

The women wore floor-length gowns that were tight about the waist and billowed to the floor. Their sleeves were long, the fabrics were glossy, their necks were covered up to their chins, and most of their bosoms boasted cameos. And let me tell you, a lot of birds gave up their lives to embellish their hats. I asked the woman to my left why she liked the Victorian Society. "I love playing dress-up," she said. "The clothes are so feminine," she added. "I feel very pretty wearing them." With her gloves on, I realized that the only part of her that was unadorned or uncovered was her face, so I was surprised to learn later that she also loved attending Renaissance fairs as a wench.

For two hours I sipped tea from a floral print porcelain tea service, ate little square sandwiches, and consumed enough truffles and tea cakes to give me diabetes on the spot. It was a Victorian gathering that would not have been out of place in an ABC tea-room. After lunch, we were entertained by a man who imperson-ated Winfield Scott Stratton, the mining district's first millionaire. Then the new owner of the Carr Manor inn sang two operatic show tunes that brought the house down. I was impressed that he could sing anything 9,500 feet above sea level. To close the program, Steve Smith invited me to the front of the room to deliver my spiel. I explained my search for the origins of a sourdough starter, up to how it came into my possession, and asked if anyone in the room could provide any clues. About half a dozen people gave me sug-gestions, and I spent the next couple of days following up on them.

Someone suggested I ask at the Gold Camp Bakery, where I found Gertrud, the baker, sitting by herself reading a book. Ger-trud got it. She knew exactly why I'd be looking for an old sour-dough starter. The problem was that she and her husband were German immigrants and had owned the Gold Camp Bakery for only three years. She couldn't help, so she sent me to her friend Sylece on the edge of town.

Sylece and her mother, Terra, invited me into their kitchen, which was decorated with icons of Jesus, Moses, Isis, Shiva, Buddha, and other gods. There were tapestries, busts, statues, carvings, paintings, batiks, and silk screens. When I asked about them all, Terra said, "I believe in God so much, I believe in everyone's God." Then she gave a big throaty laugh. Terra knew about the biology of sourdough starters. Within minutes after I explained the reason for my visit, Terra was telling me how the low humidity and high altitude of Cripple Creek would have created a unique local assem-blage, and together we wondered if that group of organisms now in my Pennsylvania kitchen might have changed in the past 117 years.

Terra's daughter, Sylece, was a local historian, and she had writ-ten and published two books of oral history about Cripple Creek's mines. It took quite a while for her to admit this, but she was also the mining district's poet laureate. Sylece had come to town in the early 1970s when Cripple Creek was all but deserted, a period when readily accessible gold had been exhausted and before new technologies allowed the multinational Newmont Corporation to resume mineral extraction. Forty years later, she was still fit, strong, and ruggedly outdoorsy. Back when she first came to town, the population had crashed to five hundred people—or maybe fewer; it depended on who I asked. Abandoned homes and storefronts crumbled in what was once one of the wealthiest boomtowns in America. "I remember one beautiful Victorian," Sylece said, "you know, with the swirling staircases, that had an open jar of mayo, a spreading knife, and bread still on the table. It had been there for twenty years." Because the average humidity almost never rises to double digits, the bread and mayo were petrified in much the same way Egyptian loaves were preserved inside their tombs. Terra and Sylece were terrifically insightful and pleasant hosts but were unable to provide any concrete leads.

I followed another tip gleaned from the Victorian tea party: Valdean Petri, District II warden of the neighboring city of Victor. When I asked Valdean if she knew anything about a historical sourdough, she didn't hesitate. Back in the early 1970s, her friend Dudley Weltz, Jr., gave her some sourdough. Though she didn't have it any longer, Valdean recalled that Dudley had told her a story about the starter when he gave it to her. Only thirty years later, she couldn't recall the story. Dudley was an exceptional cook, she said.

I returned to Terra and Sylece to get their thoughts. Terra had been very good friends with Dudley, it turned out, and it seemed entirely possible to her that Dudley was a sourdough maven who might have given some sourdough starter to a visiting hiker. Sylece, who had spoken to a lot of the people who lived through Cripple Creek's worst years, thought it was completely likely that someone

---

in town was baking sourdough bread in the 1960s. Based on her deep knowledge of Cripple Creek's history, Sylece said that giving a sample of starter to Dale Noyd, a wandering backpacker, would have been axiomatic.

Though both men had died by the time I learned of them, I imagined that the meeting of Dale Noyd and Dudley Weltz, Jr., went something like this. Dale Noyd was a recently convicted resister of the Vietnam War when he encountered Dudley Weltz in what was left of downtown Cripple Creek. Weltz and Noyd struck up a conversation that must have continued for a couple of days. You don't just hand an heirloom starter to a stranger. Moreover, it takes at least a day to grow up a batch large enough to give away a glob and still have some in storage to use in your next bake. Dudley Weltz relished Dale Noyd's independent spirit and bright intellect and invited Dale to visit his home. Dudley would have cooked something special, and according to Dale Noyd's son, Erik, his father would have reveled in it. Erik told me, his dad adored "bread *eating*, preferably heated and smeared with butter, accompanying a nice medium rare rib eye steak and a glass of cabernet sauvignon." Noyd would have made his joy known, and Dudley was exactly the type of person to share his starter and take the time to show Dale how to manage it. In the early 1970s, if you wanted to bake sourdough bread, it helped if somebody showed you how.

Close as I was to having credible evidence that my starter's roots were really in Cripple Creek, I immediately stumbled over a branch fallen from my starter's family tree. According to Valdean Petri, Dudley Weltz was new to town himself. Weltz did not come from a long line of Cripple Creek bakers. She thought that Dudley moved to Cripple Creek around 1970, so someone must have given Dudley Weltz a local starter not long after he had arrived in town. If Weltz gave it to Noyd, he had simply passed it along.

While Valdean Petri and I discussed Dudley and the sourdough starter now in my possession, we were joined in conversation by Mary Bielz, who shared an office with Valdean. Mary, chair of the regional social services organization, was a vibrant woman. She had gray hair and reading glasses perched near the very tip of her nose and was wearing red Converse sneakers. While Mary answered my questions with her own theories regarding my starter's history, she simultaneously managed three teen assistants, answered phone calls, photocopied documents, and waited on a client with a prosthetic leg.

Mary told me about a bakery in Victor, seven miles away. According to Mary, the owners baked bread in the 1930s and were still in business in the 1970s, but I began to feel my supply line growing recklessly thin. I could not persuade myself that I would be able to find evidence of a sourdough culture from 1893 that traveled to a bakery in 1930, went to a newcomer to town seven miles away in 1970, and was then given to Dale Noyd. It's possible that Dudley Weltz talked someone in the bakery into giving him some starter, but I could not figure out how I would ever know.

In midflurry, Mary pulled from beneath her work desk a well-loved cookbook that she had helped her grandmother put together in 1981. Anna Lillian Bielz, to whom the family cookbook was dedicated, was born October 3, 1903, to an original pioneer family in Cripple Creek, making Mary a fourth-generation Cripple Creek resident. The book's binding was long gone, but Mary insisted I borrow it because it had black-and-white pictures of her relatives and a recipe her grandmother had used for making yeast from local hops. It was called *Mom Bielz's Family Cookbook*.

The uneven lines of type, the reliance upon a single font, and the first twenty pages carefully written in pen and pencil clearly indicated that the book had been created before the age of home computers. There was a handwritten copyright mark, dated 1981.

The author was Peggy Bielz Cox; a hand-drawn asterisk referred to "art by Mary Bielz." It was "printed in the World's Greatest Gold Camp. Cripple Creek, Colorado." Just below "Cripple Creek" was a stain, perhaps a drop of something delicious. It was the size of a thumbprint and the shape of Greenland. Mary and I riffled pages, hoping the family heirloom might hold a recipe for sourdough bread.

There was no table of contents, though there was an index and there were handwritten page numbers at the center bottom of each page. The first section was "Soups and Salads," and section two was "Breads."[43] According to notes in the book, Anna Bielz had baked bread every week. On the day she baked bread, the family ate it fried with homemade butter and homemade jam or jelly. Anna Bielz made enough bread to feed a dozen and a half people, plus as the cookbook made quite clear, many additional guests routinely brought home by Anna Bielz's husband.

The first line in the chapter on bread was "Living Bread," and it cited John 6:51. Jesus said, "I am the living bread which came down from heaven: If any man eat of this bread, he shall live forever; and the bread that I will give is my flesh, which I will give for the life of the world." Two thousand years later, in the remote mountains of Colorado, bread was still the staff of life. "Happy eternity," says the cookbook.[44]

But none of the recipes were for sourdough. The old-fashioned white bread recipe called for three packages of dried yeast, and the whole wheat bread called for two packages of dried yeast. Those Fleischmanns were good. Even in a down-on-its-luck mining town high up in the Rocky Mountains, packaged yeast must have been available.

There was a yeasted dill bread, a beer bread made with self-rising flour, and recipes for several quick breads, muffins, rolls, and biscuits. On page twenty-eight, however, in a pullout box with a strong hand-drawn arrow pointing toward it, was a recipe called "How to Make Yeast." The recipe was attributed to Mrs. Julia C. Richardson, of North Grove, Indiana. It was typical of turn-of-the-nineteenth-century recipes. A half-pint of good strong hops was boiled for half an hour in half a gallon of water. A quart of flour and some cornmeal were added, the mixture was cooled to finger-bearing temperature, and then one teacupful of good yeast was added. The dough was kneaded, rolled, and cut into cakes. "Spread the cakes on a cloth over an old table or board, where the wind will blow over it, and turn it often during the day till it is thoroughly dried," the recipe read. "If used two months after making it will be good as when first made."[45]

Was there sourdough in Cripple Creek, Colorado, in 1893? In 1849, sourdough was raising loaves at the Boudin Bakery in San Francisco. Jack London, Robert Service, and Alaskan lore all pointed to the availability, if not the prevalence, of sourdough bread in Alaska during the last decade of the nineteenth century, just a few years after miners started excavating gold in Cripple Creek, Colorado. While the Fleischmann brothers were touting manufactured yeast and cookbooks for women with access to yeast provided recipes for making more yeast, in 1893, sourdough was not gone yet. There were still people far enough away from an increasingly urbanizing America who continued to bake with sourdough. Think of Montana ranchers or the wives of Oklahoma cattlemen. Some people simply preferred the taste, while others were just plain stubborn and insisted upon sticking to the old ways. These were the people who preserved a few living cultures. Though I have no indisputable evidence, it certainly seems possible that a bakery or a housewife in Cripple Creek, Colorado, used sourdough in 1893.

Figuring out how a sourdough culture got to Cripple Creek is mostly conjecture. The possibilities include someone from France, a French Canadian, a master baker trained in San Francisco, a housewife with a starter she brought with her when she moved with her family to the booming city, a German immigrant like Gertrud, Cripple Creek's baker, or even an immigrant from one of the more than thirty countries whose origins are listed in the area census of 1900. Sourdough might have traveled along all these paths or none of them. Or a fresh culture could have been created on the spot. Even more mysterious is who among Cripple Creek's residents continued to make sourdough, using the same starter, through the decades between Womack's discovery of gold and Dale Noyd's discovery of homemade bread around the year 1970.

When sourdough starters are given to a friend, they generally arrive in a small container accompanied by a story; they do not bear certificates of provenance. I departed Cripple Creek, Colorado, believing it possible, even likely, that the story of a sourdough starter from 1893 eventually making its way to me was true. I ended my hunt for the lineage of my starter with the following pieces of its parentage arrayed this way. There was probably at least one sourdough bread maker among Cripple Creek's fifty thousand residents and numerous bakeries at the time of its gold rush. Someone, I will never know who, continued to bake with a gold rush starter even as gold became less profitable to mine and the town slowly withered away. That someone gave some starter to Dudley Weltz, Jr., with an account of its 1893 origins, around 1970 or so. From there, the trajectory toward Meadville, Pennsylvania, is clearer: Weltz to Noyd to Steeples to Mamula to me at a picnic in 1989.

I still had a chance to establish a genetic connection to Cripple Creek using modern techniques of DNA analysis of my yeast and bacteria, but the more valuable discovery for me was confirmation that, even during the decades when commercial yeast became king, sourdough was championed by an intrepid few. To them, sourdough culture represented more than sustenance. Their adherence to a tradition of making bread whose origins covered much of the history of Western civilizations prepared sourdough for a resurrection beginning in the 1960s.

SOURDOUGH FLAPJACKS
Yield: About 18 flapjacks

Modern baking formulae depend upon precise weights of starter, water, flour, and salt. They are reliable and delicious but often suggest that unused starter be tossed out. This recipe can be made with fresh starter or starter discarded from another recipe you are making. There are as many recipes for sourdough pancakes as there are cooks, so feel free to improvise on this one. If you want to feel like a grizzled Alaskan miner celebrating the warmth of some summer sun, sprinkle some blueberries on your pancakes right after they have hit the pan but before you flip them.

> Sourdough starter, refrigerated
> ¾ cup water
> 2½ cups flour of choice, divided (I like whole wheat, but
>   all-purpose flour, rye, spelt, or any flour will do)
> 1½ cups milk
> 1 cup rolled oats
> 2 large eggs
> ¼ cup vegetable oil or melted butter
> ¼ teaspoon kosher salt

Evening, Day 1. The night before you make the pancakes, take your starter from the refrigerator. To the jar of cold starter, add the water and shake or stir to disperse it. Add 1 cup of the flour and shake or stir until the newly added flour is combined and no lumps remain.

Transfer 1 cup of the starter to a medium bowl. *Loosely* screw on the lid of the mason jar of the remaining starter and set it aside to grow overnight.

To the medium bowl of starter, add the milk, oats, and remaining 1½ cups of flour, stirring to create a batter with a thick porridge-like consistency. Cover with plastic wrap and leave until morning. If you like your starter less sour, add the flour on the morning of day 2, instead of the night before.

Morning, Day 2. Return the mason jar of starter to the refrigerator.

Separate the eggs and add only the yolks to the batter. Add the vegetable oil and salt, and stir to combine. Beat the egg whites until stiff, then fold them into the batter.

Heat a large lightly oiled cast-iron skillet over medium heat. Add the batter, ¼ cup at a time, to the skillet, and cook until bubbles begin to burst on the surface. Flip each flapjack and cook until the bottom is golden brown. Transfer to a covered plate to keep warm, and repeat this process with the remaining flapjacks.

CHAPTER 7

MODERN BREAD

T HE RESTORATION OF SOURDOUGH IN THE LATE
1960s and early 1970s was related to revolutions underway
across American society: uprisings against America's war in
Vietnam, demonstrations in support of wider civil rights, the wom-
en's liberation movement, a riot at the Stonewall Inn, strikes by the
United Farm Workers of America, the first Earth Day, and what was
called in those days a "health food craze." Caught among the swell
of Americans who questioned their country's involvement in the
Vietnam War and what felt like to some the especially stale decade
of the 1950s were sourdough bread, Dale Noyd, and my father.

In the 1960s, when Wonder Bread reigned in America, sourdough bread was a form of protest—as was, come to think of it,
simply baking a loaf at home. My father's plan to take up baking
was reinforced by my pediatrician, who reasoned that my hands
turned icicle blue without warning because the food I ate had
additives in it. If I consumed only "natural" food, he told my parents—it was the first time in America when *natural* food had to be
distinguished from, what, unnatural food?—my cold hands would
be cured.

Dad was a self-taught polymath who thought like a scientist, cooked like a chemist, and liked an explanation that included the word *vasoconstriction*. He purchased a book called *Bake Your Own Bread and Be Healthier* by Stanley and Floss Dworkin that soon became known in our house by the nickname Flossie. As in, "Flossie says, 'Always put your bread into a cold oven.'" Or "Flossie says, 'You can tell if your bread is done if it sounds hollow when you thump the bottom.'" Flossie bread was intended to displace Wonder Bread in my house. It did not always come out on top; well into my teens, I was partial to Wonder Bread and ketchup sandwiches. But as often happens, we rediscover foods we disdained as children, and homemade sourdough bread was one of mine.

How did Wonder Bread become so emblematic of modern, "unnatural" food? The answer came to me by way of a sourdough workshop I attended in Scotland in 2017 during my Fulbright. Andrew Whitley, author of the award-winning books *Bread Matters* and *Do Sourdough* and founder of Great Britain's Real Bread Campaign, was teaching the class, and he and I traded heirloom starters. In exchange for some Cripple Creek, Whitley handed me a rye culture from a bread factory in the former Soviet Union that was in use in 1960. Of course, Whitley's came with an origin story.

Whitley explained that in 1960, Soviet authorities demanded 1.5 million loaves a day from a factory he observed while working for the BBC. To meet their quota, managers set up many miniature bakeries inside the factory. Long conveyor belts carried thousands of loaves of handmade rye. The inability of communist economists to match supply and demand was evident at the end of every day, when five hundred thousand loaves of uneaten bread were returned to the factory, where they were boiled and added to make the next day's loaves. Reusing boiled rye bread in the next batch is worth a try if you ever have any leftovers. It is delicious.

By contrast, in the West in 1961, bread manufacturing was overtaken by something called the Chorleywood Bread Process, or CBP, named for the village of Chorleywood in the United Kingdom. The Chorleywood Bread Process contained the essence of capitalism—speed, vigor, efficiency, and profit—and in so many ways, right down to the starting ingredients, was the very opposite of sourdough bread.

To produce uniform, pale, squidgy loaves with blond, insipid crusts, food technologists eliminated bulk fermentation, the long wait for yeast to consume sugars contained in flour. CBP is a "no-time dough system." In a CBP factory, five hundred to one thousand pounds of flour and water are dumped into a high-torque mechanical mixer that takes off at several hundred revolutions per minute. It takes fewer than three minutes for the water to be absorbed.[1]

To prevent that much energy from ripping dough, oxidizing agents such as ascorbic acid (vitamin C) and emulsifiers are added to increase dough strength. To put it into perspective, the mixer imparts so much friction that if it weren't for an ice jacket around the mixing drum, the temperature of the dough would increase 50 to 60 degrees Fahrenheit.[2]

There *is* yeast in the bread, but the quantity is double what you might add to a non-CBP bread. Moreover, modern yeast is so powerful that when it is used at home, a dough must be punched to keep it under control. Sometimes it has to be punched twice. In a factory setting, bread rises in, well, no time. Yeast cells need sugar to ferment if they are to generate large volumes of carbon dioxide, so a sugar supplement is frequently used. High-fructose corn syrup works particularly well. Enzymes, minerals, and amylases hasten the process of supplying cells with energy while relaxing the dough. The net result is that cells of yeast inflate dough in much the same way that the Aerated Bread Company accomplished it by injecting carbon dioxide into aerated bread.

Modern transnational corporations grow yeast for CBP factories using techniques that descend from forebears: patent seekers at the end of the nineteenth century and marketers like the Fleischmanns. They raise strains that generate carbon dioxide with outstanding speed and maintain prototypes under tight laboratory conditions. Samples of pure culture are brought from the laboratory to sterilized vats, where yeast cells are fed copious quantities of nitrogen-enriched sugars, minerals, and vitamins. Tons—in some factories, upward of one hundred tons—of microscopic yeast cells are harvested from each batch, separated from their spent liquid, and sold to bread bakers as cream, cakes, or dried granules, very similar to yeast you buy in tiny packets in the store.[3]

Inside a CBP factory, along with yeast, water, flour, elasticizers, and dough conditioners are introduced; lactose is sometimes added because it browns nicely in the oven. Thick fats and surfactants are blended in to increase bread volume, tenderize the dough, and speed up the rate at which flour absorbs water. The resulting crumb is perforated by tiny bubbles of identical size and shape, and the crust remains soft. Calcium propionate is added to prevent mold from growing on old loaves.[4] According to the United Kingdom's Federation of Bakers, a CBP loaf takes four hours to produce, from end to end. Not quite as fast as aerated bread but still impressive, considering machines run around the clock and churn out hundreds of thousands of loaves per day.[5] Wonder Bread is a CBP loaf, and most modern American bread uses CBP technology.

A loaf of CBP bread typically has more than twenty—and frequently more than thirty—ingredients, a far cry from the basic four of history: flour, water, salt, and yeast or a sourdough culture. Commercial bread emits a vaguely chemical smell you can detect as soon as you wheel your cart into the bread aisle of your supermarket. It isn't bread you smell; nothing your nose picks up will make your taste buds spring into action the way a freshly baked sourdough can.

In the 1960s, American bread factories churned out millions of loaves, just like their Russian counterparts, but in contrast to the communist ideal of factories packed with workers, American and British planners applied technology, science, and money to factories filled with machines. Anxious though it was to compete with the West, Russia did not modernize its bread making, even while it mastered nuclear power and spaceflight. The Soviets designed factories to fit the nature of sourdough bread; America and Great Britain redesigned bread to fit their factories. Even France succumbed to mass production. After World War II, finding an authentic sourdough baguette with decent taste was nigh impossible as sourdough in France gave way to fast-acting yeast and tasteless industrial breads for all the same reasons sourdough disappeared in the United States and England.[6]

Food technicians had moved a six-thousand-year-old process from the discipline of biology to the discipline of chemistry, with the admixture of purified flour, enzymes, surfactants, oxidizers, emulsifiers, elasticizers, conditioners, colorants, and preservatives. In some ways, French chemists A. L. Lavoisier and J. L. Gay-Lussac trying to reason their way through fermentation were not so off the mark. Chemical analysis of CBP bread did lead to a reinstatement of some healthfulness, however. When nutritionists analyzed bleached white flour, pressed flat by Hungarian-inspired roller mills and mechanically separated from its bran and germ, they found it devoid of minerals and nutrients. Having removed much of the essential goodness in bread, scientists, in accordance with dietary recommendations of the day, introduced vitamins and minerals back into the mixture. They marketed bread fortification as a healthful bonus.

Like its antecedents in the textile industry, factory bread removed the production of our daily bread from the hands of humans and placed it inside whirring steel machines. The Industrial Revolution reached its bread apotheosis in the 1960s, but inside each eye-catching plastic bag, wrapped about a perfectly predictable loaf of vitamin-enriched, chemically preserved, evenly sliced white bread, lay the germ of a bread insurrection.

I FOUND MY DAD'S old copy of *Bake Your Own Bread and Be Healthier*. There is a special section on sourdough and another on whole wheat flour, both of which had become so rare in the age dominated by spongy bleached factory breads that they required special introductions. My dad made his own culture, and viscous sourdough starter regularly grew over the open top of its crock in the back of my refrigerator. My dad and Dale Noyd were not the only bakers to rediscover sourdough and so-called natural bread—and the Dworkins were not the only authors on the subject at the time.

In 1966, the Zen Center of San Francisco opened the Tassajara Zen Mountain Center. It was, and still is, a monastery for students practicing traditional Zen meditation. Students are given a simple diet of grains, beans, vegetables, and fruits. It is a testament to how processed American food had become by 1966 that consuming whole grains, fruit that was freshly harvested rather than packed in a can filled with syrup, and vegetables that required more work than defrosting and boiling was an idea waiting to be rediscovered by Buddhist monks secluded in the mountains of California.

According to Tassajara, its students were "accustomed as many have been to 'bread' being that pure white, bland, airy, unsubstantial filler that comes in plastic, cello, or wax paper." Visitors were given homemade bread at every meal. The monastery's head cook, Edward Espe Brown, published *The Tassajara Bread Book* in 1970.[7] On page one, Brown laid out two principles that still ring true fifty years after they were written. The first was a poem:

coarse, crusty
with rich true-spirited flavor
that one soon learns to love and create.

Brown's second principle was placed above a simple pen and ink drawing of three sunflowers: "Yet basically it's just you and the dough—ripening, maturing, baking, blossoming together." Four of Tassajara's ninety-eight recipes were for sourdough.

In 1973, Bernard Clayton published *The Complete Book of Breads*,[8] James Beard penned *Beard on Bread*,[9] and even *Better Homes and Gardens*, purveyor of mainstream Americana, published *Homemade Bread Cookbook*.[10] To demonstrate their authenticity, bread books of the early 1970s included a handful of sourdough recipes, but it is as if the authors failed to trust themselves or their readers. They certainly did not trust sourdough to supply sufficient oomph. Their recipes all included the addition of commercial yeast to complete the task of leavening. Three years later, Ruth Allman published ninety-five handwritten recipes in *Alaska Sourdough*,[11] and at last, along with blue whales and bald eagles, sourdough bread was on its way back from imminent extinction. The publication of half a dozen books on baking homemade bread was the decadal equivalent of a viral hashtag. "The times they are a-changing," sang Bob Dylan.

DESPITE THE PROLIFERATION of cookbooks, very few men cooked in that era. My father's commitment to the kitchen made a lifelong impression on me. I, too, love to cook, and I started baking yeasted bread soon after I moved away from home to attend college. My social anxiety also comes from him. The man could not stand crowds of any kind or even long gatherings of his good friends. This raises the question of whether my antisocial tendencies are the product of nature or nurture. Did I inherit my dad's genetic predisposition for discomfort in gatherings or simply model my behavior on his?

In the world of sourdough cultures, there is a similar question. Can the genes borne by yeast and bacteria in a sourdough culture, like those from Cripple Creek, Colorado, produce their unique flavors in a new location, even after decades have passed? Which is more important to the development of a human or a loaf of bread, nature or nurture? I admit that the production of pumpernickel and human development may not seem to have much in common, but there are some similarities.

The nature side of the debate has it that sourdough starters persist in their genetic legacies, much like a child may bear the characteristic red hair of his ancestors. In sourdoughs, some cultures are known for energetic yeast that can make a loaf rise like it is possessed by spirits. There are cultures heavily influenced by bacteria that produce buttery flavors, while others, like Cripple Creek, are more vinegary. Can microorganisms bequeath genetic characteristics from one generation to the next? Is the bread I bake in Meadville, Pennsylvania, still related to bread eaten at the end of the nineteenth century?

Another school argues that the world is not sterile. Sooner or later, the microscopic organisms from the new kitchen infect the import, and like it or not, Cripple Creek microbes are supplanted by Meadville's. Over time, the environment—and by analogy, nurture—molds a bread's final flavor. By this way of thinking, I did not inherit my dad's social anxiety any more than I inherited his love of cooking. I learned by watching. Unless, of course, some mixture of nature and nurture informs the personalities of both people and sourdough starters.

When I traveled to England in 2017, I smuggled two starters with me: my Cripple Creek and the thirty-year-old starter we call Meadville, made by my wife from local wild grapes. I wondered if transferring my starters across the ocean to a new kitchen would change them. What would they become now that they lived in Lancaster, England? On a cold day in early spring 2017, I placed samples of Cripple Creek and Meadville in my knapsack and took a train from Lancaster to Norwich, home of Great Britain's National Collection of Yeast Cultures (NCYC). I intended to ask NCYC's microbiologists if there was a way to discern whether the bacteria and yeast I bake with now were biologically related to their ancestors from more than a century ago. When it came to a loaf of sourdough bread, what mattered more: the enduring generations of endemic yeast and bacteria or the displacement of old species of microbes by new microorganisms—or perhaps the identity of bacteria and yeast species does not matter at all, so long as both kinds of organisms are present in a culture? Does the quality of a loaf of sourdough ultimately not depend upon species but rather on the nurture imparted by a baker?

Over the past sixty years, the NCYC has collected more than four thousand strains of yeast and recorded their DNA. They agreed to analyze both of my starters. When I received the results, I was initially disappointed. Much as I hoped that my starters contained some rare species, if they were present, they were certainly not dominant. *Saccharomyces cerevisiae*, the world's most common yeast in bread and beer, was also most common in both Meadville and Cripple Creek. I read through the long list of other species of yeast present in diminishing proportions and the list of bacterial species when it dawned on me that I was not really running a controlled experiment.

If, for example, Cripple Creek and Meadville were both dominated by *S. cerevisiae*, was it because both starters began their lives with mostly the same species and, rather than change over time, had actually remained very consistent kitchen to kitchen and decade to decade? Or was it because *S. cerevisiae* was most prevalent in my kitchen and the flour I used, had staged a coup d'état, and now governed both starters? Moreover, the question of whether the move to England had changed the composition of either one was unknowable since I had not preserved any pre-England samples for comparison. NCYC's scientists and I quickly concluded that the best way to confirm the longitudinal survival of species of yeast and bacteria would have required a decades-long controlled experiment, an expensive and unlikely prospect.

On the upside, NCYC was intrigued enough by the story of Cripple Creek that they placed a sample of Cripple Creek starter into their long-term storage facility, where it is preserved in liquid nitrogen in perpetuity. I also received images of my yeast and bacteria taken by NCYC's scanning electron microscope. I felt like a proud father.

A scanning electron microscope image of Cripple Creek sourdough culture. The slender rods are bacteria. The larger globular cells are yeast. You can see the yeast cells in varying stages of reproduction: they form buds, which grow, separate, and leave behind budding scars.

When I returned to the United States, I booked a trip to a microbiology lab at North Carolina State University to meet a team of microbiologists who specialized in sourdough cultures. Early in spring 2019, when North Carolina's flowering trees were showing their first blooms and the sun's rays finally felt warm, I visited Rob Dunn, professor of applied ecology, author of five books that explain how household biology relates to our daily lives, and advocate for the participation of ordinary citizens in scientific research. One of his experiments was called the Global Sourdough Project, directed by Dr. Erin McKenney, an inveterate teacher with a happy smile. Within minutes of my arrival in her windowless office, McKenney had pulled cardboard-backed posters from a pile near her desk to help answer my questions.

How did bacteria and yeast first find their way into my starter? Is the community of species inside my culture stable from loaf to loaf and year to year? Is it possible that the bacteria and yeast inside my culture are the progeny of ancestors that once leavened bread in 1893 in Cripple Creek, Colorado?

McKenney began with an explanation of how sourdough starters are first colonized by microscopic organisms before she told me what she could about the stability of the microbial assemblage once it had settled down. McKenney pointed to her first poster: a side-by-side accounting of white flour and whole wheat, each mixed with water and allowed to nourish microscopic organisms. To reveal the first homesteaders, swabs of diluted flour and water were smeared across petri dishes. If the starting medium was all-purpose flour, *Lactobacillus* bacteria began to grow, but not a single species of yeast showed its face. When the experiment was repeated with whole wheat flour, a couple of different species of yeast grew in abundance, but no bacteria. Right off the bat, choosing to start a starter with whole wheat or white flour had the potential to affect the outcome of which species of yeast and bacteria would set up residence and in which order. In the end, both yeast and bacteria would be present in the final sourdough, but the question of which got there first would have bearing on those that followed.

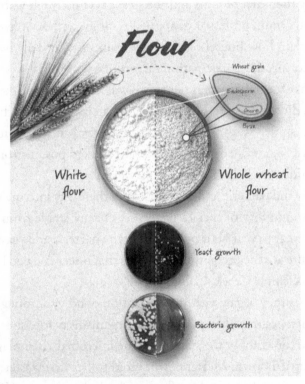

⌇⸻ On the left, white flour gives rise to colonies of bacteria, but no yeast. On the right, whole wheat flour generates the opposite: yeast cells, but no bacteria.

The answer to why a sourdough starter initiated with whole wheat flour grew yeast first and bacteria second, while a starter convened on white flour gave rise to bacteria first and yeast second, was discovered in a field of wheat. Standing waist-high in wheat, microbiologists pressed the heads of fully mature plants onto petri dishes. After a few days in a laboratory incubator, yeast colonies spread across the agar plate. The species of yeast from the field matched those identified in McKenney's whole wheat flour.

"The yeast species found in a field of wheat had traveled through the miller's stones or roller mills and lain dormant in a bag of whole wheat flour until the flour was wetted and the nutrients in the flour became available for fermentation," McKenney explained. If a starter was first generated from whole wheat, in all likelihood the yeast in it had hitchhiked its way from far-off fields of grain. But if the sourdough starter was made with white flour, cleaned not only of its bran and germ but also evidently of its field-borne yeast, then the yeast that resided in your house, in your kitchen, or on your hands was the primary colonizer.

Rob Dunn explained that yeast cells, though they are ubiquitous and can be found in nearly every environment on earth, are large enough that they do not travel far upon air currents. Each species or subspecies tends to stay close to home, making geography the primary determinant of which species are available. Yeast is so closely affiliated with its environment, Rob Dunn suggested, that given a swab from your windowsill, a petri dish to raise the yeast that is there among other particles of dust, and access to equipment to extract and analyze the DNA of your microscopic household inhabitants, scientists in his lab could determine the location of your house within fifty miles.

For six thousand years, bakers have understood that a mixture of flour and water left to stand in the open for three days or so will begin to bubble and creep up the sides of its container. Now we know that the species of yeast that causes the bubbling and rising comes from the flour itself, if it contains all the parts of the grain. Supplemental species of yeast and nearby microbes of all categories would find their way into the starter, and yet, many of the incoming species would never survive.

As proof, McKenney told me that in an experiment she was

working on to appraise the colonization of yeast on different kinds of flours, she discovered many disgusting species of yeast, mold, and fungi present in quantifiable numbers in the first day or two. Several were of the variety that infect human beings to ill end, proving in a way that if disease organisms can find their way into a scientific experiment in a university microbiology lab, then the range of critters living in my (definitely not sterile) kitchen must be countless. Fortunately, the conditions in a sourdough culture are incompatible with what we humans call germs. Instead, sourdough cultures are ideal spaces for yeast like *S. cerevisiae*. Or to put it another way, a maxim of microbiology I learned in my first class on the subject as a graduate student states: "Microbes are everywhere; their environment selects which ones survive."

Perhaps there is something to Boudin Bakery's claim, then, that its assemblage of sourdough yeast is unique. The moderate temperatures and foggy mornings common in the Bay Area are not found in many other places in the world, and if its starter was first infected with yeast from wheat grown nearby, Boudin is not incorrect. Varieties of San Francisco yeast are probably indigenous.

Before tackling the question of the endurance of yeast, I had to clarify the origin of the bacteria. McKenney's poster depicted a sourdough starter begun with whole wheat flour with yeast aplenty, but no bacteria in attendance. Bacteria, unlike yeast, are very tiny and move easily on air currents. The bacterial composition of a sourdough starter thus depends on which bacteria are present in the home, bakery, bowls, and hands of the maker. Again, the microbiologist's maxim holds true. The environment delimits which bacteria prosper. Different bacteria fly about inside a dry home in Arizona with a cat than in a house in Oregon that is damp, has no pets, but is chock-full of houseplants. McKenney and Dunn tried to correlate as many variables as they could to which species of bacteria would first establish sizable populations in recently wetted flour, but their results suggest that either chance or variables they haven't yet considered are what determine what gets there first. Their most effective model for predicting the first species of bacteria to enter a sourdough culture had an accuracy of only 13 percent.

The exploration of the microbiological ecology of sourdough cultures is very much in its infancy, and so far, McKenney had explained to me only the arrival and early establishment of yeast and bacteria. Scientific comprehension of how microbial communities change—or, as many sourdough bakers insist, do not change—in the long term still really hasn't been studied. Nonetheless, McKenney led me through some inferences that could be drawn regarding the progression of sourdough cultures from incipient to mature.

The first lesson was that early birds were not always well represented in an aged culture. Dunn and McKenney estimated that roughly four hundred species of bacteria and about half that number of yeast species were identified among all the sourdough cultures that have so far been characterized. Global diversity is fairly wide, but within an individual starter, only a very few species survive the first several weeks. That finding alone suggested that while individual starters may not have very complex combinations of yeast and bacteria, the ecosystem of species present could be dissimilar even for two sourdough cultures that developed in close proximity. Cripple Creek, therefore, might actually be distinct from any other starter in the world since my Cripple Creek starter could have begun its life in the high, dry environment of Cripple Creek, Colorado. If only we knew for certain whether a starter's flora remained consistent for decades.

Here, the science regarding Cripple Creek's longevity is actually encouraging. Microbiologists like Rob Dunn and Erin McKenney think that mature sourdough cultures are pretty stable over time, in much the same way that the microbiomes residing within our gastrointestinal tracts appear to change very little. Yes, a nasty

infection can upset the balance in your intestines or turn a sourdough starter pink, but a healthy starter, like a healthy gut, does
not appear to change either its species or the ratio of populations
of each species. The dominant species grow in roughly the same
proportions to one another each time a cup of culture is refreshed
with flour and water.

There is a scientific explanation for the persistence of microbial
communities living within sourdough cultures. Having reached an
equilibrium early in their development, dominant species of bacteria and yeast establish defenses. A healthy starter is like an armed
fortress, bristling along its ramparts with arrows, spears, crossbows,
and boiling oil. There are always invaders threatening to breach the
moat and climb the walls, but if the defenders are well-conditioned
and do not lack for food or vigor, they will hold the fort for a long
time. Bacteria and yeast in your kitchen will find their way into your
starter—none of us work in kitchens sterilized of all living things—
but to a healthy starter, the invaders appear armed for battle bearing
only pocketknives and slingshots.

If, however, the yeast and bacteria in a sourdough starter are
malnourished or exhausted, an aggressive force of invaders might
find an underdefended entryway and gain a foothold. Green
slime or pink dots might establish beachheads on its surface. The
same, of course, is true of people and the care they give to their
microbiomes.

What does this mean? It suggests that the bacteria and yeast
that leaven and flavor my loaves in Meadville, Pennsylvania,
might be the offspring of those that worked in a sourdough culture owned by a baker in Cripple Creek, Colorado, in 1893. Or,
contrary to Boudin's claim that its bread can be baked only within
sight of San Francisco's Fisherman's Wharf, anyone can bake San
Francisco sourdough. The microbes in Boudin's starter are probably still related to the microbes that were there in 1849; however,

if you were given a sample of their starter (or grew your own with flour raised in the region of San Francisco) and then took it with you to Meadville, Pennsylvania, you could make an authentic San Francisco sourdough.

But Dunn and McKenney's sense that sourdough starters can retain their microbial populations for generations, assuming they are well cared for, is refuted by a more fluid model for sourdough cultures that has been described by chefs and food scientists from the Modernist Cuisine Lab.[12] Their research proposes that long-lived starters are like large metropolises such as New York or London. Neighborhoods persist and descendants of some of the original settlers still live in grand old buildings, but new immigrants also transform old districts with new flavors. In a multi-generational starter, there are probably bacteria and yeast whose parentage can be traced thousands of generations back and others that have recently disembarked from a colony on your hands or from schmutz on the countertop. This hypothesis suggests that no starter is immutable.

There are at least three possible scenarios when it comes to sourdough cultures and the factions of microbial populations residing within them. One is that sourdough cultures undergo constant renewal. They incorporate new inhabitants when they are introduced, and in short order or over short distances, they morph into new starters. Two, the opposite is true: mature cultures are gated communities whose taste profiles remain constant over time and space. Three is that some starters are sturdy, well-built, and largely impermeable to newcomers, while others are unsteady and prone to rapid transformation in character when an influx of non-natives take up residence.

If this is all beginning to feel like lessons in urban demography, then you won't be surprised to know that a fourth outcome is also possible: new microbes still arrive, but somehow the character of the culture persists. New York City has always been a city of immigrants, but at the same time, even after wave after wave of Irish, Italian, Jewish, African American, Chinese, Puerto Rican, Dominican, Russian, Jamaican, Guyanese, and other cultures and nationalities have established neighborhoods, the taste of the city is both different and the same. New Yorkers will always be New Yorkers, projecting a gusto all their own that is recognizably distinct from that of residents in Dallas, Sarasota, Seattle, or Copenhagen. It is possible that sourdough cultures evolve and remain the same at the same time, like cities whose citizenry morphs but whose essential nature persists.

The absence of any scientific certainty leaves anyone with an heirloom starter—homemade, inherited, or acquired from a friend—in a state of scientific uncertainty. Consequently, Cripple Creek's provenance remains as gloopy as the starter is. I call my starter Cripple Creek because of the story that accompanies it, not because I can prove it. My *S. cerevisiae* may well be the great-great-great-to-the-nth-degree offspring of Colorado predecessors, or it could be the same run-of-the-mill bread yeast found everywhere in the world. Here is where the rationale for the deep-freeze storage of yeast in Great Britain's National Collection of Yeast Cultures returns to the fray.

The NCYC maintains a locked steel bin, bathed in liquid nitrogen at a temperature of approximately −330 degrees Fahrenheit, as a service to Britain's robust community of brewpubs. A dependable ale is contingent upon reliable yeast, but yeast, like other microbes, evolves both naturally and quickly. A strain of *S. cerevisiae* from the beginning of a year of brewing, after hundreds of rounds of reuse and refreshment, may undergo enough genetic change—a kind of random genetic wandering, so to speak—that an end-of-year batch of ale could taste off-color when compared with one from the beginning of the year. It is worth it for Britain's brewers to pay the NCYC to store their yeast cryogenically. Whenever they sense that it is time to go back to the original taste, they call NCYC and ask for their original yeast to be propagated. When the sample is returned, another is put into storage in its place.

The person who has come closest to producing an ancient sourdough that has not undergone the natural process of evolution is Jonathan "Seamus" Blackley, the Xbox inventor, who in 2019 repeated Ed Wood's experiment of making sourdough bread in the way of ancient Egyptians. The yeast Blackley and his collaborators scraped from an Egyptian bread pot was 4,500 years old. The desiccating conditions of Egypt induced the same microbial dormancy as NCYC's liquid nitrogen.

One additional experiment run by Rob Dunn and his associates is worth describing because it is just so confounding. In August 2017, Dunn and his associate Anne Madden traveled to the Puratos Sourdough Library in Saint-Vith, Belgium. They invited fifteen professional bakers from around the world to start sourdough cultures. In Belgium, they gave every baker identical flour, water, and sterilized glass jars, then sent them back to their home bakeries with the same directions for raising fresh sourdough cultures. When their cultures had reached maturity, they were invited back to Belgium for a bake-off. Presumably, the only difference in the cultures would be the bacteria and yeast alive on each baker's hands and any bacteria and yeast living inside their bakeries. So, before the bakers traveled back to their home countries to raise their cultures, Madden swabbed each baker's hands. Anything living atop the bakers' skin was cultured on agar-filled petri dishes and set to grow.

Once their starters were up and running, the professional bread bakers reconvened at the Puratos Sourdough Library to bake identical breads using the same flour, recipe, kitchen, and oven. Dunn and Madden identified the bacteria and yeast alive in each starter and found that some species were common in all the cultures while some were found in only a single culture. Their theory was that the first bacteria and yeast to enter a sourdough starter are, as many have speculated, from everywhere: flour, hands, kitchens, and maybe even water. It was a second observation coming to light after the scientists had an opportunity to study the populations of microbes the bakers were carrying on their hands, that astounded Rob Dunn, Anne Madden, and me.

Human hands are coated in microscopic bacteria and yeast, as are nasal cavities, digestive tracts, belly buttons, and everywhere else, private and public. During a TED Talk interview, Rob Dunn explained, "We may imagine that in washing our hands, we remove all of the microbes. We do not. If you sample the microbes on someone's hands, have them wash them, and then sample the microbes again, no change in the overall composition of the microbes occurs."[13] Consequently, it made sense that some of the bacteria Anne Madden had harvested from the hands of the visiting bakers was present in the cultures they brought with them to Belgium.

For most people, *Lactobacillus*, the species of bacteria most common in sourdough cultures, is not abundantly represented on our skin. On average, *Lactobacillus* represents only about 2 percent of the microbes on men; on women, it represents about 6 percent. Yeast can be present on skin but is rarer still and not very diverse. For the professional bakers gathered in Saint-Vith, however, *Lactobacillus* bacteria and related species made up 25 percent—and sometimes as much as 80 percent—of the bacteria alive on their hands. Moreover, nearly all the yeast found on bakers' hands was the same kind that can be found in sourdough starters, *Saccharomyces* being the most predominant.

"We had no idea this was even possible, and we don't yet fully understand it," Rob Dunn said in his TED interview, but the implications are clear. Our personal microbiomes, as well as our households, influence the microbes alive in our starters, while our starters appear to have an enormous impact on our microbiomes. Sourdough bakers and their starters share the same species of yeast and bacteria, a microbial ecosystem entirely distinct from that of non-bakers and largely unlike the microorganisms living on the hands of a baker using a different starter.[14] Sourdough cultures and their bakers look alike.

The basic findings of Rob Dunn's lab seemed to be that a baker's hands will be populated by his or her microscopic workmates, and within only a few weeks of the establishment of a new starter, the microbial makeup of a sourdough culture stabilizes under the dominance of only a few species. But the absence of any long-term experiments on how microbial populations shift with time or location leaves the question of whether my Cripple Creek starter is related to its predecessors in the realm of informal observation.

For example, I ran a very unscientific experiment of my own to test the hypothesis that sourdoughs keep their microbial cultures and hence their unique flavors. It began in 1999 when I hired Allyson Tinney as an assistant and taught her to make some sourdough bread using the Cripple Creek starter. A year later, she left for graduate school and a boyfriend, Alejandro, who later became her husband. Alejandro was working his way up Mexico's Foreign Service ladder. Together, they have moved around the world, Alejandro working for the Mexican government and Allyson working for international environmental organizations.

In the first ten years after I gave her some Cripple Creek starter in Meadville, Pennsylvania, Allyson took her starter and her developing expertise as a baker to Buffalo, New York; Mexico City, Mexico; Quito, Ecuador; and Guangzhou, China. I caught up with Allyson and Alejandro when they were stationed in Mexico's consulate in Guangzhou so that we could bake bread together. If her bread and mine tasted the same after ten years and three continents, I reasoned, then chances were pretty high that the assemblage of bacteria and yeast I handed her was still kicking in her culture. If Cripple Creek sourdough baked in China tasted the same as it did when I baked it in Meadville, it at least seemed plausible that my starter and a starter used in 1893 were one and the same, or at least very closely related.

Sitting together in her dining room one morning in Guangzhou, waiting for her bread to rise, Allyson reminded me of the day she received her starter. "You said to me that I needed to learn to make sourdough bread, and I thought it was a good idea," she recalled. "It was my last week of work, and we made some in your kitchen. My first loaf at home was terrible. Then I left for Buffalo, and I've taken that starter with me ever since." In China, Allyson used organic whole wheat flour she purchased from the Happy Home Taker store and supplemented the dough with expressed boiled soybeans. The heat and humidity of Guangzhou did wonders for the starter, and her breads rose quickly.

By midafternoon the house was infused with the smell of baking bread. Allyson made a beautiful no-knead round loaf with a crisp golden exterior and an interior crumb I envied. The bread was hardy and pungent. Cripple Creek is a rather acidic starter. Especially in a warm, humid environment like Guangzhou's, it makes bread that bites back without much subtlety. A decade of separation, a life spent in four kitchens on three continents, in cities with climatic conditions super different from mine—higher elevations, more humidity, more air pollution—that harbored very different microbes from Meadville's had not changed the flavor of a bread made from a Cripple Creek starter. Andrew Whitley, the Scot who gave me my rye starter from the former Soviet Union, reported the same observation. "In all the years I have used my rye starter," he said, "I can detect no variation in its flavor."

A second loaf that had nearly doubled its original size emerged an hour later, its four diagonal slashes bursting. Because she had extra dough, Allyson also baked five small rolls. They were smooth topped and intermediate in color between the cracked, crisp, almost burned surface of the no-knead and the pale, flour-dusted bread from the loaf pan.

Alejandro got home from work late, again. He flopped into his seat, loosened his tie, and poured himself a glass of wine. Allyson listened while Alejandro vented. It was part of their evening ritual. Soon, Alejandro would fall asleep. Alejandro inhaled the deep scent of bread in the air; the smell seemed to transport him home from his day at work. He finished talking about the office. When Allyson left the room to check on their sleeping children, Alejandro said to me, "You know, Eric, I am so glad that ever since I met her, Allyson makes homemade bread for us."

Later, Allyson explained the importance of Cripple Creek sourdough to their family. "Having chosen this quasi-nomadic lifestyle, we are armed with a certain number of tools to make the transition to a new life in a new country easier," she said. "Among those tools, my sourdough starter is definitely high on the priority list—making bread has come to mean that we are home no matter where we are." After China, Allyson, Alejandro, their sons, and their Cripple Creek starter were sent by the Mexican government to Berlin. Among her belongings, in addition to our shared sourdough culture, are probably hand coatings of bacteria and yeast that resemble mine, an infection given to both of us by our Cripple Creek starter.

HAVING DETERMINED THAT hundreds of species of yeast and bacteria can be found among the sourdough cultures around the globe, food scientists and microbiologists are now working to identify which organisms are responsible for the wide array of flavors present in sourdough breads. Artisanal bakers would love to know how to adjust flavors like tartness, fruitiness, and piquancy; industrial bakeries are anxious to learn if they can isolate a few taste-producing organisms or, better still, the chemical compounds they produce so that they can supplement their factory loaves.

The first steps toward associating microbes and flavor profiles were made in 1970, when three scientists in the USDA's Department of Food Science and Technology at the University of California investigated the microorganisms inhabiting San Francisco's sourdoughs.[15] At the time, San Francisco was home to several bakeries that used sourdough. The three microbiologists wanted to know if there was anything unique among the organisms that resided in the Bay Area. The scientists were working old school, before modern DNA technology, when picking out a species of yeast required growing it on a petri dish and comparing its form and feeding habits to photographs and reports of colonies someone else had already published.

The scientists sampled sourdough starters from five San Francisco bakeries. The first revelation was that common bread yeast, *S. cerevisiae*, was nowhere to be found. The very species of yeast used by bakers as far back as ancient Egypt, given by beer brewers to bakers across the centuries, and marketed by the Fleischmanns was absent within the five San Francisco sourdoughs they examined.

In place of *S. cerevisiae*, another species of yeast was dominant: *Saccharomyces exiguus*. *S. exiguus* was leavening San Francisco's sourdoughs. More interesting results emerged when the USDA team announced that the bacteria responsible for the sour flavor in San Francisco's sourdoughs was a heretofore unknown species. The new species was given the name *Lactobacillus sanfrancisco*, later renamed *Lactobacillus sanfranciscensis*.[16] At long last, a potential scientific discovery corresponded to the claim made by Boudin: authentic San Francisco sourdough bread depended upon local starters containing an uncommon yeast and a species of bacteria not found anywhere else.

As exciting as the early discoveries of idiosyncratic species of yeast and bacteria were, there were several shortcomings in the interpretation of what the presence of those species meant. *L. sanfranciscensis*, upon further investigation, was not uncommon. In 1970, no one had ever looked for *L. sanfranciscensis* in any sourdough cultures outside the five bakeries under study. Over the next decades, as microbiologists delineated species living in sourdough cultures around the world, *L. sanfranciscensis* turned up everywhere.

Actually, in the past couple of decades, acquisition of new information about species composition in sourdough starters has mostly served to demonstrate how much scientists do not know about sourdough. For example, as the price of analyzing DNA dropped dramatically in the second decade of the twenty-first century, the number of known sourdough species grew in number. In 2005, there were forty-six species of lactic acid bacteria and thirteen species of yeast that specialized in sourdough.[17] By 2007, three new species of lactic acid bacteria had been discovered.[18] By 2014, more than sixty species of *Lactobacilli* bacteria had been isolated, and by 2017, the number had grown to nearly one hundred.[19] In 2019, analysis of fourteen French bakeries discovered two new species of yeast.[20] Still, knowing the number of species tells only a fraction of the story. When I contacted Great Britain's National Collection of Yeast Cultures to ask how many yeast species they had cataloged, I was told the estimation was six hundred. But among those, the NCYC had accessioned more than 4,300 strains. Cripple Creek is in their catalog.

Discovering new species is only the first part of the puzzle. The influence of an individual species on flavor is another science altogether. Slowly, food scientists are making headway toward

Six starters stored by the Puratos Sourdough Library in Belgium, indicating a tiny sample of how distinct sourdough cultures can be from one another.

determining how sourdough cultures impart their flavors, beginning with sourdough's inherent sourness. Since the days of ancient Egypt, bakers have recognized that some sourdough bread tastes highly acidic, like vinegar, and some has a milkier, yogurt-like flavor. Those opposing flavors can even come from the same starter, and scientists are confident that sourness is imparted by bacteria. By contrast, bread leavened with commercial yeast is comparatively monotonic on the palate because it is devoid of bacteria. The sharpness in sourdough for most consumers is a function of acetic acid, also known as vinegar, versus lactic acid, the milder acidity associated with yogurt.

The generation of acidity inside a sourdough culture is a function of ecology. When microscopic organisms are offered moistened wheat flour, they congregate like hungry piglets at a trough. The pushing and shoving that takes place among microbes is largely chemical rather than physical. Here is how Erin McKenney described to me what happens inside a maturing sourdough culture. *Lactobacilli* bacteria dump acetic acid and lactic acid into their surrounding environment. As a growing population of bacteria acidifies its starter, most of the early-arriving yeast and bacteria are killed by the declining pH and increasing acidity. The land rush of organisms is culled as concentrations of acetic and lactic acid increase. One life-form that can continue to swim, grow, and multiply in a bacterial acid bath of sourdough cultures is yeast that specializes in sourdough environments. Though bacteria continue to outnumber them one hundred to one, *S. cerevisiae* thrives.

A technique that reliably ratchets up or down the acidity of a loaf would be nice to have in any baker's toolbox. I have scoured the internet, quizzed professional bakers, and consulted sourdough cookbooks to see if I could establish a clear correlation between simple practices and the sourness of a cooked loaf. The chefs at Modernist Cuisine, perhaps one of the best noncommercial test kitchens I know, insist that the more liquid the culture, the sourer the loaf, and that warmer temperatures increase production of lactic acid over acetic acid.[21] However, other bakers, scientists, and test kitchens suggest that a drier starter is the key to a bread rich in acids.[22] Some sources insist the trick to turning out a sourer loaf is a warmer dough, more whole grain or rye flour, and less white flour,[23] while other sources suggest a cooler or more oxygenated dough will do the trick.[24] Nearly everyone with whom I have checked is confident that their means of controlling acidity is reliable. To my eye, however, their guidance is anecdotal, not scientific.

Simple scientific procedure dictates that to test a hypothesis, you hold everything constant except one variable. Suppose, for example, that you want to prove that warm dough results in a final loaf that tastes more sour and, conversely, that a dough that rested overnight in the refrigerator will taste more creamy and less acidic. There is good reason to believe that warmer temperatures cause bacteria to reproduce more quickly and that faster-growing colonies produce more acidic outcomes: a sourer loaf.

To test the hypothesis, a baker could place some starter in an insulated container set to 70 degrees Fahrenheit and a separate sample of the same starter in another container dialed up to 78 degrees Fahrenheit following a first refreshment. At the end of a predetermined period of time, the baker could measure pH and something that professionally trained bakers call total titratable acidity. If she were really curious and had access to a high-performance liquid chromatograph, she could even measure the relative quantities of acetic versus lactic acid. If her experiment proved her suspicion correct, could the results be broadcast to bakers around the world?

Maybe and maybe not, for here are all the variables that were not controlled in the hypothetical experiment I just described and that would almost certainly be different in someone else's kitchen: the age of the starter, its ancestry,[25] the species of bacteria and yeast in the starter, the relative abundance of each species, and the starter's feeding history—daily or weekly? Was the starter kept in the fridge or on the countertop prior to the experiment? For how long before the experiment began was the starter allowed to reach a starting temperature of 70 degrees Fahrenheit? Was the hydration level before the refreshment the same as in the experimental setup? Did the experimenter stir vigorously, thereby altering the oxygen levels in the starter, or simply give the starter a swish with a spoon? Did the water have the same mineral content as the water used in the experiment? (My tap water, for example, contains such a high concentration of dissolved minerals that our household water filter clogs in two weeks, rather than the prescribed three months.) Was any chlorine in the water given time to evaporate, or was there still some chlorine present that might have inhibited microbial growth? Did the flour used to feed the microbes have the same nutrient content as the experimental flour? Was it milled to the same degree of fineness? Finely milled flour is far more readily consumed by bacteria and yeast than flour that is coarse.

To complicate matters further, acetic and lactic are not the only acids produced by sourdough bacteria. In addition to acidifying its surroundings with acetic and lactic acids, *L. sanfranciscensis* lays down a defensive ring of caproic, formic, porionic, butyric, and n-valeric acids, a solution deadly to most competing bacteria, yeast, and mold.[26] This is why a sourdough bread remains mold-free far longer than any bread leavened by commercial yeast and absent some synthetic antimolding agent, like sodium benzoate. Mold spores cannot blossom in acid. That soup of acids is also part of the complex of ingredients that makes sourdough bread so much more engaging than a bread leavened by yeast alone.

In addition to a broth of bacterial acids discharged into sourdough, both yeast and bacteria also expel gases: nearly two hundred flavor-inducing gases have already been identified by food scientists.[27] Depending upon their concentrations, their mixtures, and our personal ability to distinguish aromatic molecules, each gas might affect the final flavor of a loaf of bread. Even that is debatable, as most gases dissipate to a greater or lesser extent in the heat of the oven. Breads leavened with commercial yeast alone have been far more studied than sourdoughs, and more than 540 volatile compounds have been measured emanating from a loaf of just plain yeasted bread.[28] Add to this list more than one hundred flavor-inducing chemicals, which are not gaseous, found within bread, and farming an individual species of *Lactobacillus* to create a particular flavor profile grows increasingly difficult.

Not all hope is lost, however. If there is one thing that does work, it is consistency. If you discover a recipe that produces a loaf from your sourdough that tastes great—say, you like your bread when the crumb is airy, the flavor is mildly acidic, rich, and buttery, and the crust is crisp—chances are excellent that if you repeat the recipe, the result will be the same. Usually. Experienced bakers have excellent technique honed by years of practice. They are as consistent as star athletes, quick to react to unforeseen conditions, reliable in the clutch, and resilient following failures.

To see if I could manipulate flavors generated by my starters, I enlisted my daughter. Leah is an accomplished sourdough baker in her own right, having invented new creations from Cripple Creek that I never dreamed were possible. When she came to Meadville to visit for a weekend in 2019, she and I set up a Breadsperiment. In one weekend we baked eight loaves of bread using the Cripple Creek and Meadville starters. We used two kinds of whole wheat flour (King Arthur and freshly milled hard red winter wheat) and two baking methods (a steam-filled oven and covered cast-iron Dutch oven). We used identical formulae, making every loaf with 50 percent whole wheat flour (King Arthur or freshly milled) and 50 percent King Arthur Special Patent white flour.

We took our loaves to some professional coffee tasters at Happy Mug Coffee Roasters. Happy Mug's employees regularly travel the globe for what are called cuppings. They might taste one hundred or two hundred coffees at a cupping and judge varieties, elevations, farms, modifications in postharvest berry fermentation, and roasting temperatures. We told them how each loaf was prepared and asked them for tasting notes.

They sampled each of our breads, wandering their shop deep in concentration. They told us that they could taste clementine, mud, clarity, marzipan, earthiness, freshly cut grass, sawdust, toast, nuts, smoked jerky, mild sweetness, tart finish, apple cider vinegar, satisfyingly bitter crust, snappiness, subtle bitterness, fresh mustard, tart yogurt, cream, milk, buttermilk, sweet cream cheese, bleu cheese, cherry, cranberry, grape, apple, potato, banana, acetic acid, caramel, sour cream, sharp cheddar, brightness, session beer, flatness, consistency until the end, and fermentation.

What we did not expect was that different people tasting the same bread would call out such different flavors. Some of the tasters described vinegar flavors, while others claimed the bread tasted of buttermilk. Both lactic acid (buttermilk) and acetic acid (vinegar) were undoubtedly present, but evidently, we humans can be as variable in our perceptions as the diversity of microscopic organisms are in creating flavor compounds. Coffee tasters, like wine tasters, have a certification program designed to train professionals and unify their perceptions and language. Bread tasters, not yet.

What most people, professional tasters or not, can agree upon is that sourdough bread is distinctive from bread leavened by yeast alone. Large bread companies have taken notice of growing public demand for sourdough and are rushing to capitalize. Bread manufacturers, for example, can purchase commercially prepared sourdough starters containing a single strain or blend of microbes. Starters arrive after they have been liquified, frozen, spray-dried, or freeze-dried, whereupon food scientists prescribe the right quantity for floor workers to add to huge vats of dough about to become hundreds of loaves of bread. Their goal is to generate precise levels of acidity (species are usually selected for their speediness), produce very specific flavor compounds, reduce staling in the final product, increase bread volume, or improve mouthfeel and softness.[29]

Manufacturers can also purchase flour supplemented with dried pasteurized sourdough. Industrial bakers procure sourdough powders cultured in swimming pool–size vats. Sourdough bacteria and yeast are harvested, dried, and extinguished. The powder is not living and will not under any circumstances come to life. Rather, factory technicians add powdered sourdough because it is a quick method to modify flavor, improve texture, impart antifungal properties without the use of preservatives, and perhaps supply health benefits to assembly-line bread.[30] Critics argue that a factory-produced loaf, leavened with commercial yeast but supplemented with inanimate sourdough powder, should not bear a sourdough label, but that is a debate I will let you resolve on your own.

No matter how you measure it, sourdough bread is back. On my computer, it took Google six-tenths of a second to point to forty-eight million links for "sourdough bread." Search Google for "sourdough blog," and you will find nearly as many entries. On Instagram, #sourdough returned more than two million posts and suggested I check out #sourdoughclub, #sourdoughbread, #sourdoughbaking, #sourdoughstarter, #naturallyleavened, #realbread, #artisanbread, #crumbshot, and #breadporn. Eight months into 2020, as the COVID-19 pandemic spread around the world, the number of #sourdough Instagram posts closed in on four million.

There are sourdough scenes in Australia, New Zealand, Israel, Malaysia, Finland, Denmark, and most of the rest of western Europe. The United Kingdom, home of the original Chorleywood Bread Process, is also home to the Real Bread Campaign, Chorleywood's archenemy. In most American cities and a surprising number of small towns, you can find an artisanal bakery, and chances are it sells at least one type of sourdough bread.

Big industrial producers of bread are watching closely; the predicted growth rate in sourdough sales between 2018 and 2023 is 6.9 percent per year. That would double global consumption in just over a decade. Naturally, the United States and Europe are the largest markets, but China and India are also expected to explode.[31] Sourdough bread, probably containing a heck of a lot more than four ingredients, will likely soon take up more shelf space in supermarkets.

Advertisements touting the health benefits of sourdough will certainly be used to drive sales. When I teach sourdough classes, for example, there are always a significant number of participants who have heard that sourdough is easier to digest, particularly for people who have difficulty with wheat or gluten. Others tell me they eat sourdough bread to nourish their microbiome. There is preliminary evidence that they may be right,[32] and to be sure, large industrial producers of sourdough bread are strongly suggesting that their sourdough bread will make you healthier. The battles of Sylvester Graham, Sarah Josepha Hale, Antoine-Augustin Parmentier, and Fleischmann's Yeast live on. If you have read this far, you know by now that I am a skeptic. Even while many claims may ultimately withstand intense scientific scrutiny, the efficacy and reversibility of nutritional studies are so fraught that I have stuck with the principle that first got me into sourdough: eat sourdough bread because you like it.

While industrial producers of bread expand their sourdough facilities, the next wave in artisanal sourdough is following trends set by local brewers, vintners, and coffee roasters assiduously coaxing out subtle variations in flavor. Artisanal bakers are turning to locally grown heirloom varieties of grain. They partner with nearby millers with slow millstones that keep flour temperatures low during the milling process. They bake in wood-fired ovens capable of blasting heat at hand-shaped dough. And stencilers! Stencilers are decorating crusts of sourdough bread with patterns so intricate that, if they were tatted with lace, they could be framed. Experimenters are pushing exciting ingredients like seaweed, nettles, and purple sweet potatoes. There are some fine recipes for sourdough tortillas, crepes, crackers, cakes, and cinnamon buns.

To make bread the way our ancestors made bread in the Fertile Crescent, a practice that hasn't changed much since its discovery six thousand years ago, requires comparatively little equipment as hobbies go. Rather, an investment of all five of your senses is what is needed. You must feel dough with your hands, observing when it is time to knead, stretch, or fold. While it is baking, your nose will tell you that a moment of deep satisfaction is nearing, and a well-practiced thump on the bottom of a loaf will confirm to your ears that your bread is finished. Your eyes will send a message to your stomach and salivary glands to begin their entreaties. Finally, after you have waited as long as humanly possible for what is one of the most appreciated aromas on the planet, there is tasting.

A bread made with sourdough bears more than six thousand years of history. Deep inside its warm interior there is love, which, like the culture it comes from, is best if shared.

CHAD ROBERTSON'S TARTINE COUNTRY BREAD
Yield: 2 large loaves

A recipe for Chad Robertson's country bread is available on the Tartine Bakery website[33] and has been featured in the *New York Times*.[34] With Tartine's permission, I have simplified and adapted it slightly for this book. This recipe makes a lot of bread and can be halved. Begin feeding your starter the day or night before you want to bake. You will need only about 1 cup of starter, but you will want it ready and active when it is time to assemble. Feel free to substitute other flours, such as spelt, buckwheat, rye, and so on, for the whole wheat.

> 200 grams mature sourdough starter
> 750 grams warm water, divided
> 900 grams white bread flour
> 200 grams whole wheat flour, divided
> 20 grams salt
> 100 grams rice flour

Make the dough. In a large bowl, combine the 200 grams of starter with 700 grams of water and stir to disperse.

Add the white bread flour and 100 grams of the whole wheat flour, and use your hands to mix until no traces of dry flour remain. The dough will be sticky and ragged. Cover the bowl with a towel or plastic wrap, and let rest for 25 to 40 minutes at room temperature.

Add the salt and the remaining 50 grams of warm water to the bowl. Use your hands to thoroughly integrate the salt and water into the dough. The dough will begin to pull apart, but continue mixing; it will come back together.

Cover the bowl with a towel or plastic wrap. About every half hour, stretch and fold the dough: dip your hands in water and, with a wet hand, grab the underside of the dough, stretching straight up until the point just *before* the dough rips. You are extending strands of gluten but do not want to tear them. Fold the stretched portion of dough over the remaining bulk. Rotate the bowl a quarter turn and stretch and fold from each quadrant. As you stretch and fold, the dough will become more resistant to stretching. Each time you return, as the gluten builds, the dough will stretch farther. It really is kind of amazing.

After 5 to 8 folds (about 2½ to 3½ hours), the dough will become noticeably less sticky and puffier. It might even begin to form bubbles at the surface. That's a good sign.

Transfer the dough to a work surface and dust the top with flour. Divide the dough into two equal pieces and work into taut rounds, folding the cut side of each piece up onto itself so that the flour on the surface remains entirely on the outside of the loaf; this will become the crust. Place the dough rounds, seam-side down, on a work surface, cover with a towel, and let rest 30 minutes.

In a bowl, mix the remaining 100 grams of whole wheat flour and the 100 grams of rice flour (or just use 200 grams of rice flour). Line two 10- to 12-inch bread-proofing baskets or mixing bowls with towels. Use some of the flour mixture to generously flour the towels.

Shaping is difficult, and learning it from written instructions is a bit like learning to tie shoelaces from a verbal description. The goal is to create a tightly stretched surface that will become the bread's top. Begin with the floured side of your dough down on your work surface. Pat the dough gently to flatten it a bit, take the side closest to you, and pull two corners of the dough toward yourself. Fold them up *one-third* of the dough's length so that the edge lands roughly in the middle of the dough. Repeat this motion on the right, left, and top of the dough, so all the folds cover one another in the center of the dough. Flip the dough so that the creases are now on the bottom. Do your best to stretch the dough now on top, pinching the pulled dough together underneath.

Transfer the rounds, seam-side up, to the floured baskets. Cover with a towel and let the dough rise for 3 to 4 hours at room temperature (or 10 to 12 hours in the refrigerator, bringing the dough back to room temperature before baking).

About 30 minutes before baking, place a Dutch oven or cast-iron pot in the oven and heat to 500°F. Remove the heated pot from the oven and spray with cooking oil, and/or dust the tops of the raised dough with more of the flour mixture. Turn the loaf over into the pot, seam-side down. Score the new top several times with a lame, razor blade, or serrated knife to allow room for oven spring. If the pot is too deep and you are worried about burning yourself or if you find that scoring deflates the dough too much, skip it. Your bread will be fine and turn out very rustic looking.

Reduce the temperature to 450°F. Bake, covered, for 20 minutes, then uncover and bake for 20 minutes more, until the bread is golden brown and sounds hollow when you thump its bottom. Transfer to a rack to cool for at least 30 minutes before diving in.

Increase the oven temperature to 500°F, clean the pot, and repeat for the second loaf.

FINAL PROOF

THE LAST RISE BEFORE BAKING IS CALLED THE final proof. Dough swells in a banneton, a towel-lined bowl, a loaf pan, a linen couche, or parchment paper. The baker pokes the dough with her forefinger to see if the depression rebounds too quickly or too slowly. Having chosen her moment, the baker slashes the surface of the dough to leave room for oven spring, the expansion of superheated gases deep within the crumb. Once it is in the oven, there is nothing to do but wait for the answer. Will this be a "good bake"?

I searched for a final proof to the question that began this book. Is the starter I call Cripple Creek really more than a century old? I've written a whole book and I still don't know, but a second question follows quickly on the heels of the first. Does the precise age of Cripple Creek matter? To the final quality of any bread I make, probably not. In fact, compared with my other three starters, Cripple Creek is the sourest, not because it is old but because it just happens to contain a combination of yeast and bacteria that makes sour bread. Honestly, if left to proof too long, it can be a bit skunky.

Yet even if the age of a starter does not carry much influence into a baked loaf, history does matter. Does a watch that your father once wore keep any better time than a watch you purchased online? Is that diamond engagement ring that was once given by your grandfather to your grandmother any more valuable than a ring you selected in this moment of commitment? No and yes. To some, sentimentality is no more than baggage, an accumulation of things laden with responsibility for care, upkeep, and protection. Heirlooms can feel like obligations, sometimes. And yet the opposite is also true. Without ancestry and history, who are we? The people who have enabled us to become who we are might be biologically related or, like some sourdough starters, given to us. Keeping their warm embraces alive in our minds is neither a burden nor a sacrifice. Rather, checking the time on Dad's old watch, glancing at the diamond, or feeding your sourdough is a brief reminder of who we are and why.

Embedded in the culture of Cripple Creek are the stories of a glutinous web of Americans who have all used the same culture to leaven bread since 1893. More to the point, whether a starter is a family heirloom or something you assembled for the first time this week, making any sourdough bread connects each baker to a history of sustenance and pleasure, revolution and self-sufficiency, scientific discovery and creativity that stretches back to early human settlements in the Fertile Crescent. Baking with sourdough is a commitment to a living companion, to billions of microscopic workmates, within which lies the ability to recover parts of life too quickly being displaced by speedy machines and addictive digital technologies.

Soon after the manuscript for this book was delivered to its publisher, a widespread, apparently latent desire among thousands of self-isolating citizens to bake sourdough bread was awakened. Another microscopic organism—a virus called COVID-19, related more by size than biology to the yeast and bacteria I use to leaven my bread—made a global dash around the planet. In its wake, the

COVID-19 pandemic left illness, despair, isolation, death, and a yearning, among many, to meet a sourdough culture for the first time. I have tried to discern what it was about the menace of one invisible, and very threatening, organism that turned the attention of so many people to a different set of microscopic beings, in this case untamed yeast and bacteria. Yes, commercial yeast was in short supply in stores, but widespread adoption of sourdough microbes was not simply a question of frugality and scarcity or simply a function of having additional time at home, though time was surely a benefit.

Homebound bakers around the world launched sourdough starters and reported about them in blogs and newspapers in Russia, England, New Zealand, Singapore, Chile, Finland, and Brazil. Social media feeds were flooded with the slashed tops of sourdough loaves. Rob Dunn's research team at North Carolina State University started a citizen science project for people to create sourdough starters at home. More than one thousand people participated. Why respond to an existential threat by baking bread?

For six thousand years, the staff of life has been made by hand from only four ingredients: flour, water, salt, and a sourdough culture of wild yeast and bacteria. Workers who built the Egyptian pyramids received the bulk of their calories from bread, some or all of which was probably sourdough. Ancient Rome imported wheat from across its empire to turn into sourdough loaves it distributed to Roman citizens. Survival through the Middle Ages depended upon preparation of sourdough bread baked in communal ovens. Perhaps without even being aware of it, new bakers were searching for foundations.

Beyond history there is also a magical, and in many ways religious, transformation that occurs when dough going into an oven emerges as bread. In a quarantine-inspired seminar series called Fermentology,[1] Peter Reinhart, bread expert, author, and chef on assignment at Johnson & Wales University, put it this way: bread begins as a living organism, wheat. Seeds of wheat die when they are milled into flour. Flour is resurrected by an infection of yeast and, in the case of sourdough, bacteria, too. Bacteria and yeast grow, reproduce, and respire, leavening the dough until the moment they perish in the oven. While dough enters the oven, something else entirely emerges: bread. Sustenance for human life. Maybe baking was providing an affirmation of life, a hope for rebirth after weeks and months of numbing isolation.

In a COVID-19 world of sensory deprivation—no hugging, no kissing, where even a gentle hand on a shoulder signified that you were too close—perhaps dough acted as an imperfect replacement. A baker touched dough, kneading invisible strands of gluten until the dough felt as soft and supple as human skin. A bread that is finished baking can be discerned with our ears when a gentle thump on its base resonates like a kettledrum. The aroma of a browned crust and the chewy interior of a freshly baked sourdough bread cause most of us to salivate in anticipation. Very few slices taken from a colorful plastic bag invoke the same response.

In a pre-COVID world, a hastily eaten sandwich on Chorleywood Bread Process white bread provided uninspired calories, while office coffee reinforced our fortitude as we endured crashing waves of deadlines. Commercial yeast, liquid caffeine, and factory bread are tools and fuel for a hasty world. Sourdough bread, in contrast, is a reminder that part of what it takes to enjoy a festival of the senses is the time required to slow down enough to savor them.

Undoubtedly, by the time this book is printed and distributed, many sourdough bakers will have moved on to other pastimes, leaving behind a jar of culture to languish in the back of the fridge. Perhaps bread making was too much work, or the results were imperfect. Yet even great bakers perform postmortems on their fresh loaves, and they are almost always slightly disappointed. From the second a finished bread comes from the oven, bakers begin their inspections. Does the bread smell sweet? Earthy? Can the special aroma of roasted wheat flour be detected in the rising steam? How is the color of the crust? Has it taken on the glow of hazelnuts? Did the slashes open, or has the crust torn somewhere unexpectedly? Is the crust firm? The glaze shiny? Are seeds or nuts still happily submerged, or have they become burned exfoliants? Are the sides cooked evenly? Does the baker's tap on the bottom resonate like timpani?

The first slice tells a fuller story. Does it slice readily and evenly? Does it tear? Does the top crust stay with the rest of the slice, or does it rip away? Is the inside gummy? Is the knife clean? Now the baker inspects the crumb. Does the baguette display a crazy quilt of dissimilar holes? Did the rye rise enough? Is the crumb finely perforated and perfect for a sandwich? Are the myriad laminations in the croissant—yes, you can make outstanding croissants entirely with sourdough—discernible? Will the sourdough croissant swirl with enough integrity that it can soak up a healthy level of coffee when dunked?

At last comes taste. Sour enough, or too sour? Is the crust suitably crunchy? Is the interior cooked through? Is it too much work to chew? Are the flavors of bacterial acids balanced by the right amount of salt and yeastiness? Does the flour taste fresh? Can you sense the balance of wheat and rye? What would you like to be different the next time you make this bread?

Assessing loaves, particularly those whose growth depends on a consortium of wild organisms, can be learned by experience. Like playing the violin or swimming, the more you practice the better you get. A baker must make a lot of bread, caress every dough, and analyze each loaf. Making good bread is a delicate balance of experimentation, scientific understanding, artistry, and history.

The joy comes in eating the results.

Freshly baked sourdough bread made with Cripple Creek starter.

ACKNOWLEDGMENTS

JESSICA EASTO IS MY SUPERHERO. ASSIGNED TO me by Agate Publishing, she epitomizes the ideal editor. She employed an unearthly ability to look at my manuscript as a whole book while paying attention to each of its individual words. She encouraged me to move paragraphs, expand explanations, excise gibberish, and streamline recipes, and she advocated for word changes whose replacements had the ability to realign the arc of the story I wanted to tell. Jessica made at least six passes through the manuscript, applying a comb with finer and finer tines, a feat of concentration every bit as difficult as it sounds. My name appears on the cover of this book, but Jessica Easto deserves far more credit than this short acknowledgment allows.

My rise to publication has been slow, but as they say in the baking world, a slow rise results in better flavor. Stephany Evans of Ayesha Pande Literary has my enduring gratitude for becoming my agent and for helping me cut the fluff. This book would not be possible without Doug Seibold, founder and president of Agate Publishing, Morgan Krehbiel, for her aesthetic judgment, cover design, and assistance with the numerous images and maps,

Jane Seibold, Naomi Huffman, Jacqueline Jarik, Helena Hunt, Judy Kip, and hidden members of Agate's excellent staff who have made publication of my book a wonder and a joy. Chris Shaffer stepped up at the last minute to create the three maps in this book, without using any colors. Thank you all.

Sourdough Culture unifies stories from the separate domains of history, microbiology, and baking, none of which fall within my mastery. I have done my utmost to cite original sources and report what I have uncovered with objectivity. Undoubtedly, there are errors and oversights contained within these pages. I already regret them. Additionally, most of the recipes in this book, especially those more than one hundred years in age or those I created myself, should be treated as approximations, rather than strict formulae. I make no promises that if you prepare bread for your book club from one of these recipes that everyone will fawn over it. Still, it is likely to be better than anything you could purchase at a supermarket. It will certainly be more interesting.

Research for this book was supported by the Fulbright Scholar Program, the National Collection of Yeast Cultures, the Great Lakes Colleges Association, and my home away from home for more than three decades, Allegheny College in Meadville, Pennsylvania.

Thanks are also due to professional bakers and writers who have encouraged my entry into their coveted ranks: Peter Reinhart, Andrew Whitley, Rob Dunn, and Stanley Ginsberg.

Many have assisted me in various levels of editing. Your honesty and attention to detail have improved this book. In advance, my apologies to those of you whom I have inadvertently forgotten to include in this list: Brynya Bowden, Rich Bowden, Stephanie Bramwell, Beth Choate, David Dawson, Ellis Giacomelli, Simon Gray, Patrick Jackson, Lindsay Kelley, Bailey Kozalla, Kristen Locy, Erin McKenney, Kerry Neville, Amy Ochsenreiter, Marley Parish, Delaney Rohan, Sarah Swartz, Gavrielle Winer. Thanks also to

John Mangine for your incomparable photographs and enthusiasm. And thank you to Allyson Tinney and Karl DeSmedt for all of your bread assistance.

I am beyond fortunate that my son, Isaac, has become the King of Sandwich and my daughter, Leah, the Queen of Sourdough. Across thousands of breads, my wife, Susan, the best challah baker on the planet, has honestly assessed every one of my loaves. More importantly, she has encouraged me to "run your own race, sweetie." For their collective patience and unwavering support, I am indebted.

ENDNOTES

CHAPTER 1: IN THE BEGINNING

1　Julio Mercader, "Mozambican Grass Seed Consumption during the Middle Stone Age," *Science* 326, no. 5960 (2009): 1680–1683, doi:10.1126/science.1173966.

2　Anna Revedin, Biancamaria Aranguren, Roberto Becattini, Laura Longo, Emanuele Marconi, Marta Mariotti Lippi, Natalia Skakun, et al., "Thirty Thousand-Year-Old Evidence of Plant Food Processing," *Proceedings of the National Academy of Sciences of the United States of America* 107, no. 44 (November 2, 2010): 18815–18819, doi:10.1073/pnas.1006993107.

3　Ehud Weiss, Dolores R. Piperno, Dani Nadel, and Irene Holst, "Processing of Wild Cereal Grains in the Upper Palaeolithic Revealed by Starch Grain Analysis," *Nature* 430, no. 7000 (August 5, 2004): 670–673, doi:10.1038/nature02734.

4　Weiss, et al., "Processing of Wild Cereal Grains," 670.

5　Weiss, et al., 671.

6　Walt Newman and Rosemary Newman, "A Brief History of Barley Foods," *Cereal Foods World* 51, no. 1 (2006): 4–7, doi:10.1094/CFW-51-0004.

7　Rivka Elbaum, Liron Zaltzman, Ingo Burgert, and Peter Fratzl, "The Role of Wheat Awns in the Seed Dispersal Unit," *Science* 316, no. 5826 (2007): 884–886, doi:10.1126/science.1140097.

8　Mark Nesbitt and Delwen Samuel, "From Staple Crop to Extinction? The Archaeology and History of the Hulled Wheats," In *Hulled Wheats [Proceedings of the First International Workshop on Hulled Wheats]*, ed. S. Padulosi (Rome: IPGRI, 1996): 58–59.

9　Nesbitt and Samuel, "From Staple Crop," 62.

10　Ken-Ichi Tanno and George Willcox, "How Fast Was Wild Wheat Domesticated?" *Science* 311, no. 5769 (March 31, 2006): 1886, doi:10.1126/science.1124635.

11　Terence A. Brown, Martin K. Jones, Wayne Powell, and Robin G. Allaby, "The Complex Origins of Domesticated Crops in the Fertile Crescent," *Trends in Ecology & Evolution* 24, no. 2 (2009): 103–109, doi:10.1016/j.tree.2008.09.008.

12　Avi Gopher, Shallal Abbo, and Simcha Lev Yadun, "The 'When,' the 'Where' and the 'Why' of the Neolithic Revolution in the Levant," *Documenta Praehistorica* 28 (2001): 49–62, doi:10.4312/dp.28.3.

13　Francesco Salamini, Andrea Brandolini, Ralf Schäfer-Pregl, Hakan Özkan, and William Martin, "Genetics and Geography of Wild Cereal Domestication in the Near East," *Nature Reviews Genetics* 3, no. 6 (June 2002): 429–441, doi:10.1038/nrg817.

14   Uzi Avner, Patricia Chabot-Anderson, Bui-Thi Mai, Jacques Chabot, and Linda
     Scott-Cummings, "Ancient Threshing Floors, Threshing Tools and Plant Remains
     in Uvda Valley, Southern Negev Desert, Israel, a Preliminary Report," In *Le Trait-
     ement des Récoltes: Un Regard sur la Diversité du Néolithique au Present* (Antibes,
     France: Éditions APDCA, 2003): 455–476.

15   Uzi Avner, "Current Archaeological Research in Israel: Ancient Agricultural Set-
     tlement and Religion in the Uvda Valley in Southern Israel," *The Biblical Archaeol-
     ogist* 53, no. 3 (1990): 125–141.

16   Avner, "Current Archaeological Research," 125–141.

17   Avner, et al., "Ancient Threshing Floors," 455–476.

18   Avner, et al., 455–476.

19   Ronald Wirtz, "Grain, Baking, and Sourdough Bread," In *Handbook of Dough
     Fermentations*, eds. Karel Kulp and Klaus Lorenz (Boca Raton, FL: CRC Press,
     2003): 16–36, doi:10.1201/9780203911884.

20   Delwen Samuel and B. J. Kemp, "Their Staff of Life: Initial Investigations on
     Ancient Egyptian Bread Baking," In *Amarna Reports* (London: Egypt Exploration
     Society, 1989): 253–290.

21   Peter R. Shewry, "Do Ancient Types of Wheat Have Health Benefits Com-
     pared with Modern Wheat?" *Journal of Cereal Science* 79 (2018): 469–476,
     doi:10.1016/j.jcs.2017.11.010.

22   Nesbitt and Samuel, "From Staple Crop," 77.

23   Samuel and Kemp, "Their Staff of Life," 253–290.

24   Nesbitt and Samuel, "From Staple Crop," 51.

25   F. Filce Leek, "Teeth and Bread in Ancient Egypt," *The Journal of Egyptian Archae-
     ology* 58 (August 1, 1972): 126–132.

26   Leek, "Teeth and Bread in Ancient Egypt," 126–132.

27   Delwen Samuel, *Brewing and Baking* (Cambridge: Cambridge University Press,
     2000): 547.

28   Delwen Samuel, "Investigation of Ancient Egyptian Baking and Brewing Methods
     by Correlative Microscopy," *Science* 273, no. 5274 (1996): 488–490, doi:10.1126
     /science.273.5274.488.

29   Samuel, *Brewing and Baking*, 559.

30   Samuel and Kemp, "Their Staff of Life," 270.

31   Samuel and Kemp, 253–290.

32   Nicholas J. Conard and Mark Lehner, "The 1998/1999 Excavation of Petrie's
     'Workmen's Barracks' at Giza," *Journal of American Research Center in Egypt* 38
     (2001): 21–60; Mark Lehner, "The Pyramid Aged Settlement of the Southern
     Mount of Giza," *Journal of American Research Center in Egypt* 39 (2002): 27–74;
     Mark Lehner, "Pyramid Aged Bakery Reconstructed," *Aeragram* 1 (Fall 1996): 6–7.

33   Conard and Lehner, "The 1998/1999 Excavation," 21–60.

34   Letter to Eric Pallant, "Re: Scooping Dough," August 31, 2017.

35   Letter to Eric Pallant, "Re: Scooping Dough," September 2, 2017.

36   Ed Wood, *World Sourdoughs from Antiquity* (Berkeley: Ten Speed Press, 1996): 185.

37   Mark Lehner, "Feeding Pyramid Workers," AERAWeb, Ancient Egypt Research
     Association, 2020, http://www.aeraweb.org/lost-city-project/feeding-pyramid-
     workers/.

38 Luke Fater, "How the Man Who Invented Xbox Baked a 4,500-Year-Old Egyptian Sourdough," Atlas Obscura, April 2, 2020, https://www.atlasobscura.com/articles /what-bread-did-ancient-egyptians-eat.

CHAPTER 2: BREAD AND HUNGER

1   Thomas Braun, "Barley Cakes and Emmer Bread," In *Food in Antiquity*, eds. J. Wilkins, D. Harvey, and M. Dobson (Exeter, UK: University of Exeter Press, 1995): 32.

2   Marcus Terentius Varro, "On Agriculture," *De Re Rustica*, Book I, accessed March 7, 2021, http://penelope.uchicago.edu/Thayer/E/Roman/Texts/Varro /de_Re_Rustica/1*.html; Virgil, *Georgics*, Oxford's World Classics [10], trans. Peter Falon (Oxford: Oxford University Press, 2006): 520; Lucretius, *De Rerum Natura*, Book V, accessed March 7, 2021, lines 1370–1371, http://www.perseus .tufts.edu/hopper/text?doc=Lucr; Lucretius, *De Rerum Natura*, lines 405–409.

3   Lucretius, *De Rerum Natura*, lines 405–409.

4   Braun, "Barley Cakes and Emmer Bread," 33.

5   Juvenal, *Satire*, 10, trans. Lewis Evans, accessed March 7, 2021, lines 77–81, http://pages.pomona.edu/~cmc24747/sources/juvenal/juv_10.htm.

6   Geoffrey E. Rickman, "The Grain Trade under the Roman Empire," *Memoirs of the American Academy in Rome* 36 (1980): 261–275.

7   Rickman, "The Grain Trade," 261–275.

8   Rickman, 261–275.

9   Rickman, 261–275.

10 Rickman, 261–275.

11 Rickman, 261–275.

12 Bernard DuPaigne, *History of Bread* (New York: Harry N. Abrams, 1999): 23.

13 Gaius Plinius Secundus, "The Method of Baking Bread: The Origin of the Art," In *Pliny's Natural History*, trans. John Bostock, vol. 18 (London: Taylor and Francis, 1855): chapter 27.

14 Secundus, "The Method of Baking Bread," chapter 27.

15 Betty Jo Mayeske, *Bakeries, Bakers, and Bread at Pompeii* (Ann Arbor: University of Michigan Press, 1972): 55.

16 Haraldur Sigurdsson and Steven Carey, "The Eruption of Vesuvius in AD 79," In *The Natural History of Pompeii*, eds. Wilhelmina Mary Feemster Jashemski and Frederick Gustav Meyer (Cambridge: Press Syndicate of the University of Cambridge, 2002): 37–64.

17 Sigurdsson and Carey, "The Eruption of Vesuvius," 42–43.

18 Mayeske, *Bakeries, Bakers, and Bread at Pompeii*, 1–252.

19 L. A. Moritz, *Grain Mills and Flour in Classical Antiquity* (Oxford: Clarendon Press, 1958): 76.

20 Mayeske, *Bakeries, Bakers, and Bread at Pompeii*, 26.

21 Mayeske, 26.

22 John 6:33–35 (NRSV).

23 John 6:33–35 (NRSV).

24 Luke 11:1; Matthew 6:9–15 (NRSV).

25 Philip Schaff, *Ante-Nicene Fathers*, eds. A. Roberts and J. Donaldson, vol. 1
    (Grand Rapids, MI: Christian Classics Ethereal Library, 1885), https://www.ccel
    .org/ccel/schaff/anf01.v.v.vii.html.

26 James Thomas O'Connor, *The Hidden Manna: A Theology of the Eucharist*
    (San Francisco: Ignatius Press, 2005): 5.

27 O'Connor, *The Hidden Manna*, 18–25.

28 "History of the Nestorian Church," Nestorian.org, accessed March 7, 2021,
    http://www.nestorian.org/history_of_the_nestorian_church.html.

29 "History of the Nestorian Church."

30 Geoffrey Roper, "George Percy Badger 1815–1888," *British Society for Middle
    Eastern Studies Bulletin* 11, no. 2 (1984): 140–155.

31 William Wright, *A Short History of Syriac Literature* (London: Adam and Charles
    Black, 1894): 261.

32 Roper, "George Percy Badger," 153.

33 George Percy Badger, *The Nestorians and Their Rituals*, vol. 2 (London: Joseph
    Masters and Co., 1852): 152.

34 Badger, *The Nestorians*, 152.

35 Badger, 153.

36 Koen de Groote, Dries Tys, Marnix Pieters, and Dave H. Evans, "A Good
    Riddance of Bad Rubbish? Scatological Musings on Rubbish Disposal and the
    Handling of 'Filth' in Medieval and Early Post-medieval Towns," In *Exchanging
    Medieval Material Culture*, Relicta Monografieën, vol. 4 (Brussels: Vlaams Inst.
    voor het Onroerend Erfgoed, 2010): 267–278.

37 Kathy L. Pearson, "Nutrition and the Early-Medieval Diet," *Speculum* 72, no. 1
    (1997): 1–32.

38 Pearson, "Nutrition and the Early-Medieval Diet," 1–32.

39 Richard C. Hoffmann, "Medieval Origins of the Common Fields," In *European Peas-
    ants and Their Markets* (Princeton, NJ: Princeton University Press, 1975): 38–43.

40 Pearson, "Nutrition and the Early-Medieval Diet," 1–32.

41 Nesbitt and Samuel, "From Staple Crop," 76–77.

42 Pearson, "Nutrition and the Early-Medieval Diet," 1–32.

43 John Fitzherbert, *The Boke of Husbandry* (London: Thomas Berthelet, 1533): 61–63.

44 Jeffrey L. Singman, *Daily Life in Medieval Europe* (Westport, CT: Greenwood
    Press, 1999): 80.

45 Singman, *Daily Life in Medieval Europe*, 83–86.

46 Ruth Goodman, *How to Be a Tudor: A Dawn-to-Dusk Guide to Everyday Life*
    (New York: Penguin Books, 2016): 150–174.

47 Goodman, *How to Be a Tudor*, 150–174.

48 Bernhard Hendrich Slicher van Bath, *The Agrarian History of Western Europe*,
    A.D. 500–1850, trans. Olive Ordish (London: Edward Arnold, 1963): 182, 335.

49 H. H. Lamb, *Climate, History and the Modern World* (London: Methuen Publish-
    ing, 1982).

50 C. Pfister, J. Luterbacher, G. Schwarz-Zanetti, and M. Wegmann, "Winter
    Air Temperature Variations in Western Europe during the Early and High
    Middle Ages (AD 750–1300)," *The Holocene* 8, no. 5 (1998): 535–552,
    doi:10.1191/095968398675289943.

51 Pearson, "Nutrition and the Early-Medieval Diet," 1–32.

52 Melitta Weiss Adamson, *Food in Medieval Times* (Westport, CT: Greenwood Press, 2004): ix.

53 Adamson, *Food in Medieval Times*, ix.

54 Peter Brown, *The Body and Society: Men, Women and Sexual Renunciation in Early Christianity* (New York: Columbia University Press, 1988): 224.

55 Goodman, *How to Be a Tudor*, 34–36.

56 Pearson, "Nutrition and the Early-Medieval Diet," 1–32.

57 Goodman, *How to Be a Tudor*, 1–320.

58 Goodman, 124–125.

59 Pliny the Elder, *The Natural History*, trans. John Bostock and H. T. Riley, (London: Taylor and Francis, 1855): 18.27, http://data.perseus.org/citations /urn:cts:latinLit:phi0978.phi001.perseus-eng1.

60 Pliny the Elder, *The Natural History*, 18.29.

61 Oakden, "Maslin Bread," accessed November 23, 2020, https://oakden.co.uk /maslin-bread-recipe/.

CHAPTER 3: THE FRENCH CONNECTION

1 Peter Tamony, "Sourdough and French Bread," *Western Folklore* 32, no. 4 (1973): 265–270.

2 Steven Laurence Kaplan, *The Bakers of Paris and the Bread Question 1700–1775* (Durham, NC: Duke University Press, 1996): 23.

3 Kaplan, *The Bakers of Paris*, 23.

4 Kaplan, 26.

5 Jeffrey L. Singman, *Daily Life in Medieval Europe* (Westport, CT: Greenwood Press, 1999): 1–10, 105–138.

6 Hilton Lewis Root, "Challenging the Seigneurie: Community and Contention on the Eve of the French Revolution," *The Journal of Modern History* 57, no. 4 (1985): 652–681, doi:10.1086/242899.

7 Cynthia A. Bouton, *The Flour War: Gender, Class, and Community in Late Ancient Régime French Society* (Philadelphia: Pennsylvania University Press, 1993): 6.

8 Bouton, *The Flour War*, 7.

9 Bouton, 7.

10 Bouton, 6.

11 Steven Laurence Kaplan, "Policing the General Subsistence, 1771–1774," In *Bread, Politics and Political Economy in the Reign of Louis XV* (Dordrecht, Netherlands: Springer, 1976): 555–613.

12 Kaplan, "Policing the General Subsistence," 555–613.

13 Christopher Hibbert, *The Days of the French Revolution* (New York: William Morrow Paperbacks, 1999): 96.

14 Hibbert, *French Revolution*, 97.

15 Hibbert, 98.

16 Hibbert, 99.

17 Hibbert, 99.

18 Hibbert, 100.

19 Hibbert, 101.

20 Hibbert, 101.

286   ENDNOTES

21   Antonia Fraser, *Marie Antoinette: The Journey* (New York: Anchor Books, 2002): 135.
22   Hibbert, *French Revolution*, 104.
23   Hibbert, 105.
24   Judith A. Miller, "Politics and Urban Provisioning Crises: Bakers, Police, and Parlements in France, 1750–1793," *The Journal of Modern History* 64, no. 2 (1992): 227–262, doi:10.1086/244479.
25   Kaplan, *The Bakers of Paris*, 61.
26   Kaplan, 61.
27   Kaplan, 67.
28   Kaplan, 70.
29   Kaplan, 71.
30   Kaplan, 73.
31   Roger D. Reid, "Studies on Bacterial Pigmentation," *Journal of Bacteriology* 31, no. 2 (1936): 205–210.
32   Reid, "Studies on Bacterial Pigmentation," 207.
33   Reid, 205–210.
34   Robert Hooke, "The Discovery of Microorganisms by Robert Hooke and Antoni Van Leeuwenhoek, Fellows of the Royal Society," *Notes and Records of the Royal Society of London* 58, no. 2 (1665): 187–201, doi:10.1098/rsnr.2004.0055.
35   J. R. Porter, "Antony van Leeuwenhoek: Tercentenary of His Discovery of Bacteria," *Bacteriological Reviews* 40, no. 2 (1976): 260–269.
36   Antonie van Leeuwenhoek, *Arcana Naturae Detecta* (Delft, Netherlands: Henrik van Kroonevelt, 1721).
37   J. A. Barnett, "A History of Research on Yeasts 1: Work by Chemists and Biologists 1789–1850," *Yeast* 14, no. 16 (1998): 1439–1451.
38   Barnett, "A History of Research on Yeasts," 1441.
39   Barnett, 1442.
40   Barnett, 1442–1443.
41   Barnett, 1444–1445.
42   Jamie Wisniak, "Antoine-Augustin Parmentier," *Revista CENIC Ciencias Biologicas* 41, no. 2 (2010): 142.
43   Wisniak, "Antoine-Augustin Parmentier," 141–148.
44   Wisniak, 146.
45   Simon Schama, *Citizens: A Chronicle of the French Revolution* (London: Penguin Books, 1989): 186.
46   Kaplan, *The Bakers of Paris*, 51.
47   Kaplan, 52.
48   Kaplan, 67.
49   Kaplan, 67.
50   Kaplan, 67.
51   Kaplan, 68.
52   Kaplan, 38.
53   Kaplan, 38.
54   Kaplan, 68.
55   D. Leader, *Local Breads* (New York: W. W. Norton & Company, 2007): 124–128.

CHAPTER 4: SOURDOUGH GOES TO AMERICA

1   Kate Caffrey, *The Mayflower* (Lanham, MD: Rowman and Littlefield, 2014): 73.

2   Auguste Jal, *Documents Inedits* (Whitefish, MT: Kessinger Publishing, 1841): 44–45, quoted in Samuel Eliot Morison, *The European Discovery of America: The Northern Voyages A.D. 500–1600* (Oxford: Oxford University Press, 1971): 276.

3   Morison, *The European Discovery*, 131; J. R. Tanner, ed., *A Descriptive Catalogue of the Naval Manuscripts in the Pepysian Library at Magdalene College, Cambridge* (London: Naval Records Society, 1903): 165–167.

4   Dudley Pope, *Life in Nelson's Navy* (Annapolis, MD: Naval Institute Press, 1996): 70–71, Google Books.

5   William N. B. Watson, "Alexander Brodie and His Firehearth for Ships," *The Mariner's Mirror* 54, no. 4 (1968): 409–412.

6   Watson, "Alexander Brodie," 410.

7   John Cochrane, *The Seaman's Guide: Shewing How to Live Comfortably at Sea. Containing, among Other Particulars, Complete Directions for Baking Bread, . . . Recommended Also to Public Bakers, as well as to Private Housekeepers*, vol. 12 (London: J. Murray and S. Highley, 1797), Google Books.

8   Abraham Edlin, *A Treatise on the Art of Breadmaking* (London: J. Wright, 1805), Internet Archive.

9   Edlin, *A Treatise*, 63.

10 Edlin, 72.

11 William Bradford, *Of Plymouth Plantation, 1620–1647: The Complete Text with Notes and an Introduction*, ed. Samuel Eliot Morrison (New York: Alfred A. Knopf, 2002): 25.

12 Azel Amez, *The Mayflower and Her Log* (Boston and New York: Houghton, Mifflin, and Company, 1901): 198–199, Internet Archive.

13 Jeremy Hugh Baron, "Sailors' Scurvy before and after James Lind—A Reassessment," *Nutrition Reviews* 67, no. 6 (2009): 315–332, doi:10.1111/j.1753-4887.2009 .00205.x.

14 George B. Cheever, *The Journal of the Pilgrims at Plymouth, in New England, in 1620* (New York: John Wiley, 1848): 48, Internet Archive.

15 Cheever, *The Journal of the Pilgrims*, 34.

16 Keith Stavely and Kathleen Fitzgerald, *America's Founding Food* (Chapel Hill and London: University of North Carolina Press, 2004): 11.

17 John Gerard, *The Herball or Generall Historie of Plantes* (London: Norton, John, 1597): 77.

18 Gerard, *The Herball*, 77.

19 Edward Johnson, *Johnson's Wonder-Working Providence: 1628–1651*, ed. John Franklin Jameson (New York: Charles Scribner's Sons, 1910): 115, Google Books.

20 Denis Wall and Virgil Masayesva, "People of the Corn: Teachings in Hopi Traditional Agriculture, Spirituality, and Sustainability," *American Indian Quarterly* (2004): 435–453.

21 Stavely and Fitzgerald, *America's Founding Food*, 24.

22 Robert C. Winthrop, *Life and Letters of John Winthrop* (Boston: Ticknor and Fields, 1864): 312, Google Books.

23 Francis J. Bremer, *John Winthrop: America's Forgotten Founding Father* (Oxford: Oxford University Press, 2005): 314, ProQuest Ebook Central.

24 Fulmer Mood, "John Winthrop, Jr., on Indian Corn," *The New England Quarterly* 10, no. 1 (1937): 125.

25 Mood, "John Winthrop, Jr.," 125.

26 Mood, 130.

27 Joel Perlmann and Dennis Shirley, "When Did New England Women Acquire Literacy?" *The William and Mary Quarterly* 48, no. 1 (1991): 50–67, doi:10.2307/2937997.

28 Stavely and Fitzgerald, *America's Founding Food*, 26.

29 Mood, "John Winthrop, Jr.," 131–132.

30 Winthrop, *Life and Letters of John Winthrop*, 221.

31 Stavely and Fitzgerald, *America's Founding Food*, 13.

32 Perlmann and Shirley, "When Did New England Women Acquire Literacy?" 50–67.

33 Stavely and Fitzgerald, *America's Founding Food*, 26.

34 Jean-François Blanchette and Lise Boily, *The Bread Ovens of Quebec* (Ottawa: National Museum of Canada, 1979): 76.

35 Blanchette and Boily, *The Bread Ovens of Quebec*, 76.

36 Blanchette and Boily, 76.

37 Blanchette and Boily, 5.

38 D. Diderot and J. L. d'Alembert, *Encyclopédie, ou Dictionnaire Raisonné des Sciences, des Arts et des Métiers* 15, no. 2 (Lausanne: Société Typographique, 1782): 1751–1765.

39 Diderot and d'Alembert, *Encyclopédie, ou Dictionnaire Raisonné des Sciences*, 1751–1765; Blanchette and Boily, *The Bread Ovens of Quebec*, 22.

40 Blanchette and Boily, 44.

41 Blanchette and Boily, 81.

42 Blanchette and Boily, 87.

43 Blanchette and Boily, 91.

44 Carole Shammas, "How Self-Sufficient Was Early America?" *The Journal of Interdisciplinary History* 13, no. 2 (1982): 247.

45 Matthew Carey, "The American Museum, or Universal Magazine: Containing Essays on Agriculture, Commerce, Manufactures, Politics, Morals and Manners: Sketches of National Characters, Natural and Civil History, and Biography: Law Information, Public Papers, Intelligence: Moral Tales, Ancient and Modern Poetry," *American Museum* I (Philadelphia, 1787): 11–13, Hathi Trust Digital Library.

46 Shammas, "How Self-Sufficient Was Early America?" 253.

47 Shammas, 255.

48 Bettye Hobbs Pruitt, "Self-Sufficiency and the Agricultural Economy of Eighteenth-Century Massachusetts," *The William and Mary Quarterly* 13, no. 2 (1984): 333–364.

49 Edward Hopkins Jenkins, *A History of Connecticut Agriculture* (New Haven: Connecticut Agricultural Experiment Station, 1926): 308, Internet Archive.

50 S. W. Fletcher, "The Subsistence Farming Period in Pennsylvania Agriculture, 1640–1840," *Pennsylvania History: A Journal of Mid-Atlantic Studies* 14, no. 3 (1947): 185–195, http://www.jstor.org/stable/27766803.

51 Barbara Clark Smith, "Food Riots and the American Revolution," *The William and Mary Quarterly* 51, no. 1 (1994): 3–38.
52 Kyla W. Tompkins, "Sylvester Graham's Imperial Dietetics," *Gastronomica* 9, no. 1 (2009): 50–60.
53 Sylvester Graham, *A Lecture to Young Men on Chastity: Intended Also for the Serious Consideration of Parents and Guardians*, 4th ed. (Boston: George W. Light, 1838): 20, Google Books.
54 Tompkins, "Imperial Dietetics," 50–60.
55 Graham, *A Lecture to Young Men on Chastity*, 145.
56 Graham, 145.
57 Graham, 148.
58 Sylvester Graham, *A Treatise on Bread and Bread-Making* (Boston: Light & Stearns, 1837), Internet Archive.
59 Graham, *A Treatise on Bread and Bread-Making*, 106.
60 Graham, 76.
61 Graham, 85.
62 Cindy Lobel, "Sylvester Graham and Antebellum Diet Reform," Gilder Lehrman Institute of American History, accessed May 5, 2017, https://www.gilderlehrman.org/history-by-era/first-age-reform/essays/sylvester-graham-and-antebellum-diet-reform.
63 Peggy M. Baker, "The Godmother of Thanksgiving: The Story of Sarah Josepha Hale" (Plymouth, MA: Pilgrim Society & Pilgrim Hall Museum, 2007), accessed March 7, 2021, https://www.pilgrimhall.org/pdf/Godmother_of_Thanksgiving.pdf.
64 Sarah J. Hale, *The Good Housekeeper: Or, the Way to Live Well and to Be Well While We Live: Containing Directions for Choosing and Preparing Food, in Regard to Health, Economy and Taste*, 6th ed. (Boston: Weeks, Jordan and Company, 1839), Google Books.
65 Hale, *The Good Housekeeper*, 11.
66 Hale, 21.
67 Sarah J. Hale, *Mrs. Hale's New Cook Book: A Practical System for Private Families in Town and Country; with Directions for Carving, and Arranging the Table for Parties, Etc. Also, Preparations of Food for Invalids and for Children* (Philadelphia: T. B. Peterson and Brothers, 1857): 424, Hathi Trust Digital Library.
68 Hale, *Mrs. Hale's New Cook Book*, 424.

CHAPTER 5: A REIGN OF YEAST

1 William G. Panschar, *Baking in America*, vol. 1 (Evanston, IL: Northwestern University Press, 1956): 31.
2 H. G. Muller, *Baking and Bakeries* (Aylesbury, UK: Shire Publications, 1986): 11.
3 Elizabeth Wayland Barber, *Prehistoric Textiles: The Development of Cloth in the Neolithic and Bronze Ages with Special Reference to the Aegean* (Princeton, NJ: Princeton University Press, 1992): 9–27, Google Books.
4 R. L. Hills, "Hargreaves, Arkwright and Crompton. Why Three Inventors?" *Textile History* 10, no. 1 (2013): 114–126, doi:10.1179/004049679793691321.

5   Melvin Thomas Copeland, *The Cotton Manufacturing Industry of the United States* (Cambridge, MA: Harvard University Press, 1912): 6–7.

6   R. A. Arnold, *History of the Cotton Famine from the Fall of Sumter, to the Passing of the Public Works Act* (London: Saunders, Otley, and Co., 1865): 36–37.

7   Claire Hopley, "British Textiles Clothe the World," British Heritage Travel, July 29, 2006, https://britishheritage.com/british-textiles-clothe-the-world/.

8   E. Parkinson, *The Complete Confectioner, Pastry-Cook, and Baker* (Philadelphia: J. B. Lippencott, 1864): 154, Michigan State University Libraries Digital Repository.

9   Parkinson, *The Complete Confectioner*, 130.

10 John Bickerdyke, *The Curiosities of Ale and Beer: An Entertaining History* (London: Field and Tuer, 1886), Google Books.

11 Parkinson, *The Complete Confectioner*, 135.

12 Parkinson, 135.

13 J. Crowley, *Jenny June's American Cookery Book* (New York: American News Co., 1870): 400, Michigan State University Libraries Digital Repository.

14 L. Hearn, *La Creole Cuisine* (New Orleans: F. F. Hansell & Bro., Ltd, 1885): 280, Michigan State University Libraries Digital Repository.

15 "Our Rich Heritage," Carlsberg Group, accessed March 9, 2021, https://www.carlsberggroup.com/who-we-are/about-the-carlsberg-group/our-rich-heritage/.

16 Richard N. Hart, *Leavening Agents: Yeast, Leaven, Salt-Rising Fermentation, Baking Powder, Aerated Bread, Milk Powder* (Easton, PA: Chemical Pub. Co., 1914): 22, Google Books.

17 Hart, *Leavening Agents*, 26.

18 Hart, 21–35.

19 P. Gelinas, "Mapping Early Patents on Baker's Yeast Manufacture," *Comprehensive Reviews in Food Science and Food Safety* 9 (2010): 483–497.

20 Muller, *Baking and Bakeries*, 14.

21 Robert Henry Thurston, *Reports of the Commissioners of the United States to the International Exhibition Held at Vienna, 1873* (Washington, DC: US Government Printing Office, 1876), Google Books.

22 Eben Norton Horsford, *Report of Vienna Bread* (Washington, DC: US Government Printing Office, 1875), Google Books.

23 Horsford, *Report of Vienna Bread*, 87.

24 Gelinas, "Mapping Early Patents," 483–497.

25 L. Stephen, ed., *Dictionary of National Biography* (London: Smith, Elder, and Co., 1888): 96–97, Google Books.

26 J. Dauglish, *Improvements Machinery for the Manufacture of Aerated Bread* (Washington, DC: US Patent and Trade Office, 1865): US48534 A, https://www.google.com/patents/US48534.

27 Stephen, *Dictionary of National Biography*, 96–97.

28 A. Broomfield, "Soldier of the Fork: How Nathanial Newnham-Davis Democratized Dining," *Gastronomica* 12, no. 4 (2012): 46–54.

29 Hart, *Leavening Agents*, 69–74.

30 Charles W. Forward, *Fifty Years of Food Reform: A History of the Vegetarian Movement in England* (London: Ideal Publishing Union, 1898): 83, Internet Archive.

31 Benjamin Ward Richardson, *On the Healthy Manufacture of Bread* (London: Bailliere, Tindel, and Cox, 1884): 68, Google Books.

32 A. H. Church, "Aerated Bread," *Nature* 19 (1878): 174–175, Google Books.

33 Richardson, *On the Healthy Manufacture of Bread*, 72–80.

34 Richardson, 82.

35 Church, "Aerated Bread," 174–175.

36 Richardson, *On the Healthy Manufacture of Bread*, 84.

37 "Manufacture of Aerated Bread," *New York Times* (June 20, 1895): 3.

38 Scott Svenson and Alley Svenson, "Our Story," Seattle Coffee Company, https://www.seattlecoffeecompany.co.za/our-story/.

39 "It's Official, Britons Now Prefer COFFEE to TEA, according to New Research," *FMCG Magazine*, September 29, 2017, http://fmcgmagazine.co.uk/official -britons-now-prefer-coffee-tea-according-new-research/.

40 P. Christiaan Klieger, *The Fleischmann Yeast Family* (Mount Pleasant, SC: Arcadia, 2004): 9.

41 Horsford, *Report of Vienna Bread*, 1.

42 Klieger, *The Fleischmann Yeast Family*, 15.

43 Klieger, 16.

44 Joseph Arthur Le Clerc and Robert Wahl, "Chemical Studies of Barleys and Malts" (Washington, DC: US Government Printing Office, 1909): bulletin 124:115, Google Books.

45 Bruno Giberti, *Material Worlds: Designing the Centennial: A History of the 1876 International Exhibition in Philadelphia* (Lexington: University Press of Kentucky, 2002): 145, ProQuest Ebrary.

46 *The Stranger's Pocket Guide to Philadelphia and the Centennial Exhibition* (Philadelphia: Central News Co., 1876): 6, Hathi Trust Digital Library.

47 Klieger, *The Fleischmann Yeast Family*, 17.

48 Klieger, 17.

49 Klieger, 27.

50 "The Lightest Food," *Times Dispatch* (February 7, 1913), https://chroniclingamerica.loc.gov/lccn/sn85038615/1913-02-07/ed-1/seq-3/.

51 Klieger, *The Fleischmann Yeast Family*, 53–54.

52 "Embarrassed by Horrid Pimples?" *Popular Mechanics* (November 1938): 615, Google Books.

53 Advertisement for Fleischmann's Yeast from Standard Brands, *Good Housekeeping* (1932): 105, https://commons.wikimedia.org/wiki/File:Fleischmann%27s_ Yeast_advertisement,_1932.jpg.

54 Catherine Price, "The Healing Power of Compressed Yeast," Distillations: Science, Culture, and History, Science History Institute, 2015, https://www.chemheritage .org/distillations/magazine/the-healing-power-of-compressed-yeast.

55 Charles Scott and James Scott, *Vienna Bread: Instructions and Recipes* (London: Baker and Confection Ltd., 1909), Internet Archive.

CHAPTER 6: HOW MUCH BREAD CAN YOU BUY WITH GOLD?

1   John Sutter, "The Discovery of Gold in California," *Hutchings' California Magazine* XVII (November 1857): 193–198, https://www.yosemite.ca.us/library/hutchings _california_magazine/17.pdf.

2   Hubert Howe Bancroft, *History of California* (San Francisco: History Company, 1888): 30, Internet Archive.

3   Bancroft, *History of California*, 52.

4   Bancroft, 59–61.

5   Richard J. Orsi, Kevin Starr, and Malcolm Rohrbough, *Rooted in Barbarous Soil: People, Culture, and Community in Gold Rush California* (Berkeley: University of California Press, 2000): 25.

6   Malcolm J. Rohrbough, *Rush to Gold: The French and the California Gold Rush 1848–1854* (New Haven, CT: Yale University Press, 2013): 7–20.

7   Rohrbough, *Rush to Gold*, 95.

8   Rohrbough, 106.

9   Joseph Robert Conlin, *Bacon, Beans, and Galantines: Food and Foodways on the Western Mining Frontier* (Reno: University of Nevada Press, 1987): 102.

10   Conlin, *Bacon, Beans, and Galantines*, 96.

11   Rohrbough, *Rush to Gold*, 114.

12   Conlin, *Bacon, Beans, and Galantines*, 103.

13   *LeCount & Strong's San Francisco City Directory for the Year 1854: Embracing a General Directory of the Citizens: And a Street Directory, with an Appendix, Containing All Useful and General Information Appertaining to the City, an Almanac, etc 1854* (San Francisco: San Francisco Herald Office, 1854): 153–154.

14   *Colville's San Francisco Directory*, vol. 1: *For the Year Commencing October, 1856; Being a Gazetteer of the City . . . Prefaced by a History of San Francisco, and Reviews of Industrial Enterprises, Associations, Etc.* (San Francisco: S. Colville, 1856): 14, 124, 131.

15   Peter Tamony, "Sourdough and French Bread," 265–270.

16   T. F. Sugihara, "Commercial Starters in the United States," In *Handbook of Dough Fermentations*, eds. Karl Kulp and Klaus Lorenz (Boca Raton, FL: CRC Press, 2003): 145–157.

17   Michael Bauer, "Boudin's Sourdough Is a Lot More Than a Tourist Attraction," *San Francisco Chronicle*, January 10, 2014, https://www.sfgate.com/restaurants /article/Boudin-s-sourdough-is-a-lot-more-than-a-tourist-5132404.php.

18   Eric P. Jensen and Mark D. Barton, "Geology, Petrochemistry, and Time-Space Evolution of the Cripple Creek District, Colorado," In *GSA Field Guide 10: Roaming the Rocky Mountains and Environs: Geological Field Trips*, ed. R. G. Reynolds (Boulder, CO: Geological Society of America, 2007): 63–78.

19   Lynn Colip, *Colorado's Gold Cone: A Hundred Year Beehive* (self-published, 1996): 41.

20   Elizabeth Jameson, *All That Glitters: Class, Conflict, and Community in Cripple Creek* (Urbana: University of Illinois Press, 1998): 30.

21   Thomas J. Noel, *Colorado: A Historical Atlas* (Norman: University of Oklahoma Press, 2019): 109.

22 Sharon Vail, "Sourdough: More Than a Bread," Kitchen Window, NPR, September 12, 2006, https://www.npr.org/templates/story/story.php?storyId=6061648; Kat Eschner, "Gold Miners Kept Their Sourdoughs Alive by Cuddling Them," *Smithsonian Magazine*, March 31, 2017, https://www.smithsonianmag.com/smart -news/gold-miners-kept-their-sourdough-starters-alive-cuddling-them-180962689; Avital Unger, "The Definitive History of San Francisco Sourdough Bread," *SF Travel*, July 16, 2015, https://www.sftravel.com/article/definitive-history-san-francisco-sourdough-bread.

23 Sharon Smulders, "'A Man in a World of Men': The Rough, the Tough, and the Tender in Robert W. Service's Songs of a Sourdough," *Studies in Canadian Literature* 30, no.1 (January 2005): 34, https://journals.lib.unb.ca/index.php/SCL/article /view/15270/16349.

24 Robert W. Service, "Songs of a Sourdough by Robert W. Service," Project Gutenberg (May 20, 2008): 31–32, Project Gutenberg.

25 Jack London, "A Klondike Christmas," In *The Complete Short Stories of Jack London*, eds. Earle Labor, Robert C. Leitz, and I. Milo Shepard, vol. 5 (Stanford, CA: Stanford University Press, 2013): 150.

26 Service, "Songs of a Sourdough by Robert W. Service," 42.

27 Jameson, *All That Glitters*, 37.

28 Jameson, 37.

29 Marshall Sprague, *Money Mountain: The Story of Cripple Creek Gold* (Detroit: University of Michigan, 1953): 133–162.

30 Jan Mackell, *Cripple Creek District: Last of Colorado's Gold Booms* (Mount Pleasant, SC: Arcadia, 2003): 59.

31 Brian Levine, *Cripple Creek: City of Influence* (Cripple Creek, CO: Historic Preservation Department, 1994): 32.

32 Leland Feitz, *Myers Avenue: A Quick History of Cripple Creek's Red-Light District* (Colorado Springs, CO: Little London, 1967): 5.

33 Jan Mackell, *Brothels, Bordellos, & Bad Girls: Prostitution in Colorado 1860–1930* (Albuquerque: University of New Mexico Press, 2004): 168.

34 Jan Mackell, *Red Light Women of the Rocky Mountains* (Albuquerque: University of New Mexico Press, 2009): 151.

35 Feitz, *Myers Avenue*, 5.

36 Anne Seagraves, *Soiled Doves: Prostitution in the Early West* (Hayden, ID: Wesanne Publications, 1994): 60–61.

37 Cripple Creek District Directory Co's Directory of the Cripple Creek Mining District for 1896 (Cripple Creek, CO: Cripple Creek District Directory Company, 1896); Cripple Creek District Directory Co's Directory of the Cripple Creek Mining District for 1900 (Cripple Creek, CO: Cripple Creek District Directory Company, 1900).

38 "City Directory" (Cripple Creek, CO, 1896); "City Directory" (Cripple Creek, CO, 1900).

39 Douglas Martin, "Dale Noyd, Vietnam Objector, Dies at 73," *New York Times*, January 28, 2007, https://www.nytimes.com/2007/01/28/us/28noyd.html.

40 David A. Anderton, *North American F-100 Super Sabre* (London: Osprey Publishing, 1987): 136–145.

41   Jeremy Larner, "The Court-Martial of Captain Noyd," *Harper's Magazine* (June 1968): 78–85.
42   Captain Dale E. Noyd, Petitioner v. Major General Charles R. Bond Jr., et al., 830 (S. Ct. 1969).
43   Peggy Bielz Cox, *The Mom Bielz's Family Cookbook* (Cripple Creek, CO World's Greatest Gold Camp, 1981): 23–39.
44   Bielz Cox, *The Mom Bielz's Family Cookbook*, 24.
45   Bielz Cox, 28.

CHAPTER 7: MODERN BREAD

1   M. Collado-Fernández, "Bread: Breadmaking Processes," In *Encyclopedia of Food Sciences and Nutrition*, 2nd ed., eds. Benjamin Caballero, Luiz Trugo, and Paul M. Finglas (Amsterdam: Academic Press, 2003): 627–634.
2   Collado-Fernández, "Bread: Breadmaking Processes," 627–634.
3   P. Saranaj, P. Sivasakthivelan, and K. Suganthi, "Baker's Yeast: Historical Development, Genetic Characteristics, Biochemistry, Fermentation and Downstream Processing," *Journal of Academia and Industrial Research* 6, no. 7 (2017): 111–119; Dallas Safriet, "Emission Factor Documentation for AP-42" (Research Triangle Park, NC: US Environmental Protection Agency, 1994), https://www3.epa.gov/ttn/chief/ap42/ch09/bgdocs/b9s13-4.pdf; "Bakers Yeast Production and Characteristics," Lallemand, accessed March 9, 2021, https://www.lallemandbaking.com/wp-content/uploads/2018/04/3_4YEAST.pdf.
4   Collado-Fernández, "Bread: Breadmaking Processes," 627–634; Weibiao Zhou, Yiu H. Hui, and Noel Haegens, *Bakery Products Science and Technology* (Oxford: Wiley-Blackwell, 2014): 309–324; "Chorleywood Baking Process," BakerPedia, accessed January 19, 2020, https://bakerpedia.com/processes/chorleywood-baking-process.
5   "Production Methods," Federation of Bakers, February 11, 2020, https://www.fob.uk.com/about-the-bread-industry/how-bread-is-made/production-methods/.
6   Steve Murez, "His Daily Bread," *Princeton Alumni Weekly*, Princeton University, April 11, 2018, https://paw.princeton.edu/article/his-daily-bread.
7   Edward Espe Brown, *The Tassajara Bread Book* (Berkeley: Shambhala, 1970).
8   Bernard Clayton, *The Complete Book of Breads* (New York: Simon and Schuster, 1973).
9   James Beard, *Beard on Bread* (New York: Knopf, 1973).
10   *Better Homes and Gardens Homemade Bread Cookbook* (New York: Meredith Corporation, 1973).
11   Ruth Allman, *Alaska Sourdough: The Real Stuff* (Portland, OR: Alaska Northwest Publishing Co., 1976).
12   "Sourdough Science," Modernist Cuisine, September 21, 2020, https://modernistcuisine.com/mc/sourdough-science/.
13   Rob Dunn, "Inside the Fascinating (and Delicious!) Science of Sourdough Bread," Ideas TED, TED Conferences, LLC, December 19, 2018, https://ideas.ted.com/inside-the-fascinating-and-delicious-science-of-sourdough-bread/.
14   Dunn, "Inside the Fascinating (and Delicious!) Science."

15 T. F. Sugihara, L. Kline, and M. W. Miller, "Microorganisms of the San Francisco Sourdough Bread Process. I. Yeasts Responsible for the Leavening Action," *Applied Microbiology* 21 (1971): 456–458.

16 Sugihara, et al., "Microorganisms of the San Francisco Sourdough Bread Process," 459–465.

17 W. P. Hammes, M. J. Brandt, K. L. Francis, J. Rosenheim, M. F. H. Seitter, and S. A. Vogelmann, "Microbial Ecology of Cereal Fermentations," *Trends in Food Science & Technology* 16 (2005): 4–11.

18 L. De Vuyst and M. Vancanneyt, "Biodiversity and Identification of Sourdough Lactic Acid Bacteria," *Food Microbiology* 24 (2007): 120–127.

19 L. De Vuyst, S. Van Kerrebroeck, H. Harth, G. Huys, H.-M. Daniel, and S. Weckx, "Microbial Ecology of Sourdough Fermentations: Diverse or Uniform?" *Food Microbiology* 37 (2014): 11–29, doi:10.1016/j.fm.2013.06.002; L. De Vuyst, S. Van Kerrebroeck, and F. Leroy, "Microbial Ecology and Process Technology of Sourdough Fermentation," *Advances in Applied Microbiology* 100 (2017): 49–160.

20 C. Urien, J. Legrand, P. Montalent, S. Casseregola, and D. Sicard, "Fungal Species Diversity in French Bread Sourdoughs Made of Organic Wheat Flour," *Frontiers in Microbiology* 10, no. 201 (2019): 1–17, doi:10.3389/fmicb.2019.00201.

21 "Sourdough Science."

22 "Tips for Manipulating the Sourness of Your Sourdough," Culture for Health, January 17, 2020, https://www.culturesforhealth.com/learn/sourdough/how-to-make-truly-sour-sourdough-bread/.

23 "Part I: How to Make Sourdough More (or Less) Sour," Brod and Taylor, January 17, 2020, https://brodandtaylor.com/make-sourdough-more-sour/.

24 Aysha Tai, "18 Ways to Make Sourdough Bread More (or Less) Sour," TrueSourdough.com, January 17, 2020, https://truesourdough.com/18-ways-to-make-sourdough-bread-more-or-less-sour/.

25 Jonas Warringer, Enikö Zörgö, Francisco A. Cubillos, Amin Zia, Arne Gjuvsland, Jared T. Simpson, Annabelle Forsmark, et al., "Trait Variation in Yeast Is Defined by Population History," *PLoS Genetics* 7, no. 6 (2011), https://journals.plos.org/plosgenetics/article?id=10.1371/journal.pgen.1002111.

26 Aldo Corsetti and Luca Settanni, "Lactobacilli in Sourdough Fermentation," *Food Research International* 40, no. 5 (2007): 539–558, https://www.sciencedirect.com/science/article/pii/S0963996906001979; Aldo Corsetti, M. Gobbetti, J. Rossi, and P. Damiani, "Antimould Activity of Sourdough Lactic Acid Bacteria: Identification of a Mixture of Organic Acids by *Lactobacillus sanfrancisco* CB1," *Applied Microbiology and Biotechnology* 50 (1998): 253–256; Johan Schnürer and Jesper Magnusson, "Antifungal Lactic Acid Bacteria as Biopreservatives," *Trends in Food Science & Technology* 16 (2005): 70–78; Brenna A. Black, Emanuele Zannini, Jonathan M. Curtis, and Michael G. Ganzle, "Antifungal Hydroxy-Fatty Acids Produced during Sourdough Fermentation: Microbial and Enzymatic Pathways, and Antifungal Activity in Bread," *Applied Environmental Microbiology* 79, no. 6 (2013): 1866–1873.

27 Cécile Pétel, Bernard Onno, and Carole Prost, "Sourdough Volatile Compounds and Their Contribution to Bread: A Review," *Trends in Food Science & Technology* 59 (2017): 105–123.

28   Pétel, et al., "Sourdough Volatile Compounds," 105–123.

29   De Vuyst, et al., "Microbial Ecology and Process Technology," 63; E. K. Arendt, Liam A. M. Ryan, and Fabio Dal Bello, "Impact of Sourdough on the Texture of Bread," *Food Microbiology* 24 (2007): 165–174; G. Lacaze, M. Wick, and S. Cappelle, "Emerging Fermentation Technologies: Development of Novel Sourdoughs," *Food Microbiology* 24 (2007): 155–160.

30   M. Gobbetti, C. G. Rizzello, R. Di Cagno, and M. De Angelis, "How the Sourdough May Affect the Functional Features of Leavened Baked Goods," *Food Microbiology* 37 (2014): 30–40; De Vuyst, et al., "Microbial Ecology and Process Technology," 49–160; M. J. Brandt, "Sourdough Products for Convenient Use in Baking," *Food Microbiology* 24 (2007): 161–164.

31   "Sourdough Market Growth, Trends and Forecasts (2019–2024)," Mordor Intelligence, January 17, 2020, https://www.mordorintelligence.com/industry-reports /sourdough-market; Nico Roesler, "Is Sourdough Experiencing a Resurgence?" BakingBusiness.com, March 8, 2019, https://www.bakingbusiness.com/articles /48166-is-sourdough-experiencing-a-resurgence.

32   "Sourdough Nutrition and Digestibility," Sourdough School, accessed March 7, 2021, https://www.sourdough.co.uk/category/sourdough/sourdough-nutrition -digestibility/.

33   "Country Bread," Tartine, accessed March 7, 2021, https://tartinebakery.com /stories/country-bread.

34   Chad Robertson, "Tartine's Country Bread," *New York Times Cooking*, January 17, 2020, https://cooking.nytimes.com/recipes/1016277-tartines-country-bread.

CONCLUSION: FINAL PROOF

1   Peter Reinhart, "The Fundamentals of Bread Baking Science: Fermentology Mini-Seminars," YouTube, Applied Ecology: Wild Sourdough Fermentology Mini-Seminars, May 7, 2020, https://youtu.be/Nm1ht7v1SYQ.

ILLUSTRATION CREDITS

———•———

INDEX

ABOUT THE AUTHOR

John Mangine

ERIC PALLANT is a serious amateur baker, a two-time Fulbright Scholar, an award-winning professor, and the Christine Scott Nelson Endowed Professor of Environmental Science and Sustainability at Allegheny College. He is acknowledged for his skill in weaving research narratives into compelling stories for TED-like talks (Gresham Lecture Series, London), bread symposia, podcasts, and articles for magazines such as *Gastronomica, Sierra*, and *Science*. More information on Pallant and his sourdough cultures, including a map of bakers around the world using Cripple Creek sourdough, can be found at EricPallant.com. He lives in Meadville, Pennsylvania, with his wife, a cat he did not expect, and three active sourdough starters.